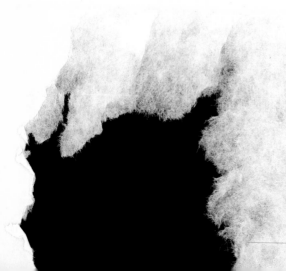

The Emergence of
the NIEO Ideology

Also of Interest

The Challenge of the New International Economic Order, edited by Edwin P. Reubens

Threat to Development: Pitfalls of the NIEO, William Loehr and John P. Powelson

U. S. Foreign Policy and the New International Economic Order: Negotiating Global Problems, 1974-1981, Robert K. Olson

U. S. Foreign Policy and Multilateral Development Banks, Jonathan E. Sanford

International Financial Cooperation: A Framework for Change, Frances Stewart and Arjun Sengupta, edited by Salah Al-Shaikhly

Development Financing: A Framework for International Financial Cooperation, edited by Salah Al-Shaikhly

The Lending Policy of the World Bank in the 1970s: Analysis and Evaluation, Bettina S. Hurni

Debt and the Less Developed Countries, edited by Jonathan David Aronson

The Economics of Foreign Aid and Self-Sustaining Development, Raymond F. Mikesell with Robert A. Kilmarx and Arvin Kramish

Comparative Development Perspectives, edited by Gustav Ranis, Robert L. West, Cynthia Taft Morris, and Mark Leiserson

The Challenges of South-South Cooperation, edited by Breda Pavlic, Raul R. Uranga, Boris Cizelj, and Marjan Svetlicic

From Dependency to Development: Strategies to Overcome Underdevelopment and Inequality, edited by Heraldo Muñoz

The Economics of New Technology in Developing Countries, edited by Frances Stewart and Jeffrey James

Information, Economics and Power: The North-South Dimension, edited by Rita Cruise O'Brien

The Foreign Policy Priorities of Third World States, edited by John J. Stremlau

*Available in hardcover and paperback.

Westview Special Studies in Social, Political, and Economic Development

The Emergence of the NIEO Ideology
Craig Murphy

This study traces the political history of the ideas underlying Third World calls for a New International Economic Order. Filling a significant gap in the literature, the book shows that NIEO ideology has a direct, unbroken line of development extending back to World War II, when a "new international economic order," the Bretton Woods system, was created. Dr. Murphy maintains that NIEO ideology is not rooted only in Third World acceptance of Prebisch's views on trade; rather, it evolved from Third World attempts to cope with problems and opportunities that emerged as the Bretton Woods system was created, operated, and began to break down. By the 1970s, the ideology had become a complex and coherent analysis of the economic position of Third World states, including a *political* analysis of how Third World views could be made dominant.

Many of Dr. Murphy's conclusions challenge the conventional wisdom about the Third World position of the NIEO. In addition, his study offers insight into the relatively unexplored area of how changes in political and social consciousness affect international systems, and provides grounds on which officials from both the South and the North can see the others' views as less alien.

Craig Murphy is assistant professor of political science at Wellesley College. He is the author of numerous journal articles in *International Interactions, International Studies Quarterly,* and *The Legion Observer* (in Ghana).

The Emergence of
the NIEO Ideology

Craig Murphy

Westview Press / Boulder, Colorado

Westview Special Studies in Social, Political, and Economic Development

Copyright © 1984 by Westview Press, Inc.

Published in 1984 in the United States of America by
  Westview Press, Inc.
  5500 Central Avenue
  Boulder, Colorado 80301
  Frederick A. Praeger, President and Publisher

Library of Congress Catalog Card Number 83-50979
ISBN 0-86531-664-3

Composition for this book was provided by the author.
Printed and bound in the United States of America.

Contents

Acknowledgments ix
List of Abbreviations x

INTRODUCTION: THE IDEOLOGY'S ROLE IN THE
NORTH-SOUTH CONFLICT 1

    Notes 10

1 THE ALTERNATIVE TO BRETTON WOODS BEFORE 1960 11

    Consensus on Global Management, Disagreement
      Over Regulation of Trade 13
    Economic Rights and Duties of States 28
    Third World Industrial Development 41
    Completing Bretton Woods and Moving On to
      Development 48

    Notes 52

2 THE "NEW" IDEOLOGY IN THE 1960S 59

    From Trade Issues to the Group of 77 62
    The Group of 77's Politics 73
    More New Economic Issues for the South 77

    Notes 86

3 1970-1974: CRACKS IN THE OLD ORDER AND CALLS
FOR THE NEW 91

    The Third World Divided 93
    The Third World Reunited 96
    Theory as a Source of Unity 105
    Leadership and the 1974 NIEO Program 112
    Responses to Northern Initiatives 116

    Notes 119

4 THE DEBATE SINCE 1974 125

   The North-South Dialogue Since 1974 127
   The Debate and NIEO Goals 137
   The Debate and NIEO Policy Proposals 142
   The Debate and the Group of 77's Political
   Analysis 147

   Notes 152

5 THE NIEO IDEOLOGY AS IDEOLOGY 157

   Key Elements of the New Order Ideology 158
   Interests Underlying the NIEO Ideology 166

   Notes 177

AFTERWORD: HOW IDEAS CAN HELP RESOLVE THE
NORTH-SOUTH CONFLICT 181

   Notes 184

Index 185

Acknowledgments

This book began as a doctoral dissertation in political science at the University of North Carolina at Chapel Hill. My advisor, Andrew Scott, both suggested the original idea and gave me help throughout my doctoral research. The other members of my dissertation committee, Enrique Baloyra, Claudio Cioffi-Revilla, Fredrico Gil, and Jeffrey Obler, provided me with detailed comments and suggestions. I also received suggestions and support from other graduate students working on dissertations in international relations at the same time, Bobby Childress, Tom Havener, Roseanne Lipe, and especially Doug Nelson. Paul Streeten and Margaret de Vries generously answered my initial naive questions about the workings of the Bretton Woods institutions. The documents librarians at the University of North Carolina and at Wesleyan University constantly found ways to make my research easier. Elizabeth Grover, the secret reason why so many of the political science faculty at the Johns Hopkins University write well, did much more than type my dissertation.

Ernst Haas, Jeffrey Hart, Stephen Krasner, Wentworth Ofuatey-Kodjoe, and two anonymous reviewers read and commented on my manuscript as I rewrote it. My senior colleague at Wellesley College, Linda Miller, gave me moral support throughout the process. The editors of International Studies Quarterly helped me refine arguments that appear in chapters 1 and 2 as well as in an article in their journal, "What the Third World Wants: An Interpretation of the Development and Meaning of the NIEO Ideology," vol. 27 (March 1983): 54-76.

My sister, Claire Wilhelm, and parents, Arthur and Florence Murphy, encouraged me throughout the whole project. JoAnne Yates, my wife, tried valiantly to give me some of her writing skills. She succeeded, instead, in giving me much more.

Craig Murphy

ix

Abbreviations

CIEC	Conference on International Economic Cooperation
DMC	Developed Market Country
ECLA	Economic Commission for Latin America
GATT	General Agreement on Tariffs and Trade
IDA	International Development Association
IFC	International Finance Corporation
IMF	International Monetary Fund
IPC	Integrated Programme for Commodities
ITO	International Trade Organization
LDC	Less Developed Country
LLDC	Least Developed Less Developed Country
NIEO	New International Economic Order
OECD	Organization for Economic Cooperation and Development
SDR	Special Drawing Right
SUNFED	Special United Nations Fund for Economic Development
TNC	Transnational Corporation
UNCTAD	United Nations Conference on Trade and Development
UNIDO	United Nations Industrial Development Organization
UNRRA	United Nations Relief and Rehabilitation Administration

Introduction:
The Ideology's Role
in the North-South Conflict

. . . any talk of giving "cultural autonomy" to the
smaller countries while transferring their right of
regulating their economic affairs (within the limits
imposed on all international intercourse) to some
laisser-faire mechanisms of a larger area is
nonsense. If we mean by "cultural autonomy" something more than the preservation of picturesque
costumes and out-of-date traditions which delight
the traveller, then we must realize that it cannot
develop unless a certain economic environment is
given.

-- K. W. Rothschild, 1944

The complaint of the poor nations against the
present state is not only that we are both poor in
absolute and relative terms and in comparison with
the rich nations. It is also that within the
existing structures of economic interaction we must
remain poor, and get relatively poorer, whatever we
do . . . The demand for a New International Economic
Order is a way of saying that the poor nations must
be enabled to develop themselves according to their
own interests, and to benefit from the efforts they
make.

-- Julius K. Nyerere, 1974(1)

Between the end of the second world war and the
beginning of the 1970s an originally obscure set of ideas
became central to one of the most important modern global
conflicts. In the 1940s these ideas reached print only
rarely, for example when a relatively eclectic British
economist like K. W. Rothschild decided to work out some
of the less popular implications of Keynesian economic
theory. By the 1970s scores of books and thousands of
pages of documents advanced the same views. The obscure

notions of the forties had become the organizing ideology
of the largest alliance of nations ever assembled. This
book is a political history of that new ideology, the New
International Economic Order (NIEO) ideology. It
describes where the ideology came from and how it became
a force in international relations.

Like some older economic ideologies influencing
international relations -- mercantilism, laissez faire
liberalism, Keynesian liberalism, and Leninism -- the
NIEO ideology defines an ideal system of global economic
relations. But the new ideology is not mercantilism;
advocates of the new order support conscious international management of global economic relations. It is
not Keynesian liberalism; the new ideology's supporters
reject creation of international institutions with powers
limited only by the rational dictates of economic
science. And the new ideology is neither laissez faire
liberalism nor Leninism; new order advocates reject the
idea that a single type of domestic economy need be
imposed worldwide before a just system of international
economic relations can exist.

One thing distinguishes the new order ideology from
all of the older major ideologies that have influenced
international economic relations: The new ideology is
concerned with alliance politics. New order advocates
explicitly attempt to enlist international institutions
behind their program to structure the world economy.
Their ideology governs the behavior of the alliance of
third world nations within international organizations.
As an alliance's political ideology, the new order
beliefs resemble the "free world" doctrine of the United
States and its allies and the "socialist" doctrine of the
Soviet Union and its allies: All define positions taken
in global political conflicts. The NIEO ideology
underlies the proposals for a New International Economic
Order made by the Group of 77 less developed countries
(LDCs)(2) and their supporters. It is one part of the
current north-south conflict's visible, ideological face.

In tracing the development of this ideology, I begin
in the 1940s, when the current north-south conflict over
how the global economy should be structured first
appeared. To the extent that the world economy is
structured by any conscious public decisions, three
international economic management institutions established then have the most influence: the International
Monetary Fund (IMF), the World Bank, and the General
Agreement on Tariffs and Trade (GATT). Each works
alongside the agencies with trade, aid, and monetary
powers that are parts of the governments of major
developed market countries (DMCs). Not only were all
three of these global organizations created in the 1940s;
the ideologies framing the current economic policies of
most DMCs were invented or revitalized then.

Following current convention, throughout this book I

refer to the three international agencies and the
national actions which support those agencies as "the
Bretton Woods system," even though only the IMF and World
Bank were negotiated at Bretton Woods. The GATT's legal
status, organization, and operations also differ from
those of the two other agencies. The IMF and the Bank,
more than the GATT, are true international governmental
organizations having their own chartered powers, their
own staffs, and (at least potentially) their own independent operational ideologies. The GATT is a contract
among states; it does not require the staff and autonomy
of the other agencies. All three institutions, plus the
agencies of the dominant governments that provide crucial
support for the institutions' goals, can be considered
together for analytical purposes because the creation of
those international organizations was informed by the
dominant ideology of the powerful nations.

In the forties K. W. Rothschild characterized this
dominant ideology as a desire for a weak global feder-
ation dedicated to laissez faire economics, a system
where international management of the world economy would
lead to free trade and free enterprise economies everywhere. This fundamental vision continues to inform many
of the policies of the Bretton Woods institutions as well
as many of the aid, trade, and monetary policies pursued
by the major DMC governments. The dominant ideology's
fundamental vision runs completely counter to a major
theme that advocates of the NIEO reiterate constantly:
their belief that the structure of the world economy
should impose no economic principles (like laissez faire)
upon nations. Rather, they believe that the international
economy should be structured to help any nation achieve
its development plans whatever the principles guiding
that plan might be.

We can understand why third world leaders talk about
their "rights" to "develop themselves according to their
own interests" by seeing the new order ideology as a
response to the dominant ideology and the system of which
it is a part. Recent references, like Nyerere's, to
development rights based upon a more fundamental right of
cultural autonomy just reiterate Rothschild's view,
thirty years after the system he criticized was created.

In its simplest form, then, my thesis is that the
New International Economic Order ideology developed as an
understandable response to real problems experienced by
third world states as a result of the Bretton Woods
system's creation and operation. The analyses the new
order advocates offer of the economic problems they face
may or may not be the most accurate ones, and the
policies they advocate many or may not be the best; I am
offering an analysis of the ideology's development, not a
critique of it validity or value. Therefore I do not use
the word "ideology" as a pejorative. Most practical human
consciousness, including most scientific thinking, is

just as "ideological." NIEO advocates simply countered
one ideology with another.

On one level, the development of the new order
ideology looked like this: Each of the positions added to
the developing ideology was adopted because it was the
most satisfactory of all the available ways for new order
advocates to understand a new, shared problem. While they
sought the most accurate or "scientifically" correct of a
set of ideas available for apprehending the new problem,
that set was bounded by an "ideological constraint." This
constraint ruled out any new ideas that contradicted any
part of the previous new order consensus. Over time,
under the ideological constraint of their prior
consensus, the ideas third world governments adopted to
apprehend and cope with their old and new problems under
the Bretton Woods system became an ideology as
comprehensive and coherent as the ideology that was part
of the dominant system.

Together, the two ideologies constitute the ideological face of the current north-south conflict. That
ideological conflict appears throughout statements made
by the advocates of the new order and those made on
similar topics by the people who want to continue the
present system. On its face, the conflict is one between
two specific conceptions of how international economic
relations can and should be governed. The dominant
ideology and the NIEO ideology both identify a proper
realm for international, rational management of the world
economy. The ideologies differ in the ways they define
the boundaries of that realm, the main goals of such
management activity, and the policies that should be
employed.

The area of agreement between the two ideologies,
between statements by DMC spokesmen about international
economic matters and those made by third world spokesmen,
tell us the current north-south conflict is ostensibly
about the management of international economic relations.
Both north and south believe in conscious governmental
intervention in the economy at the national and international levels. Adherents to both ideologies agree that
governments and international organizations should have a
role in setting economic goals and attempting to achieve
those goals through policy. Moreover, both positions
identify the international economic policy-making process
as one that should be essentially rational; policy makers
should analyze all variables that may influence a chosen
goal, and they should choose policies to maximize that
goal.

The differences between the two ideologies show up
when we examine the limitations on the realm of rational
economic policy making that each considers essential. The
dominant ideology suggests that international economic
policy making should never penetrate a realm of
international economic relations defined by the entitle-

ments and duties of private property ownership. Property owners must have the right to use their property in ways they see fit. They must be compensated when property is expropriated. Contracts must be enforced. The realm of property must be protected no matter how irrational private uses, policies of compensation, and the consequences of some contracts may be in terms of achieving international economic goals. In contrast, the new order ideology affirms that entitlements and duties associated with national sovereignty define the only proper limitations upon international economic policy making. Nations must have the right to use their geographically defined resources in any way they see fit, and national governments have the duty to respect and even foster the form of economic relations adopted by the governments of every other country despite irrational effects those policies may have on international economic goals.

The two ideologies also differ in terms of the specific concepts necessary for rational economic planning -- goals, economic analysis, and ideas about policies that could achieve those goals in light of that analysis. The dominant ideology places maximization of the world's production of goods and services as its central and primary goal and considers subordinate goals -- such a encouraging world political cooperation, full employment, and economic security for individuals -- as inevitable consequences of maximized production. The new order ideology also emphasizes production, peace, full employment, as well as some ecological goals, but it does not necessarily see them as correlated. Supporters of the new order emphasize trade-offs, yet say one goal, industrial development in the third world, should have the highest priority.

The two analyses of international economics differ even more when we look at the variables that are said to influence these goals. The NIEO ideology presents a picture of the world divided between economically central and economically peripheral countries in which the level of employment and level of production in the periphery are dependent on decisions made at the center. The dominant ideology presents a world of economic actors -- firms and individuals -- that merely happen to be circumscribed by certain national laws; it argues that correctly perceived national interests never contradict free market policies. Consequently, the adherent to the dominant ideology calls for reciprocal concessions by all nations to make a world free market and prescribes ways that intergovernmental organizations should intervene in economic relations to make such concessions likely. New order advocates say that nonreciprocal policies allowing certain national restrictions on exchange are essential if we want to achieve the highest possible levels of production and welfare.

While the differences between the ideologies are

great, they would be less important if advocates of both
could agree upon a way to settle disputes about principles, goals, and analyses. The desire for rational
economic management expressed by both ideologies provides
one means to resolve disputed economic analysis: empirical scientific study. Yet both ideologies suggest
additional, conflicting means to resolve intergovernmental economic disputes. Adherents to the dominant
ideology say that conflicts over goals and analyses
should be resolved by direct bargaining between national
governments. Implicitly, they affirm that in such
bargaining all elements of national power -- diplomatic,
economic, and military -- should be allowed to come into
play; therefore, the outcomes of such bargaining must be
weighted toward the self-defined interests of the most
powerful nations. The new order ideology says that
binding decisions over disputed goals and analyses should
be made by majority rule or consensus of national
governments, each government having an equal voice to
reflect its equal sovereignty. This conflict over the
right way to resolve differences keeps the sides apart
even when new events force them to amend their views. The
north-south conflict has gone through many changes
without being resolved.

I organize my analysis around the five distinct
phases in the north-south conflict:

1944-59 before the Bretton Woods system began
to operate the way it was designed to

1959-64 after the system began to operate normally
but before third world states made their
alliance formal

1964-71 while the system continued to operate
normally and after the formal alliance

1971-75 after the system began to break down but
before third world adversaries provided
opportunities for compromise

1975 - after the first opportunities for
compromise appeared

Andrew Scott's theory of managing international interdependence and David Apter's theory of stages in the
development of domestic mobilizing ideologies in new
nations(3) suggest these phases and accurately predict
the innovations that occurred during each. The validity
of these combined theories, in turn, supports the thesis
that the NIEO ideology developed in response to the
creation and operation of the Bretton Woods system.

Scott explains that the history of consciously
created systems for structuring human relations, like the

Bretton Woods arrangements, can be described in three stages: formation, operation, and breakdown. To form the system, those who will be affected by the structure or regime must resolve conflicts over what relations should be governed and how that should be done. Some of the actors that will be affected by the regime may have doubts that are not resolved simply because they do not have the power to make their interests salient to others. Of course that would only happen if the regime-formation conflicts were resolved through direct bargaining, subjection, or some other process that takes all forms of power into account. The actors whose interests are not considered, therefore, have automatic grounds for grievances with the new regime. As Apter suggests, their grievances can provide them with the basis for a new shared moral code and a new, separate identity.

My first chapter covers the long period during which the Bretton Woods system was formed, the 1940s and 1950s. Asian, African, and Latin American interests in postwar regimes that would foster economic development through coordinating national trade regulations were excluded from the postwar institutions. Those third world interests became the basis for principles, goals, and symbols of identity first adopted by third world governments in the forties and fifties, core elements of the new order ideology that they still reiterate today.

As the Bretton Woods system became more and more of a reality, third world spokesmen began to offer analyses of the world economy that did more than reiterate their initial grievances with the Bretton Woods system. For example, in the fifties third world governments began to charge DMCs with manipulating the terms of trade for third world goods through cold war policies of stockpiling raw materials and through exceptions to GATT rules that DMCs granted to themselves in order to allow special trade alliances including the European Community.

Scott's theory of managed international interdependence explains why new problems occurred and how they were linked back to the Bretton Woods system itself. With his theory we can explain all of the new economic analysis the third world adopted as part of the new order ideology in the 1960s, the only decade during which the Bretton Woods system operated in anything close to the way its founders intended. Scott argues that even consciously managed interdependence regularly produces distressing results that no one ever intended. Most of the early unintended consequences of the operation of the Bretton Woods system could be ignored by the system's most important backers. At first the unexpected events only harmed the interests of the less developed countries that had never really backed the system anyway.

Chapter 2 covers the 1960s, the period when the Bretton Woods system operated most normally. This decade was marked by unintended results of growing international economic interdependence that were harmful to third world nations but not to others. Ironically, partially as a result of the successes of the Bretton Wood system, the third world's share in world trade declined, differences in standards of living between third world and developed nations and among third world nations grew, some capital and skilled manpower left the third world, and trans-national firms in the third world increased their influence over local economies. Throughout the sixties third world governments barely amended the principles and goals they had agreed upon previously. Yet they expanded the new order ideology's policy analysis rapidly as they adopted new ideas to apprehend and explain the new economic problems they encountered.

Apter's theory makes me divide this decade during which the Bretton Woods system functioned the most successfully into two phases of the north-south conflict. With his theory we can understand the one set ideological innovations in the sixties that Scott's ideas cannot clarify. Apter suggests that a conflict enters a new phase when aggrieved parties develop a new, collective political identity. The third phase in the emergence of the New International Economic Order ideology began halfway through the 1960s when the Group of 77 formed. After that, the group confronted the political problem of making its ideology dominant. Throughout the late sixties the members of the alliance tested proposals for projecting what influence they had over DMCs. In the course of doing so the alliance added a political analysis to the economic analysis, principles, and goals which had previously made up the New International Economic Order ideology.

This third phase was far from smooth. Not all inter-third world dissent on global economic principles ended with the formation of the Group of 77. Chapter 3 begins in 1970, after the third world governments had agreed upon the notion that a new international economic order should be formed, but while the third world alliance still remained divided between two groups, each advocating economic duties under the NIEO. Initially these differences were based upon the different interests of the recently independent third world nations, on the one hand, and older members of the group, on the other. The differences disappeared from official statements before the south presented the new order program at the General Assembly Special Session in 1974. By that time all third world governments had consented to having the principles first adopted by the older group members in the forties as the single set of principles governing the duties of wealthy states to aid poorer ones. The key principle they affirmed was a permanent duty of all wealthy states to aid the economic development programs of poorer states. In contrast a historical duty based upon restitution for colonialism, advocated by the newer states, never obtained a similarly central a position in the ideology.

The bulk of chapter 3 discusses the proximate cause of the most recent third world convergence upon this key principle, the first signs of the Bretton Woods system's breakdown, in 1971. Extending Scott's argument, we can distinguish a period of breakdown in a regime as one that begins when the inadvertent consequences of management start to harm the actors whose support the regime needs. When the DMCs started to refuse obligations under Bretton Woods in the wake of global stagflation, mounting trade deficits, and approaching energy limits to growth, the fourth phase in the development of the New International Economic Order ideology began. Third world ideologists had something new to discuss after 1971, the attempts to reform the Bretton Woods system engineered by DMCs in the wake of the system's crises.

At the time the new order ideology could be characterized by that Apter calls "hortatory realism."(4) That is, while the ideology certainly contained many objectively accurate propositions arrived at through attempts to correctly understand real problems, the ideology's primary function was to keep the alliance directed toward its fundamental goals. New order advocates were ideologically constrained to repeat all the untested propositions in their earliest consensus. They did so, in part, because no opponents had expressed enough sympathy with the ideology for NIEO advocates to begin the sort of dialogue that could bring some of their untested assumptions into question. Consequently, in the early seventies new order advocates tended to limit their innovations to adding analyses of ways to exploit the DMCs economic vulnerabilities that had been exposed as the Bretton Woods system started to break down.

In 1975 the north-south conflict entered a new political phase, the fifth phase in the development of the new order ideology. By then many of the major developed states had accepted some new order proposals as the agenda for further north-south discussions. According to Apter, such a development should allow the third world's economic and political realism to turn from being "hortatory" to being "practical" as opportunities for realistic compromise appear. The actual record since 1975 is mixed. Compromises between north and south have been reached, but, in the main, third world states continue to support goals and principles for a new order that is anathema to at least the most powerful DMCs. Chapter 4 discusses the increasingly substantive new order debate in light of the few changes in the third world position since 1974.

Chapter 5 summarizes my conclusions about the origin of the new order ideology and then looks both at and below the level of the global system to find out why all third world governments, which differ so much one from another, can share some underlying interests that the ideology helps them understand and pursue. Even a superficial global view of the ideology suggests how complex the network of interests supporting the new order might be. The new order ideology sanctions all the different development doctrines around the world, doctrines that differ enough to satisfy the scores of different domestic political coalitions of classes and sectoral groups backing different third world governments. Chapter 5's analysis of the new order ideology as ideology suggests some simple patterns underlying the apparent complexity of domestic interests in the south. It also discusses how common individual experiences of members of the third world elite contributed to the ideology's development.

Both chapters 4 and 5 suggest reasons for being optimistic that the current north-south conflict can be resolved through further negotiated reforms of the Bretton Woods system that would satisfy some of the interests underlying the NIEO ideology. In order for the conflict to be resolved parts of the NIEO ideology itself would have to begin to guide the policies the international institutions follow. But in addition to better satisfying some third world interests, the operational ideology of an actual new international economic order would also have to reflect the self-defined economic interests of the governments of developed states more fully than the new order ideology does at present. The Afterword looks at this problem and at other impediments to a "debated" or "idea-generated" resolution to the current north-south conflict. It illustrates something hopeful in the fact that, even on its own terms, the NIEO ideology would be inadequate as the operational ideology for an actual new international economic order.

NOTES

(1)K. W. Rothschild, "The Small Nation and World Trade," Economic Journal 54 (Apr. 1947): 35. Julius K. Nyerere quoted in Anthony J. Dolan and Jan van Ettinger, eds., Partners in Tomorrow (New York: E. P. Dutton, 1978), p. 129.
    (2)The group now includes well over a hundred members and some of them, like the oil producing states, are countries where people, on average, are now quite wealthy.
    (3)Andrew M. Scott, "The Logic of International Interaction," International Studies Quarterly 21 (Sept. 1977): 429-60; David E. Apter, "Ideology in Modernizing Societies," in his The Politics of Modernization (Chicago: Univ. of Chicago Press, 1965), pp. 313-56.
    (4)Apter, p. 320.

1
The Alternative to
Bretton Woods Before 1960

Bretton Woods:

. . . typified by the dollar sign, gold at Fort
Knox, international cartelism, and a spider-web of
Shylocks squeezing out the heart of hungry
multitudes.

-- Diego Luis Molinari of Argentina, 1948

And the alternative:

The undeveloped countries seek industrialization by
some simple and quick route. By obtaining large
loans with no strings attached and by offering
enterprisers a monopoly of local markets they hope
to build factories overnight. They do not believe
that they must creep before they can walk.

-- Clair Wilcox of the United States, 1949(1)

Molinari and Wilcox represented their respective
governments at meetings called to create a world trade
organization following the second world war. Their
comments foreshadow the ideas and emotions expressed in
the north-south conflict now, in the eighties. Moreover,
they reflect the actual roots of that conflict, the
issues that first divided north and south over thirty
years ago.
Throughout the decade and a half following the
second world war governments worked to establish a new,
postwar economic order. The war ended with little
consensus on the nature of the new order aside from
agreement that there should be some sort of intergovernmental management to facilitate expansion of global
production. The American government wanted regimes that
would eliminate national regulation of trade. In

contrast, most other governments wanted international
regimes to approve and coordinate national trade regulations. Eastern European governments wanted provisions
encouraging bilateral trade agreements. Western European
governments and Commonwealth members felt that proposals
mooted by the United States during the war failed to
respect worthwhile regulations that could be used to
reduce unemployment. Many leaders of what we now call the
third world were convinced, like Molinari, that American
plans would enhance the economy of the United States at
the expense of Latin American, Asian, and African plans
for industrialization, plans belittled by Wilcox and
other advocates of the American proposals.

In 1959, when the IMF and GATT both celebrated their
first year of normal operation, the system had become
something less than most of its founders had envisioned.
Most east European governments had rejected the new
economic system. Western European governments and those
of developed Commonwealth countries had ceased to raise
the issue of creating an international employment regime.
Yet African, Asian, and Latin American governments had
neither muted their doubts about the Bretton Woods
institutions nor withdrawn from the system. They
expressed their doubts through proposals that granting
aid to other nations be considered a duty of statehood
and through an economic analysis which said that
industrialization was desirable and viable everywhere. By
1959 governments in the south had adopted a core of
concepts around which proposals for reforming the postwar
economic order could be organized and through which those
governments would come to recognize one another as
potential allies.

The history of the New International Economic Order
ideology of the 1980s begins, then, in the 1940s when the
issue of creating regimes to help manage world economic
relations first appeared on the international agenda. It
begins with the worldwide acceptance of the conception
that advocates of the NIEO still share with the framers
of Bretton Woods, the belief that some degree of intergovernmental economic management is desirable. Only after
the first Bretton Woods agreements did the south
articulate a new ethic of international economic relations. This notion of economic rights and duties of
states that morally grounded the specific global policies
desired by the poorer states outside of Europe during and
immediately after the war -- technical assistance,
commodity pricing agreements, and multilateral aid.

With this ethic the founders of the new order
movement presented a policy analysis justifying the
reforms they proposed in terms of goals they shared with
leaders of both the developed nations and the nations
that had once been developed, before they were impoverished by the war. The new analysis said that a
historically determined structure of the world economy

impeded optimal economic growth. This analysis began and remained controversial and distinct from the analysis that came to guide day to day policy making within postwar regimes. Yet the analysis was always politically significant. Through the new analysis, African, Asian, and Latin American governments could see each other as sharing economic problems distinct from those of industrial nations. The analysis explained the division of the world into rich north and poor south; it pointed to a concrete reality behind the symbol of the "third world."

This chapter relates the history of the first period in the emergence of the new order ideology, emphasizing that it developed around southern grievances with the emerging Bretton Woods regimes. Those grievances explain the focus of the new order ideology on global management and the south's state-centered ethic of rights and duties as well as the structural policy analysis accepted by many Asian, African, and Latin American governments. They adopted the ethic and analysis to frame specific grievances which precluded the adoption of other contemporary theories about international economic relations, including the slightly modified laissez faire theory underlying the Bretton Woods institutions. Throughout this chapter I compare that dominant ideology, which emerged as part of the Bretton Woods system in the forties and fifties, to those concepts that came to form the base of the new order ideology.

CONSENSUS ON GLOBAL MANAGEMENT, DISAGREEMENT OVER NATIONAL REGULATION OF TRADE

The intergovernmental institutions involved in the management of economic relations after the second world war came about through negotiation. Admittedly, Americans set the agendas for international conferences and used threats and promises backed by American economic power to preclude some options championed by other states. Nonetheless, ultimately postwar institutions were not created by dictatorial fiat of a single power but by agreement of all the nations that signed their charters. Given that the founders had to resolve disputes among people with fundamentally different visions of what the world economic order should be, it is remarkable that the postwar system developed at all. Consensus was reached only because the Americans raised the least controversial issues about postwar regimes first and then helped resolve them by pointing to ways that institutions proposed by the U.S. would expand production throughout the world, a paramount concern for most governments.

When the Americans finally raised the issue of creating an international organization to coordinate national regulation of trade and, ultimately, left it unresolved because consensus could not be reached, most nations had already agreed upon some institutions that had the ability to restrict such national regulation. An American desire for free trade thus became a principle of actual postwar regimes as if by default, and the governments that remained unconvinced that a free trade system would allow them to achieve their economic goals, yet accepted the new regimes, found themselves arguing against a status quo assumption that global management should be constrained by free trade principles. In addition, by accepting the new regime's rules for amendment, those governments opposing free trade made it impossible for themselves to effectively express their grievances within the system. Under the rules of the IMF, World Bank, and GATT, the governments opposing free trade had little voice. Their grievances with the new system were left to be expressed within the United Nations General Assembly and the short-lived conference on creating an international trade and employment regime, arenas in which all governments were granted equal power.

The early consensus on the postwar institutions that were created reflected general agreement among scholars and policy makers throughout the world that it was folly to allow the global economy to be ungoverned by some notion of the common good. They considered this a lesson of the two world wars.

By the early 1940s the intellectual sources of that lesson were myriad. Some democratic socialists in the early part of the century had predicted and supported a universal alliance among empires in which the inevitable conflicts of their expanding economies would be resolved.(2) Studies of business cycles pointed to the interdependence of national economies and the desirability of coordinating anticyclical policies.(3) Scholars joined policy makers in blaming restrictive trade practices for setting the conditions for the second world war, such as the dependence of east European economies on Germany.(4) And Keynes's polemic, The Economic Consequences of the Peace, written in 1919, with its forecast of vindictive trade and monetary policies and the ultimate collapse of the European economy, read like prophecy. Policy makers even accorded Keynes's solution -- for governments to agree to jointly undertake the benign international management functions performed by City of London bankers in the nineteenth century -- the respect a prophet's vision deserves.(5)

In countries with market economies, where government intervention was usually questioned, mobilization for the war brought officials practical experience in using economic controls. Mobilization also brought economists into government in greater numbers than ever before. An explosion of innovative exchange and production policies resulted, some with international implications. They ranged from the marketing boards for primary commodities in the British colonies to lend-lease arrangements for financing expanded American production and Allied war needs.(6)

Governments throughout the world helped manage economies during the war; increased intervention occurred even outside the combatant states. If anything, the British government more strictly managed the economies of its colonies and dependencies for the war effort than it did the economy of the home country. Native adminis- trators, who would later become leaders of independent nations, learned the tools of economic planning during the war.(7) Throughout the war, Latin American nations even received U.S. support for internal policies of economic diversification and industrialization in exchange for both their political and economic support of the Allies. Latin American governments attempted to negotiate international agreements that would help assure stable terms of trade for the goods they exported. They also demanded to be allowed to protect infant industries with tariffs and to receive global support for their import substitution policies. Throughout the war the United States supported such suggestions despite ideo- logical objection to them by the highest policy makers. As the State Department put it in 1941, American free trade principles were "moderated in practice" to support the international agreements desired by Latin America.(8)

Nonetheless, when most American policy makers thought about postwar institutions they rarely moderated their advocacy of liberal principles. The State Depart- ment under Cordell Hull consistently maintained that "free trade" and "free enterprise" should define moral boundaries circumscribing the role of any postwar intergovernmental economic organization. The depart- ment's notion of "free enterprise" involved both support for market-oriented internal policies and strong oppo- sition to "monopolistic practices," partially of firms but more especially of national governments. This included opposition to most tariffs, quantitative restrictions upon amounts of goods imported or exported, multilateral interference in the market to support the price of certain goods (commodity agreements), and special bilateral trade agreements -- all of which American policy makers considered means of giving monopoly-like advantages to national firms.(9) The State Department supported global regimes that would create conditions under which unrestricted trade was possible, a system whose goals would include abolition of just the sort of international economic arrangements toward which the Americans had agreed to negotiate with Latin American states during the war. While Latin American policy makers were more typical of others throughout the world in envisioning postwar institutions as regulating the way national governments regulated trade, the State Depart- ment envisioned a world federal government dedicated to removing all barriers to trade erected by national governments.

Commercial Affairs Division Chief Herman Geist accurately reflected this vision and the feelings of those who held it when he said:

Let me warn against the futile speculations of theorists who would have us deviate from sound principles in international trade and espouse methods of dealing repugnant to our way of life. If in the international sphere we reject political and social systems harmful to mankind, we must also repudiate the economic practices upon which they are based. If we hold fast to our destiny we shall create an indivisible and advancing civilization upon the foundation of our prosperity and rear a new edifice where enlightenment based on material, moral, and spiritual progress will finally decide the future of mankind.(10)

From this point of view, international trade deviating from the ideal of free enterprise domestically and internationally -- the ideal Roosevelt was to call a basic economic right in 1943(11) -- was anathema. Rejection of fascism implied rejection of the restrictive trade practices employed by fascist states. Governments that rejected restrictive trade practices could expect a wealthy, moral world in return. They even could expect conditional American assistance to aid economic development. As one official put it:

Plans for investing in developing the resources and diversifying underdeveloped areas must have as an outstanding object the promotion of international trade in the interests of all countries providing the help as well as in the interests of the countries receiving it. It makes little sense if governments maintain or impose new obstacles to trade which is sought to develop, thereby destroying the trade and investment as well. In the last analysis, every problem in the field of economic relations resolves itself into a problem of trade.(12)

This statement could be read as a promise of American aid and investment in exchange for adoption of free trade and free enterprise policies. Geist's "foundation" of American "prosperity," the wealth of the United States, assured that there would be investment in poorer countries as long as they did not impose obstacles. In 1941 when Dean Acheson spoke of this State Department vision of a federated world dedicated to free trade and formed under American leadership through promises of American investment, as the "last best hope of mankind."(13)

As Geist makes clear, some economic theorists in the early forties did not welcome this proposed "edifice" of international government dedicated to free trade and free enterprise. Not all of those theorists were apologists for totalitarian regimes. Because of the reputation of Keynes's work, which influenced many policy makers in the United States as well as in the Commonwealth and Latin America, and because of Keynes's own role as the major negotiator for Great Britain at early conferences called to create postwar regimes, the most serious challenge to the State Department vision was Keynesian.

Keynes supported the formation of intergovernmental organizations that would be more limited in their effects on existing restrictive national trade policies, yet more interventionist than those envisioned by the American State Department. Keynes wanted to give latitude to governments to regulate their trade and the use of their currency when the absence of such regulation might result in unemployment. Yet, Keynes wanted intergovernmental organizations to have the financial capability to support full-employment policies, a management role that went far beyond the one envisioned by the State Department.(14)

In his seemingly prophetic 1944 article, British economist K. W. Rothschild laid out what he believed to be the fundamental differences between Keynesians and free enterprise advocates over matters of international trade. Rothschild called the free enterprise "federal solution" to problems of trade and the global economy in general, ". . . a remnant of the idea that the mere removal of regulation and interference will give us paradise on earth." Rothschild rejected that idea:

> The frequent abuse of tariffs, quotas, and monetary methods for aggressive purposes and "beggar-my-neighbor" policies has clearly shown that the absence of this type of regulation would be beneficial to the vast majority of people. But the fact that certain tools are misused does not justify us jumping to the conclusion that the removal of tools is preferable to their proper use.

Rothschild's Keynesian position had it that the potentially beneficial effects of international trade restrictions should be studied rather than ruled out in principle. The Keynesians considered ruling restrictive policies out "in principle" to be either an unscientific response to a few cases where restrictive policies had proved to be detrimental or else an uncritical acceptance of theories which ignored significant elements of the actual world economy. Rothschild continues:

> That the complete removal of tools is so widely accepted as the best solution is probably also due to the fact that the two most outstanding modern

books on the theory of international trade exclude
monopolistic phenomena and problems connected with
the trade cycle from the larger treatment of the
subject. Will a consideration of them not necessitate a modification of the conclusions which were
based on the assumption of perfect competition and a
highly flexible economic system in which frictional
forces play only a minor part?(15)

The Keynesians thought, of course, that such explicit
consideration of monopolies and trade cycles would
necessitate new policy conclusions.

American officials were concerned with the ways
business cycles affected trade, but when making foreign
policy they rarely worried about how the investment
decisions made by private firms affected those cycles.
American officials downplayed the significance of firms
that had monopoly powers in their own right, considering
monopoly powers to be a global problem only when they
were created by the trade practices of states. Consequently, had they further investigated "monopoly
practices," as they understood them, American policy
makers still would not have reached new policy
conclusions.

Americans based their insistence upon the mutual
desirability of both global free trade and the creation
of free enterprise economies around the world on
something more than generalization from the results of
restrictive practice prior to the war. Their views
reflected something more than uncritical acceptance of
abstract trade theories. Praise of free trade and free
enterprise reflected convictions developed while guiding
the United States out of the depression. Adherents
reasonably could say that these beliefs were prudent,
altruistic, and proven in practice -- if not always
consistent one with another.

To justify that free trade could be good in itself
supporters could point to the abstract theories. Those
theories demonstrated, at the very least, that if a free
trade system meeting their assumptions could be created,
there would be opportunities for greater production
worldwide.

Yet extensive government intervention in the status
quo world economy would be needed just to create such a
system. Intervention would be needed, on the one hand, to
dismantle existing restrictive trade practices, and, on
the other, to assure that the nations which could make or
break the system had the financial wherewithal to benefit
from the new export opportunities that the system would
give them.

American policy makers saw creating such a system as
a political task similar to the one confronted by the
Roosevelt administration in bringing the U.S. out of the
slump in the thirties: They had to get powerful economic

actors who supported the status quo of inefficient,
restricted trade together with those who desired greater
redistributive intervention in the economy to work
together to increase production and support the growth-
rather than redistribution-oriented interventionist
policies of the government. During the depression the
government's partial reliance on free enterprise to
expand the economy was essential to get business support
for the interventionist programs of the Roosevelt
administration. Expanding production, not redistribution
of economic goods or the power to produce them, was the
key to that program. As Charles Maier puts it, members of
the Roosevelt administration sought to transform the
class-based political problem of the depression and,
"adjourn class conflict for consensus on growth."(16)

Their success makes it not surprising that they
brought the same focus on economic growth to debates over
international economic relations. Under conditions that
still had to be created through intervention in the
postwar world economy, free trade could assure growth.
But it was just as politically important during those
debates that the principled insistence upon free trade by
men like Hull, Geist, and Acheson served to enlist the
support of much of the American business community behind
new international institutions that would intervene in
the world economy to help it expand. State Department
support of free trade even helped legitimize the least
market-oriented parts of the postwar order -- like the
system of fixed exchange rates for national currencies
under the eye of international financial institutions
controlled by governments rather than by private
interests. This system was first championed by the
Treasury Department, which was more influenced by
Keynesian concerns than the State Department was. The
State Department explained the interventionist financial
institutions as a necessary support system for an
ultimately noninterventionist free trade regime. In doing
so they created business support for the leadership role
that the U.S. government would take in making all the
postwar regimes work, including business acceptance of
the financial burden of that leadership, the massive aid
and investment needed to assure that many nations could
expand production.

Of course, American officials expected that ultimately such an open international economic system would
further American interests. It would open avenues for
exports that would quell the American fears in the early
1940s of postwar overproduction and recession.(17) An
open international system would assure U.S. firms access
to foreign raw materials, again helping to assure further
U.S. economic growth. But, because they considered
expansion of the American economy necessary if the goods
needed by war-devastated poorer countries were to be
produced, American policy makers could find a large

element of altruism in their insistence upon the free
trade principles that would serve American interests.(18)
    At first, in the early 1940s when intergovernmental
consultation was mostly limited to monetary and financial
matters, Americans placed more emphasis on adjourning
global economic conflict for consensus on growth than
they did upon the principles of free trade and free
enterprise. The American emphasis on expansion in general
helped international consensus on financial and monetary
matters to be reached quickly, if slightly imperfectly;
the organizations created were unacceptable to the Soviet
Union and many of its allies. The liberal Keynesians,
like the free market theorists, accepted facilitating
growth as the central goal for postwar institutions.
Growth had been the goal of liberal economics since
Smith. In the world depleted by the war, policy makers,
not surprisingly, accepted the economists' focus on
growth. Even in the countries least affected by the war,
like the Latin American states, the central national
economic goal was growth. That was the point of
industrialization and diversification. Only in the
socialist countries, where policy makers had a super-
ordinate concern with maintaining socialist national
economies in a capitalist world, did national goals
preclude acceptance of international organizations
designed to coordinate monetary and financial matters in
order to facilitate economic growth.
    In addition to the general prevalence of expanding
production as a top-priority item on national agendas,
another thing assured that consensus could be reached
quickly in the early years: The issues addressed at the
conferences for creating monetary and financial institutions did not preclude agreement at a later date upon
the sorts of restrictive trade policies many governments
desired. And when nations had central economic goals
other than maximizing production, governments tended to
relate those goals more to trade than to monetary or
financial policy. When they agreed upon the charters of
the IMF and the World Bank, all governments expected that
a third institution, the International Trade Organization
(ITO) would later be created to join the fund and the
bank as centers of the intergovernmental regimes managing
postwar economic relations.
    Keynes's ideas illustrate why those governments
which remained uncommitted to free trade considered this
trade organization to be so important. They expected the
ITO to offer an international framework for dealing with
trade-related unemployment problems and for coordinating
government programs of restricting trade to encourage
domestic investment in countries where powerful foreign
firms would not invest. Keynesians felt that these issues
had to be resolved both because a framework was needed to
maximize growth and because full employment and national
programs for economic development were good in

themselves.

Keynesians believed that in a world governed by free trade principles, national programs to maintain full employment, and hence full use of productive factors, could become unworkable due to foreign recession. A country whose exports suddenly became less valuable because of the economic difficulties of nations importing those items would also suffer from the slump. Production in the export sector would be limited, and there would be unemployment unless that country's government were allowed to use trade and monetary policies to cushion the impact of foreign recessions. This view reflected a major worry the British government and the governments of other developed non-Axis market nations -- especially Australia -- had throughout the war. They feared that their countries might have to suffer from further recessions in the United States where they believed anticyclical policies were less well developed than in their own countries.(19)

Keynes proposed that subsidies for affected exporters and some trade restrictions (that would, in a sense, punish the countries that had not developed anti-cyclical policies) should be allowed in such cases. He also proposed that whatever sort of international bank was created after the war be mandated to help finance national policies that would contain the international diffusion of recession. Given the importance of bringing the advanced Commonwealth countries into the postwar global system, Keynes got his way, in part. The IMF came to function as a creditor to nations experiencing problems that had foreign causes or might have foreign effects.(20)

Less effectively aired in the early forties were Keynesian proposals designed to increase the ability of smaller, less developed countries to restrict their international trade in order to diversify their economies. Rothschild outlines the justifications for such proposals by arguing that in a postwar laissez faire world, powerful, monopolistic private firms would continue to be able to decide where most investment would be made. Unlike the competitive firms of economics textbooks, real monopolistic firms would invest in such a way that the specialization resulting from free trade would fail to employ resources throughout the world with great efficiency. The conservative investment practices of industrial monopolies assured that they would only heavily invest where they had invested before:

> If a laisser-faire policy is pursued the creation of a federal union will tend to reinforce and perpetuate the economic structure of its constituent members. The greater industrial countries will become centers of heavy and other monopolistic industries, the smaller countries will find oppor-

tunities in small-scale industries and agriculture. Backward countries will remain backward just because they were backward before.(21)

This was just the sort of future feared by policy makers in Latin America and in other other independent less developed regions. For them the free trade system might mean less than optimal growth. More importantly, a free trade world would be one in which they would be allowed none of their traditional powers to compensate for a lack of foreign industrial investment.

As it was chartered, the World Bank could become a lending agency that would help poorer nations combat the parochial investment decisions of monopolistic firms. But governments in the nations with few industries felt that other policies, including internationally sanctioned tariff protection of infant industries, would be also needed. They left comprehensive international discussion of such policies to the debates over the ITO in the late forties.

Even at the beginning of those trade discussions, the less industrialized countries' negotiating position was weak. Before the discussions started, the IMF and the World Bank looked like institutions that would help recreate the prewar worldwide division of labor and maintain it. The IMF was designed to encourage nations to allow their national currencies to be freely converted into those of other nations. It would try to eliminate the possibility that a nation could use restrictions on foreign exchange to prevent the flight of capital to more lucrative investments abroad. The World Bank accepted as its first priority industrial reconstruction of the war torn regions, first in Europe, thus helping reestablish the prewar division between a relatively industrialized north and relatively nonindustrial south.

Yet statesmen in the forties saw things differently. Despite the prescience of theorists like Rothschild on other matters, the possibility that the IMF and the World Bank could help recreate and maintain the old global division of wealth and poverty was hardly recognized when those institutions were formed. Preventing the establishment of such a division, and thus accounting for the Keynesian doubts about the ultimate effects of the international investment policies of powerful firms, was, for most concerned officials, a matter of trade policy. Trade controls had been the most frequently employed policy for maintaining and enhancing the relative economic positions of particular nations since mercantilist times. The ITO negotiations appeared to most as the logical place to raise such issues.(22)

Despite the fact that creating a trade organization would remain an issue of international politics for five years after 1947, the actual intergovernmental institutions of the postwar system had all been chartered by then. The last agreement was the GATT. Taken together the IMF, World Bank, and GATT represented a consensus among market countries that global management aimed at expanding production was essential. From the standpoint of a laissez faire advocate, those regimes were complete in themselves. Had they actually appeared complete to all governments, their creation would have represented the achievement of the American goal; intergovernmental economic conflict would have been overcome through consensus on growth. The IMF provided a mechanism for dealing with short term balance of payments problems and currency conversion, thus making trade easier and encouraging growth to accommodate the new trade potential that the easing of exchange problems would create. World Bank provisions of capital would aid war torn states and allow them to productively enter the world system. The GATT defined conditions under which trade would go on. It emphasized the removal of tariffs and other restrictions thus creating new opportunities for trade and production. Free trade theories as far back as Ricardo's or Smith's could be used to show why this system was designed to facilitate growth: Specialization encouraged by increasingly free world trade would result in the more efficient and complete employment of labor and capital everywhere. From the laissez faire point of view the move to maximize global production had begun.

Nonetheless, in 1947 it would have seemed odd to the delegates at international conferences on economic matters had anyone suggested that the postwar system was fully developed. They considered the GATT only a stopgap measure to encourage trade before comprehensive agreement on the ITO could be reached. GATT was designed so that export sectors could start to function as catalysts to growth. It reflected no agreement on trade-related goals other than growth, such Keynesian goals as full employment and economic development.(23) In addition, in 1947 direct American aid to the war torn countries was becoming increasingly more important rather than less important, thus casting some doubt on the effectiveness of the Bretton Woods monetary and financial regimes. Even those regimes were still incompletely defined in an important sense: The ideas that would guide their decisions were not yet fixed.

In 1946, six weeks before he died, Keynes addressed the first meeting of the IMF Board of Governors. He encouraged them and their counterparts at the World Bank to develop independent policy analysis rather than to be tied to the policies and analyses preferred by their most powerful members. Keynes revealed some of that insight often attributed to those near death. He correctly predicted what the postwar international economic management system would become, forseeing the limited fulfillment of his vision.

IMF and World Bank charters mandated their staffs to

make decisions, in Keynes's words, "on their merits," to employ empirical analysis and rationally choose the best policies to achieve those goals all IMF members had agreed upon. Conscious, rational public management of the world economy had become a structure, a relatively permanent source of influence, in the world economy alongside the structures which emerge unconsciously from habitual market relations and the rarely coordinated interventions made by national governments. Within this unprecedented realm for making decisions in the global interest conflicts could be resolved by reference to economic theory and to empirical analysis of the ways alternative policies could be expected to affect accepted goals.

This much Keynes both knew and was glad of; yet he feared that this realm of conscious management to achieve global goals would be unduly limited by purely political decisions, decisions not reached through reference to the best economic analysis but ones reflecting only the interests of some predominant coalition of powerful governments:

> You two brats [the IMF and the World Bank] shall grow up politicians . . . everything you shall determine shall not be for its own merits, but because of something else.(24)

Of necessity, the two institutions had a specifically political element. Goals cannot be chosen by empirical analysis; they are a matter of political judgement. Furthermore, economists can disagree on the effects of proposed policies. Some extrascientific means is needed to determine whose economic analysis will guide policy making. Keynes's deep worry was that the political mechanisms in the postwar system would assure that his own sort of economic analysis would rarely be employed to solve policy problems.

He had reason to worry, given the political principle the postwar institutions would adhere to when resolving disputes that could not be resolved by referring to economic theory. This principle is that nations should be able to influence such decisions in proportion to the strength of their economies. Keynes's fears were well grounded because of the predominance of the American economy and the propensity of American policy makers to prefer laissez faire analysis. In the IMF and the World Bank the principle of granting influence in proportion to the strength took the form of voting rights weighted on the basis of a formula primarily reflecting levels of production.(25) Even under the GATT this principle was established through rules for negotiating tariff reductions which required states not to award preferential tariffs to any nation while encouraging direct bargaining between all nations.

Nations with more diverse and productive economies could make more concessions than poorer nations in order to achieve the specific liberalizations they desired, and they could stop making concessions long before reducing all their barriers to trade with poorer countries.(26)

Due to their adherence to this political principle, the IMF and World Bank could only become widely legitimate management institutions if their most powerful members sometimes acted selflessly. Wealthy members had to restrain themselves from using those institutions soley to advance their own interests and their own ideas about correct economics.

Some American actions in the forties suggest the U.S. accepted this restrained leadership role; others suggest the U.S. abandoned the role to pursue interests that were narrowly its own.

At first, in the late forties, many governments came to question the American commitment primarily because the U.S. started to insist upon its free trade principles as soon as the ITO negotiations began. Editorials in the liberal London Economist are good indications of European and developed Commonwealth doubts. During the first ITO conference in 1945 the Economist's exasperated editor wrote of the American delegate that his, "simple-minded identification of free trade with prosperity, world peace, and economic freedom sounded out of date."(27) Throughout the following two years the Economist would decry the U.S. for caring a great deal about increasing the volume of world trade while failing to recognize that a modern economy has other needs than maximizing wealth,(28) for offering much to American business in its ITO proposals while offering nothing that would aid the world's working people, and for failing to offer to redistribute the world's wealth in the face of existing global scarcities.(29) The last point reflected the fact that the Europeans' slowly growing awareness of the extent of the war's destruction made them ask that the U.S. share its wealth.

New American pledges of economic aid for postwar reconstruction of the formerly wealthy parts of the world, over and above pledges to the World Bank, certainly reflected American willingness to accept some of the responsibilities Europeans understood to be incumbent upon the world economy's leader. After the announcement of significant loans to Britain and the development of the Marshall Plan, the tone of the Economist's editorials changed. They first accepted and ultimately supported British involvement in a global economic system under American leadership. The U.S., while it called the shots, still loaned enough that others could join the game.(30)

European demands for American aid triggered similar demands from those poor nations which, like Ethiopia and a few countries in Asia, had suffered from the war as long as any other Allied state. Those countries had not been included in the American programs. Similar demands even came from poorer countries that had not been so directly affected by the war.

At the 1947 ITO conference, where the GATT was negotiated, American pledges of aid became a salient issue. Actual American pledges of aid served to diminish European and developed Commonwealth insistence upon a postwar regime that would allow wide trade restrictions. At the 1947 conference, pledges of Marshall Plan aid even created a majority behind the preliminary charter proposed by the U.S. Pledged aid could provide the capital for industrial reconstruction, including purchases from the U.S. that would serve to keep the American economy booming; the U.S. had removed the need to restrict trade in order to force domestic reinvestment, and had shown itself willing to intervene aggressively to make sure its own economy did not go into recession.(31)

In 1948, partially toward the same end of achieving agreement on free trade principles, the U.S. government offered to cooperate within the United Nations system to encourage economic development in countries that had never been industrialized. This offer was less effective than promised Marshall Plan aid in rallying support for American proposals since it was tied to the requirement that the U.S. government be allowed to evaluate the extent to which development plans were ". . . soundly conceived, mutually consistent, and effectively coordinated."(32) The second Annual Report of the World Bank, publicizing the bank's lending policies for the first time, suggested what those words might mean both to the only existing United Nations aid organization and to its most powerful member. The report stressed that governments applying for aid should encourage liberal trade and the free flow of capital within their country as well as see that all their national debts to private firms, most of which were firms in the U.S., were quickly paid.(33) Rather than construing the American offer as one of exchanging development aid for acceptance of international laissez faire, most less industrialized nations read the American offer as an attempt to prescribe internal as well as external free market economies in the interest of American firms.

Between 1947 and 1948 the ITO conference moved from Europe to Havana and expanded to include many more representatives of Asian and Latin American countries. In Havana the United States made its pledges to provide aid to poorer countries within the U.N. But throughout the conference, delegates from Asian and Latin American countries waited in vain for the U.S. to announce a program of the scale and kind of the Marshall Plan -- a program of substantial direct aid to the development projects chosen by leaders in recipient countries. A

clear American statement came only after the ITO conference. At the Inter-American conference in Bogota a
reporter confronted Secretary Marshall with the argument
that the economic need of Latin America was greater than
that of Europe because on average Latin Americans
consumed fewer calories than Europeans. Marshall answered
that the United States planned no direct aid to Latin
America. He said that the benefits of American aid to
Europe would "trickle down" to the poor of Latin America
if Latin American governments accepted free trade
principles. Increasing European demand, particularly for
agricultural (not industrial) goods, would mean economic
growth for Latin America.(34) This was the unacceptable
answer negotiators from the poorer countries had come to
expect by the end of ITO conference.

Without the promise of acceptable American aid, the
majority at the 1948 ITO conference transformed the free
trade charter into the charter of an organization that
could support some restrictive trade policies. Molinari
made his emotional statement about the U.S. position,
quoted at the head of this chapter, at this conference.
Under the leadership of the larger Latin American states
and India, the ITO conference amended the American
proposals by accepting articles governing preferential
tariffs, commodity agreements, and bilateral trade
agreements as well as by accepting the principle that the
ITO would make decisions on the basis of one nation one
vote.(35) But the fluidity of the international situation
in 1948 and the fact that the U.S. did not firmly reject
the less industrialized nations' demands for economic aid
until after the ITO conference allowed American delegates
to retain some free trade elements of their charter,
including the central position of the GATT as the basis
for tariff negotiations.(36)

The charter that came out of the Havana meeting was
a compromise only in the sense that it represented a
middle ground. It was not a compromise acceptable to most
of the governments represented at the meeting. The Havana
Charter, and with it the ITO, died of neglect in the
early fifties after the U.S. Senate and (partially in
response to the U.S. action) all but two other governments failed to ratify it. Ironically, the coalition that
killed the ITO in the U.S. included firms and unions with
protectionist interests that resembled those of the less
industrial states.(37)

In his 1949 inaugural address President Truman
reversed the U.S. position on aid to Asia and Latin
America with his "point four" promises of U.S. technical
assistance. Point four aid, like Marshall Plan aid, came
to be conditional as much upon a potential recipient's
willingness to accept the American security doctrine as
upon willingness to accept the American point of view on
economics. Given the simultaneous rise of the trade and
aid issues on the international agenda in the late

forties, followed by an apparent American willingness to
consider expanding its aid to poorer countries, aid
rather than trade became the more central issue of the
north-south economic debate in the 1950s. But the death
of the ITO was inconclusive. American willingness to aid
southern nations as part of its anticommunist policy
implied no change in American support of its free trade
principles. And Latin American, Asian, and African
acceptance of aid implied no rejection of the sort of
restrictive trade policies they had hoped the ITO would
support.

The grievances of the anti-free trade forces at
Havana did not die, but with the end of an ongoing forum
where each state had an equal opportunity to express its
opinion on trade matters those grievances were removed to
the debates in the central organs of the United Nations,
where aid matters could be discussed as well. The IMF and
World Bank continued to provide opportunities to express
grievances, but the narrow specializations of those
organizations along with their restricted membership and
voting rules made them less likely places for the poorer
countries' protests than the General Assembly. We must
turn to the debates in the General Assembly to see how
Asian, African, and Latin American leaders transformed
their grievances about one new international economic
order into the ideas underlying proposals for another.

ECONOMIC RIGHTS AND DUTIES OF STATES

When the trade issue was placed on the international
agenda in 1945, governments that wanted to retain
national trade regulations were confronted with the
problem of explaining the moral basis for their trade
restrictions. They had to counter the argument that such
regulations were unjust in principle. Within the milieu
of economic ideas in 1945 were at least three possible
"principled" justifications for regulating trade. One was
Keynes's "scientific" principle: If it could be
demonstrated, as the Keynesians felt it could, that
economic efficiency and general welfare would be enhanced
by trade regulation, then the principles of rational
economic policy making would themselves dictate such
regulation. The second possible justification required
invoking traditional ideas of national sovereignty
including the the right of sovereign nations to determine
their own economic policy. The third possible justification could be found in the more complex notion of
sovereignty found in the United Nations Charter, among
other places. One interpretation of the charter allowed
governments to argue that it was both a right of states
to regulate trade and a duty of wealthier states to aid
poorer ones. Because it justified both the trade and aid
arguments that southern nations made they chose this

third principle as the moral basis for the reforms they
requested.

The U.N. Charter barely outlines the economic roles
that the organization has acquired since its inception in
1945. Yet from the earliest meeting of the General
Assembly, the charter's preamble and its more extensive
ninth chapter have provided the sort of moral
justification needed by framers of the emerging New
International Economic Order ideology. In the early years
the charter especially appealed to governments with
little influence in the IMF and World Bank, governments
that could not expect the volume of economic aid that was
given to western Europe. The charter speaks of respecting
"equal rights" of nations large and small, of promoting
better standards of living, full employment, and
development.(38) Moreover, the ninth chapter gives the
responsibility for overseeing the economic roles of the
U.N. and its specialized agencies, like the IMF and the
World Bank, to the General Assembly.(39) In the assembly,
where all states are equally powerful, interested
governments could push for economic development programs
to be undertaken by all U.N. agencies as well as for
policies that would encourage international acceptance of
the idea that each state has the right to regulate its
international trade.

The charter is ambiguous. Its relevant paragraphs
could equally be used as moral justification for the
postwar economic regimes as they had been developed by
1947. The duty of nations to cooperate to improve
standards of living could be considered a mandate for the
cooperation needed to reduce trade barriers. The equal
economic rights of states might be understood as their
equal rights to join and receive the benefits of the IMF,
World Bank, and GATT as well as the more specific rights
to expect reciprocity and equal treatment in tariff
reductions that the GATT was meant to assure.

Governments supporting trade regulations would never
come to interpret the charter's economic principles in
that way. From the earliest negotiations on the formation of the United Nations, eastern European socialist
governments as well as most of those from the later-to-
emerge third world took the charter to grant U.N. members
the rights to choose both a domestic system of ownership
and control of property and an international orientation
of their economy, the right to choose either a more open
or more closed system. Understood in this way, the
economic rights of national governments precluded the
creation of a universal free trade and free enterprise
system so long as any state, for whatever reason,
supported a more closed or planned economy. Under this
interpretation, the charter's sections about the duties
of states could not be understood as duties to support
the postwar regimes extant in the late 1940s. U.N.
members who opposed the postwar order had to give those

sections of the charter new meaning.

In its simplest form, the interpretation third world (but not eastern European) opponents came to accept demanded that every state aid the economic development of every other state to the best of its ability and with the relative needs of all states in mind. The south understood the equal rights of states as giving each government the right to choose its own development path, while believing material support of every nation's particular development program to be an international matter.

This principle might be summarized as, "from each state according to its ability, to each state according to its need" in order to emphasize two things about the ethic the south developed from the U.N. Charter: (1) It concerned states rather than individuals or corporations as the moral agents of international economic relations, and (2) it implied aid should be awarded on the basis of need, to the extent that donors could provide it, not on the basis of mutual interest or out of charity.

This utopian principle, the ethic for a sort of global communism of nations, had a short practical life in the mid-1940s as the principle governing the policies of the United Nations Relief and Rehabilitation Administration (UNRRA), especially when it was directed by former New York Mayor Fiorello La Guardia. Because La Guardia was the first person to argue within the U.N. for the principles that would come to underlie southern demands for reformed international economic relations throughout the three decades following UNRRA's dismantling, his views are worth discussing in some detail.

La Guardia spoke before the Second (Economic) Committee at the first meeting of the General Assembly in the fall of 1946. He had directed UNRAA for less than a year but the organization was not much older. The U.S. had created UNRRA during the war to provide food and other needed goods to areas liberated from the Axis powers. Contributions from noncombatant "United Nations," the wartime allies, served to ease the economic burden of the war on the United States and firm up the commitment of the noncombatant states to the Allied effort. Latin America donated a politically significant part of UNRRA's resources.(40) Controversy marked La Guardia's short tenure at UNRRA. He wanted to assure that relief operations would continue at a time when they were becoming burdensome to American policy makers. He displeased Washington with his policy of political blindness in distributing aid. La Guardia refused to use UNRRA to punish advances by communist parties in eastern Europe. When he testified before the Second Committee he took part in a lively debate with the U.S. representative, Adlai Stevenson, about principles that should govern the postwar economic order.

La Guardia came to the General Assembly to advocate

the creation of international agencies to continue
UNRRA's work after it ceased operation in 1947.(41) He
wanted those ongoing organizations to be guided by what
he believed were UNRRA's principles. Those included a
view of nations as collections of individuals sharing
culturally distinct means of meeting common human
economic needs. While people might consent out of
conviction, indifference, or fear to different sorts of
governments, a nation's form of government (and its sort
of economic policies) could be ignored when evaluating
the extent of its economic needs. To do otherwise, for La
Guardia, would be to violate the U.N. Charter.(42)

In 1946 La Guardia saw the world's greatest economic
needs in central Europe where many people actually
starved or had no shelter. As soon as international
efforts had met those needs, other jobs would become more
important. La Guardia felt international organizations
should then begin to focus on regions of the world where
the next most crucial human needs existed, the war-
devastated areas outside Europe. Even after these areas
were rebuilt, international aid would still be needed. La
Guardia called the next most crucial needs the ones for
"public works projects and industrialization" in what in
those days were called "backward" nations.(43)

La Guardia felt this ongoing system of international
aid should always be financed by the more advantaged
nations. Given the deep poverty of many in Europe in
1946, it struck him as appropriate that UNRRA's funds
came from all other parts of the world, including from
the Latin American states which he noted gave especially
generously relative to their wealth. In the future La
Guardia hoped that those nations themselves would be
recipients of aid. He hoped that other U.N. agencies
governed by these principles would be created, a
children's fund and a basic relief agency.(44)

Stevenson adamantly rejected La Guardia's proposals
on two grounds. "The U.S.," the official U.N. summary of
his speech says, "could not participate in a plan based
on a principle of mandatory allocation," like the one
UNRRA was suppose to have followed. The U.S. rejected the
idea that every state owes something to the economic
development of all less advantaged states. Moreover, the
U.S. rejected the idea that any aid it happened to offer
-- out of charity or in line with national interests --
should be allocated by a multilateral agency on the basis
of that agency's judgement of "need." According to
Stevenson, for efficiency's sake alone donor nations had
the right to expect political and economic conditions to
be met by recipients of aid. "Delays and inequitable
distribution" would result from international management
of aid because governments with no material interest in
the productive use of funds, governments other than the
donor and recipient, would have influence over
transactions.(45)

La Guardia argued that Stevenson's rejection
reflected a selfish American desire to limit its aid
commitments in hopes that it could get political
advantages from doing what was only its duty:

If the U.S. is a country of great resources it
should be remembered that God made its citizens
trustees of His bounty. Citizens of the U.S. are
naturally generous and would disapprove of any plan
requiring a country to humiliate itself in return
for assistance.(46)

La Guardia's notion of the ethic that should guide
international assistance never became a guide for
American aid policy nor did many American citizens ever
complain about the strings attached to American aid
promises. Observers at the time did credit La Guardia
with convincing U.N. delegates to approve of UNICEF,(47)
but UNRRA itself was disbanded and not replaced by
another U.N. agency with the same operational ideology.
And even though the World Bank began to lend money to
less developed countries at the time La Guardia had
suggested it would become appropriate, after the critical
poverty in the war torn countries had been allieviated,
the bank adopted criteria other than "need" for
allocating its resources.

The significance of La Guardia's testimony comes
from the way leaders with objections to the postwar
regimes adopted UNRRA's ethic to justify their grievances. La Guardia had outlined a moral justification for
multilateral economic aid programs which Asian and Latin
American officials then joined to traditional notions of
sovereignty to create a summary of the basic economic
rights and duties of states. They linked that ethic
through the UNRRA precedent to the U.N. Charter. The
precedent also let them argue that the powerful nations
had once accepted the new ethic as legitmate, at least
when UNRRA and the U.N. were created. The ethic
sanctioned both national regulation of trade -- as a
reflection of sovereign economic rights -- and demands
for economic aid to the third world that would have no
political or economic conditions.

As early as 1946 southern spokesman justified the
reforms they wanted with this ethic. They used their
principle the same way American free trade advocates used
theirs. The new interpretation of the economic rights and
duties of states validated only one set of policies
designed to achieve the internationally agreed upon goal
of increasing production while precluding others on moral
grounds. Southern spokesmen first used their view to
justify U.N. technical assistance programs to "backward
countries;" then to explain why it was right to create
U.N. economic commissions for Latin America, Asia, and
the Middle East; and finally to argue for the creation of

a Special United Nations Fund for Economic Development
(SUNFED), all before 1960.

There is a certain neatness in these principles, at
least for governments that want international approval
for their trade regulations as well as international
support for their development programs. If, in the late
1940s, the governments that had both of these interests
had adopted either of the two other available sets of
principles, their interests would not have been as well
served.

Keynes's principle that international economic
relations should be governed by policies chosen on their
economic merits alone would have demanded that national
development programs be subject to international monitoring and evaluation. The south's proposed economic
rights and duties of states gave national governments
primary jurisdiction in deciding development goals and
evaluating the success of their own development plans.
Keynes's principles might have forced some national
governments to adopt economic development programs which
destroyed their indigenous cultural bases of support in
the name of economic efficiency, something no government
would knowingly do. By referring to the economic rights
and duties of states, the government of a country that
received aid could protect any traditional national
social institution from the impact of foreign aid,
whether that institution be as irrelevant to economic
efficiency as local habits of dress or as significant as
the power structure traditionally supporting the
government.

References to older notions of national sovereignty
could have justified southern refusal to accept
conditional international aid, but older views would not
have justified the southern premise that aid should be
forthcoming in the first place. The UNRRA precedent, and
La Guardia's view of the UNRRA and U.N. Charter
principles, provided that premise.

It would be incorrect to assume that the support
"backward" nations gave to UNRRA interpretations of the
rights and duties of states was merely "ideological" in
the pejorative sense of the term. Certainly their shared
interests "ideologically" constrained their choice among
available principles. The less industrialized nations
could have chosen no other available principles as long
as they wanted to maintain their old interest in using
some trade restrictions and still pursue their new
interest in exploiting the opportunities available in an
international system in which, for the first time, most
nations accepted that it was a duty of wealthier states
to aid at least some types of poorer states. Acceptance
of their principles would mean that, after European
reconstruction, the "backward" states would be the only
rightful recipients of material aid; nevertheless,
nothing the less industrialized states did at the time

suggests that they masked any other purposes when they
adopted their principles, nor do any of their actions
suggest that they adopted these principles without
sincerity.

In assessing southern motives we must remember that
in 1946 the distinctions between rich and poor nations,
as well as the equation of the absence of poverty and the
presence of wealth with economic development that we
commonly accept today, were not so clear. When the
Brazilian delegate rose during the first year's debate in
the Second Committee to propose a U.N. technical
assistance program to Latin America and Asia for the
first time, he represented a country that had given 1
percent of its previous year's production to European
recovery, a country that due to its overall wealth and in
spite of the poverty of most of its people and its
"backwardness" (lack of industry) Cordell Hull had wanted
to make a permanent member of the Security Council.(48)
When the Mexican delegate proposed the establishment of a
U.N. economic commission for Latin America, modeled on
one already in the works for Europe, and justified
financing his proposal out of general revenues on the
basis of U.N. Charter duties of states to aid other
states in developing economic plans, he represented a
country that, like many other Latin American countries,
had given around .3 percent of its income to the poor in
Europe during the previous year.(49) India's general
proposals for international cooperation to assure
worldwide industrialization, raised the next year, were
championed by a representative who had reason to believe
that his country's use of sterling as national reserve,
rather than some stronger medium, represented a major
sacrifice to aid British recovery, especially after
British postwar devaluations had cut India's reserves
almost in half.(50) In the earliest years of the United
Nations, the governments that said that all nations had
duties to aid the economic development of poorer nations
could point to their own example of adherence to that
principle.

In the late forties and throughout the fifties the
south employed their new principles the most persistently
when arguing for the Special United Nations Fund for
Economic Development. In 1949 India's V. K. R. V. Rao
submitted an outline of such a fund to a U.N. commission
he then headed. Little more was done with the proposal
that year.(51) While nothing was heard about it on the
floor of the General Assembly, Lebanon's George Hakim
spoke extensively about a similar proposal to the Second
Committee.(52) He outlined the need for the fund in terms
of the limitations of the World Bank. The bank, as
originally constituted, had to give assistance to
projects that would have predictable, direct economic
returns; the institutions was, after all, a bank. It
loaned money and expected repayment with interest. The

bank did not have money for infrastructure projects -- building roads and ports, for example -- that, in themselves, would not provide returns. In its early years the bank rarely provided funds for what La Guardia had called the "public works projects" needed in less industrialized countries.

All the early arguments for SUNFED linked the fund to that need and even to exact language and arguments used to support La Guardia's position during the very first meetings of the Second Committee. Hakim's first speech paraphrased a speech made by Roberto de Oliveira Campos a year earlier. In that speech the Brazilian delegate had mixed praise for existing U.N. technical assistance programs; he considered them worthwhile as the "only things the U.N. can do" for less industrialized countries because the World Bank had yet to provide significant loans to any of them and because UNRRA had been disbanded.(53) Campos's speech, in turn, reiterated the 1946 debate in which the Brazilian delegate had first proposed U.N. technical assistance as a program justified by the charter's sections on economic development as embodied in UNRRA and in which the Argentine delegate, after noting the size of his country's contribution to European recovery, had proposed that making UNRRA a permanent international organization would be the best way to institutionalize the organization's view of evolving development needs.(54)

Rao's and Hakim's proposals, and all the subsequent southern proposals based on them, were opposed by most developed states for years. In the end the U.N. institutionalized them only in part, through the creation of a small Special Fund that the U.S. proposed as a compromise.(55) In addition the World Bank created a facility which would provide loans to infrastructure projects in countries with little industry, the International Development Association (IDA).(56)

Two days after Hakim made his proposal in 1949, his colleague from Turkey proposed another type of international capital assistance, the provision of funds to private corporations through a World Bank International Finance Corporation (IFC) to encourage foreign investment in poorer nations. The IFC could be more easily reconciled to the dominant ideology's concerns with private enterprise than could SUNFED, so it was adopted much more quickly and completely. Nonetheless, despite the fact that the IFC could have been justified under the dominant ideology, the delegate who first proposed it to the Second Committee did just what Hakim had done. He pointed to the precedent of U.N. technical assistance and to the aid duties suggested in the southern view of the U.N. Charter. Ultimately, the Turkish representative linked the duty of wealthy states to provide the funds through which the IFC would insure private investment to responsibilities incumbent upon the rich just because of their wealth. For him aid was "not charity" but an affirmation of the unity of mankind.(57)

In the early fifties the south also combined the suggestion that resource owners had a duty to use their resources for the good of all with the issues of foreign investment in another way to create the most controversial application of their principles that they made before 1960. Wealthy market states firmly rejected this application even though it implied that poorer states had economic duties that most had never before conceded.

This controversial application first appeared in 1952 during the debates over the Universal Declaration of Human Rights. The Chilean representative, applying the south's new principles, proposed that states had the right of sovereignty over their natural resources.(58) DMC delegates correctly interpreted this statement as implying that governments had the right to set the level of compensation for property seized from foreign nationals. In that form the notion had a long tradition, particularly in relations between the United States and Latin American governments. Latin American lawyers first developed the idea specifically as a justification for compensating nationalized American extractive firms at levels lower than both the firms and the U.S. government thought fair. Throughout the twentieth century few Latin American governments had ever announced exceptions to this principle; even though all quietly accepted levels of compensation dictated by international arbitration and foreign governments, they always emphasized they had the right not to do so.(59)

Raising the principle of a state's right to control its resources under the broader principles of the economic rights and duties of states added a new element, however. Advocates of the principle proposed that while a nation had a right to choose how its resources were to be used it also had a duty to choose a way to use those resources that would benefit people throughout the world. When southern delegates such as the Chilean representative raised this point in the 1950s, DMC representatives considered it to be little more than a meaningless rhetorical flourish. Hindsight suggests that wealthy states missed a chance at the beginning of the New International Economic Order debate to set guidelines for the responsible use of natural resources that would have been useful to the north in the mid-seventies when southern oil owners helped make the NIEO appear new again.

In contrast to the north's failure to call upon the south to consistently recognize the limits on national action imposed by their new principles, the less developed states did call upon each other to demonstrate their complete adherence to their new principles very early on. Such demonstrations helped to strengthen the very loose southern coalition. From the mid-fifties

onward further development of the emerging ideology went
hand in hand with new concrete steps toward a formal
third world alliance.
   Treaties between India and China in the fifties
initiated this trend. Those treaties provided a new,
deeper level of moral justification for the rights and
duties of states the south demanded. Five principles of
peaceful coexistence framed the first major treaty after
the Chinese revolution between the new government and
India. Nehru would dub these the "Panch Shila" following
Sukarno's use of this Sanskrit translation of "five
principles" to identify the moral bases for his
government in Indonesia. The two sets of five principles
were similar. The international Panch Shila, in the most
limited interpretation, recognize the rights of states to
have different economic and political systems. In that
sense, an American legal scholar correctly identifies
them as the old wine of European ideas about the rights
of sovereignties placed in an eastern bottle with a
Sanskrit label.(60) But from the very beginning those who
affirmed the Panch Shila illustrated that that the
principles meant much more.
   Asian nations with radically different internal
economies first used those principles to frame pledges of
mutual aid. They said that the minimal duty of states
toward one another was mutual noninterference in their
internal affairs, i.e., mutual acceptance of differences,
and that all further cooperation must continue to develop
on that basis. Ethical international economic aid
programs, for example, could only be aimed at assuring
the success of the unique economic system that the
recipient had chosen. And the Panch Shila affirmed that
the path toward international unity was through
diversity. In the first instance, the Panch Shila
justified what, to minds schooled in the cold war ideas
of the industrialized states, seems to be an impossible
pledge of Indian aid to help China develop its radically
socialist economy in exchange for helping develop the
mixed, but still fundamentally capitalist, economy of
India.(61)
   As subsequent Sino-Indian relations illustrate, it
is difficult for states with different national economic
ideologies and long standing disputes to consistently
maintain cooperation under the Panch Shila. But
recognition of that fact should not tempt us to ignore
the political importance of those principles. With
inconsequential modifications they have been included in
all the key agreements among third world countries that
became the background for the New International Economic
Order proposals.(62) Those agreements never demanded the
impossible achievement of complete economic integration
between states with fundamentally different economic
doctrines. Rather, they demanded efforts of good faith
aimed at identifying and fostering those parts of the

economic systems within each country that could be
uniquely developed. Those who affirm the Panch Shila have
criticized both socialists and liberals, but only those
socialists and liberals who seem convinced that such a
good faith effort across systems is immoral or pointless.
    Respect for cultural differences underlies both the
Panch Shila and La Guardia's interpretation of UNRAA and
U.N. Charter principles. When Sukarno used the Sanskrit
words to label principles for Indonesian government he
made a similar point quite clear. He contrasted
"cosmopolitanism" to the "internationalism" expressed by
the Panch Shila. "Cosmopolitans" believe that
international cooperation, as well as national
integration, develop as differences between people are
abolished, when people from different cultures come to
share the same family customs, economic systems,
language, philosophy, and government. "Internationalists"
hold the view that cooperation develops when
collaboration aids the unique concerns of each
culture.(63) Similar distinctions could be made between
different views of how to develop cooperative social
relations in a large multiethnic city, like New York. On
the one hand, some say cities should serve as melting
pots, bringing people from cultures foreign to each other
together into a single culture. Others argue that
cultural diversity strengthens a city and that urban
government should foster tolerance of diversity and
further cooperation building on that tolerance and
preserving that diversity. La Guardia, of course,
advocated the latter view more than the former.(64)
    The importance of this view to international
economic relations may have little to do with the fact
that these ideas were developed by leaders of multiethnic
communities. Clearly global economic management involves
collaboration among people from very different cultures,
so that an ethic based on recognition of that fact may be
more relevant than one which ignores cultural diversity.
But to guide actual management of the global economy,
such an ethic would have to be more clearly defined than
it was, at least in the early days of the third world
alliance. It would have to pinpoint those elements of
"culture" which are to be tolerated, preserved, and
strengthened by cooperation. In most multicultural
polities, including India, Indonesia, and New York City,
leaders have simultaneously used both "internationalist"
and "cosmopolitan" ethics to justify particular parts of
the government's program.(65) The global political
importance of the "internationalist" ethic stems from the
fact that it provided a further level of ethical
grounding for the south's view of the economic rights and
duties of states. And unlike their view of the rights and
duties, the south's "internationalism" could be directly
contrasted with an element of the dominant ideology, the
"cosmopolitanism" which serves as a deeper level of

justification for the Bretton Woods system.

Many social scientists are already familiar with the "internationalist" arguments against Bretton Woods. American scholars' frequent "critiques of liberalism" in the 1960s and 1970s focused on the same pattern of beliefs that Sukarno called "cosmopolitanism" in the fifties. Robert Packenham in Liberal America and the Third World does a particularly good job of illustrating the prevalence of those beliefs among scholars and policy makers responsible for U.S. aid programs since Truman's Point Four speech.(66) But in his critique of U.S. foreign policy Garry Wills has probably appropriated the most apt name for the cluster of beliefs, "universalism," the conviction that the economic and political goals and policies which have proven to be appropriate for one nation -- in particular, American economic liberalism -- are appropriate for the rest of the world. From this universalist point of view, international cooperation builds in stages as more nations accept "universal" policies held to be worthwhile for all.(67)

Sukarno and other third world leaders in the fifties did not have the insights of later social scientists to guide them when they perceived that "cosmopolitanism" was prevalent and harmful to their interests. They did have their instructive experience with the new Bretton Woods system. Taken together, the charters of the IMF, World Bank, and GATT affirmed that international cooperation would develop as states accepted the principles of limited intergovernmental intervention in the world economy and the goal of free trade. U.S. and World Bank policies of excluding many socialist countries from the aid system demonstrated that the emerging global regimes were little concerned with cooperation that might be based upon fostering fundamental differences between states. Many of the framers of the postwar system refused to tolerate fundamental differences in economic policy. The men who most influenced the policies of the emerging system believed that, " . . . free enterprise is, or eventually will be, universal."(68) They linked this view to the one we have already seen Stevenson express, that bilateral aid was more efficient than multilateral aid because the wealth of the donors -- their mere ability to give aid -- provided prima facie evidence that they had discovered effective economic policies. The donors' wealth suggested that any restrictions they might place on the use of aid funds would, in fact, make development more efficient. The dominant ideology held that there was one best way to develop.

In a complementary view, throughout the 1950s both the U.S. government and the World Bank explained the south's lack of economic development in terms of local "cultural" constraints:

. . . lack of traditions of political responsibility, weakness of economic initiative . . . and insufficient understanding that economic progress requires patience, effort, and self-denial.(69)

While the U.S. government and the bank demanded changes in these "cultural attributes" as preconditions for the international cooperation that aid funds represented, third world governments demanded toleration and encouragement of many of the same habits the donors wished to abolish. Southern officials, of course, had very different names for the same habits referred to in the above quotation from the bank's 1953 Annual Report.

Even earlier evidence of the significance of this univeralist idea can be cited. The apparent U.S. policy of encouraging international agreement on the postwar institutions by bringing up the least controversial items first also reflected American universalist beliefs: Without recognizing the right of every state to have a different sort of economy, the United States encouraged the widest possible agreement among governments only because those agreements reflected goals and policies which the American experience had proven to be valuable.

In refusing to accept the American experience -- or any other model -- as a guide for all economic development, third world governments affirmed that a country's economic system should reflect its cultural history and, thus, should be part of its unique culture, a culture which not only had a right to exist, but which other states had a duty to foster. In addition, third world governments acted as if the only valid interpretation of a country's culture was the government's own. This assumption linked third world "internationalism" back to the economic rights and duties of states. It suggested another principle, maintaining the world's cultural diversity, as a value to be fostered by the global economic system. The conflict between "internationalists" affirming the need for cultural diversity, on the one hand, and "cosmopolitans" affirming economic policies they held to be universally valid, on the other, became one of the deepest, and least discussed, divisions underlying the current north-south conflict.

The south's increasingly complex moral position did more than help LDC governments understand their conflict of interest with the north. It allowed them to create an unusually broad alliance. In a sense, it gave prior moral justification for the inevitable disagreements that the members in the vast alliance would have. It provided a cooperative way to accept those differences.

National economic and political ideologies never became a threat to the alliance because the third world's moral principles provided a nest of justifications for those differences. When cooperation developed between third world states with conflicting national development

ideologies -- like Keynesian liberalism and Leninism --
leaders of those countries could pursue their cooperation
without cognitive inconsistency by referring to the
principle that "international cooperation develops on the
basis of mutual recognition of cultural differences."
Conflicting development ideologies just reflected
different national cultures. When everyone was aware that
the actual differences were less "cultural" than
ideological, the cooperating governments could invoke the
"right of states to choose their own development path."
      Those who apply the shared third world ideology the
most masterfully, Tanzania's President Julius Nyerere for
example, also recognize that one deeper justification for
"maintaining cultural diversity" is the fact that the
knowledge embodied in every society is limited. Thus, it
is in each society's own interest to support the very
different plans made by societies that share only some of
its goals. The knowledge embodied in the foreign culture
may turn out to be helpful to you later. Nyerere, once
one of his generation's most sincere and articulate
spokesmen for democratic socialism, has no trouble
praising the antisocialist development plans of a third
world ally like the Ivory Coast or even accepting (at
least for a while) the antidemocratic political system
established by his much closer allies in Zanzibar.(70)
      The nest of southern justifications for cooperation
between states holding different views is so deep that
members of the southern alliance have only rarely had to
invoke the condescending expedient that most states with
"universalist" ideologies use to explain why they
cooperate with states that ignore their views. Third
world states rarely have had to argue that their allies'
views are "appropriate at this time" because of the
allies' present (presumably, lower) state of economic or
cultural development in the way the democratic U.S.
sometimes argues for its authoritarian allies' views and
the way the socialist Soviet Union sometimes argues for
its nonsocialist friends' systems.

THIRD WORLD INDUSTRIAL DEVELOPMENT

      In order to maintain cooperation under their
extremely flexible moral framework, Asian, African, and
Latin American states had to share some fundamental
goals. To last as long as it has, southern cooperation
had to based on something more than the habit that
reinforced the southern desire to continue trade
restrictions after the war or the opportunism that
contributed to the first southern calls for international
aid. In addition the south's basic goals had to be ones
that international regimes could be designed to achieve
even though the Bretton Woods institutions did not accept
them.

The goals institutionalized by the Bretton Woods regimes in the late forties were simple and few: Expanding global trade and production and thus, according to many of the regimes' advocates, removing the preconditions for the world wars. Advocates of the earliest proposals for technical assistance to Latin American and Asian countries even justified that policy with the argument that the reconstruction of Europe and the expansion of world trade desired by all would be quickened if LDC agricultural surpluses could reach port more easily; technical assistance in improving internal transportation, they argued, would help expand global trade and production.(71) But even when they referred to expanding global trade and production as reasons for the reforms they proposed, southern spokesman also talked about the goal of industrializing the economies of "backward" nations. They discussed that goal more frequently and feverently.

Just as American State Department justifications for free trade rested upon both a moral theory and an economic, southern insistence upon internationally supported industrialization had the same dual ideological underpinning. The principles of states' economic rights and duties said it was the duty of industrial nations to aid the industrialization of any LDC that chose industrialization as its development path, even if that might not be the most efficient way to expand global production. In addition, governments supporting industrialization argued that it was, in fact, the most effective way to achieve maximum growth.

Since the free trade theories underlying the postwar system considered specialization rather than industrialization to be the most effective development policy conflict over goals between followers of the dominant ideology and those who invented the new alternative was inevitable. At the ITO conferences Latin American and Asian officials aimed their proposals for restrictive trade practices toward industrialization. To American ITO negotiator Clair Wilcox, southern emphasis on industrialization was a "fetish." Even if some countries that had not been industrialized before the war did have some sort of comparative advantage in producing some industrial lines, only an open world economy would encourage the foreign capital investment that would provide the most efficient way to develop that advantage. Such was the lesson of free trade theory.(72)

Unlike Wilcox, some Asians and Latin Americans began their analysis with the Keynesian fear that industrial monopolies would choose the conservative, but still profitable, strategy of investing where they had invested before in lieu of searching out more profitable investments in the "backward" countries. Others just began their analysis with the observation that industrial countries and regions were always richer than culturally

similar regions and nations without industry.
Nineteen forty-five saw the publication of two major
statistical studies highlighting this fact, one by the
League of Nations, the other by the Oxford statistical
institute. The league report advocated industrialization
in LDCs not for import substitution, as had been the
policy in many Latin American states since the 1920s, but
to raise employment levels and supplement, rather than
replace, products imported. The league report suggested
that if richer countries helped poorer ones
industrialize, the poor would have more with which to buy
things from the rich. Trade would increase.(73) The
Oxford report reached some of the same conclusions. Poor
nations had to industrialize in order to abolish
disguised rural unemployment. A free trade system without
special programs to industrialize the "backward" regions
would just maintain an existing, destructive global
division of labor and wealth.(74)
After the U.N. created economic commissions for the
developing regions, authoritative analysis praising
industrialization became commonplace. Developments in
economic analysis quickened the international debate. In
the autumn of 1948, after the Havana conference, Latin
American delegates in the General Assembly thanked the
new international professional staffs for improving the
analysis which favored their goal. These staffs had
already gone beyond the simple correlation that people in
industrial nations were richer to work toward an
explanation. They called underemployment -- habitual part
time work and inefficiently done work -- the cause of
underdevelopment in the nonindustrial nations. The Oxford
study had already said as much. The U.N. added that LDCs
specialized in high-underemployment, nonindustrial
products only as a result of colonialism.(75)
Reports of the Second Committee's annual debate in
1948 demonstrate that as soon as industrialization became
an openly discussed topic, the ideological split between
north and south became obvious. Misunderstanding
abounded. At one point the Colombian delegate requested
that the U.N. investigate why underemployment and low
wages typified agricultural countries. The American
delegate responded that the request was foolish. Low
wages just implied unproductive labor; no study needed to
be undertaken to show that. But the Colombian was
searching for some other explanation. He probably would
have accepted the thesis that industrial techniques
themselves raised productivity and hence, as further
consequence, could help raise wages. He may even have
wanted a report that actually explained the origins of
low wages in poorer countries rather than discussing
something correlated ("low productivity") or suggesting a
cure ("industrialization"). Given that he already
believed in industrialization as the cure, he probably
just wanted his thesis authoritatively affirmed. In

contrast, the American delegate's immediate thought about "low productivity" could be made part of a real (although questionable) explanation for low wages in poorer countries. To understand his view, we would need to link it to the American ideas about "cultural impediments" to development that were so popular at the time: People in poorer countries received low wages because they did not produce much; they did not produce much because their cultures did not value work.(76)

Whether primarily as a result of requests like Colombia's or because of his own research inclination, Raul Prebisch of the Economic Commission for Latin America (ECLA) worked throughout 1948 on a study that would offer a different explanation.(77) Prebisch suggested that the global division between a "core" of colonial and former colonial powers engaged in manufacturing, and a "periphery" of former colonies and colonies producing primary products be considered analytically important. He wanted to explain the low wages and disguised unemployment in the periphery, and he wanted to explain why prices of manufactured goods in international trade tended to rise (as he believed they did) and the prices of primary commodities remained constant or fell.

He offered an eminently Keynesian explanation, reflecting his background. It rested upon the powers he assumed large firms, unions, and national governments had to enforce decisions based on their parochial interests. According to Prebisch, unions and firms in industrial nations had the power to assure that what they received for their products could not decline. Production of raw materials involved no global unions. No raw material producers acted like monopolies. They competed with each other. Even whole nations dependent on the sale of a single commodity usually had many other major competitors. The price they received for their goods could, and did at times, go down. Declining LDC terms of trade with rich countries resulted. The decline meant that remuneration to the firms and workers producing southern exports could not grow. Moreover, peripheral economies found it hard to save money to invest in new enterprises to absorb the labor released from increasingly unprofitable export sectors. Industrialization for import substitution, reducing the need to buy increasingly expensive foreign goods, could help the problem. And industrialization of any form would help absorb the unused labor in the LDCs.

Prebisch's analysis later would come under significant attack from all liberal economists, despite his Keynesian roots. Frequently critics charge Prebisch with a naive belief that industrialization is a panacea. His early work leaves itself open for such criticism. Logically, his analysis points to a need for countervailing centers of power in the third world rather than an emphasis on industrialization. Industrialization was just one of many possible ways to solve that problem of employing the unproductive labor in backward countries. Industrialization, in theory, could reduce the dependence of poor countries on products from rich countries. But industrialization, in and of itself, would not neces- sarily increase the relative value of the products the south exported.

Most countries had already chosen industrialization as their first economic goal long before Prebisch published his ideas. It is hardly surprising that he would have discussed such policies or that his policy proposals for industrialization became the first part of his thesis adopted by third world governments. For a very long time, though, southern officials ignored the powers to set prices that firms and unions in industrial countries had. Instead, Prebisch's ideas first appeared in intergovernmental debate when LDCs discussed the economic effects of the rich countries' cold war "strategic stockpiling" policies.

Rearmament in the 1950s, while temporarily driving up the prices of raw materials as wealthy states pur- chased goods for their stockpiles, drove up the prices of technologically sophisticated industrial products even faster. In 1950, Brazil suggested that rearmament was really being undertaken for economic rather than strategic reasons: Rich market countries armed in order to maintain high, wartime levels of employment, a goal the Brazilian government felt could just as easily have been met by increasing production in order to help other countries industrialize.(78)

Throughout the four following years southern governments became increasingly disturbed over the military competition among wealthy states. They fore- casted inevitable declines in the prices of raw materials beginning as soon as wealthy nations began to sell from their strategic stockpiles. Early on Egypt made the position shared by other southern nations clear. Invoking the economic rights and duties of states especially as they apply to those who own resources, an Egyptian U.N. delegate said that if rich nations wanted to stockpile goods or sell from their stockpiles that was their perogative. But their duties to the other nations made it incumbent upon them to also fix the prices of indus- trial goods through similar government involvement in the market. "An equilibrium must be established between the prices of raw materials and the prices of industrial products." Commodity agreements and long term contracts could provide that balance.(79)

Cold war competition affected southern views about aid as just a much as about trade. The cold war intensified the free market bias of the Bretton Woods institutions and restricted available economic aid. The World Bank Annual Report of 1951 used the rearmament of "free nations" as an explicit reason for demanding that underdeveloped countries increase their production of raw materials rather than be concerned with industrialization. The bank, thus, reinforced the specialization argument with considerations of strategic politics.(80) Of course, after Truman's point four speech the World Bank was not the only source of aid funds that the south hoped might be used for industrialization. Other nations even joined the U.S. in establishing bilateral programs as the cold war intensified. This aid, of course, was designed to achieve strategic objectives. Southern economic goals were not always congruent with such objectives. Moreover, in the 1950s wealthy nations frequently diverted promised economic aid to their own or their recipient's military purposes in order to achieve the higher goals at stake in the cold war.

India's powerful foreign minister in the 1950s, Krishna Menon, explains that African and Asian governments called the 1955 Bandung conference in order to share such frustrations with aid programs linked to strategic objectives.(81) The conference adopted the Panch Shila as guidelines for future Afro-Asian relations and argued for the entire range of economic reforms that other southern forums had discussed since the war. At the time of the Bandung conference northern writers began to use the term "third world" to describe these nations that were determined to stay out of the cold war competition.(82) The name stuck. Along with the Panch Shila, the idea of the "third world" defined the new alliance outside the cold war as a set of nations whose economies should be aided by the international community, yet from whom no state should demand political concessions.

Meanwhile, within the General Assembly the same nations' frustrated interest in creating an international aid system not linked to the wealthy states' security goals focused debate on reforms that involved much more than changing language. Third world officials continued to say that multilateral aid was preferable to bilateral aid because multilateral institutions would be less likely to try to serve both economic and strategic goals with the same policy.

Of course, wealthy nations never made support of their cold war positions the only criteria for granting aid, even in the 1950s. They also based their policies on economic analysis designed to identify optimal growth policies. Not surprisingly, the analysis preferred by the poorer recipients and the wealthiest donors continued to differ throughout the decade. But in the fifties, when the science of development economics was in its infancy, north-south disagreements were less dramatic than the rhetoric of the the 1980s might make us think. In fact, through the decade the views of poor aid recipients and rich donors began to converge. Even the U.S. government demoted "specialization" from the central position in its growth doctrine. The U.S. began to talk about the more central roles of foreign investment and technical assistance. Third world analysis remained distinct from that preferred by most donors in only two ways: The third world saw colonialism as the source of their underdevelopment and always saw industrialization as part of the cure. Nevertheless, in the 1950s aid donors and recipients shared the same discourse about hypothetical ways to eradicate underdevelopment.

What assured that development economists as different as (say) a laissez faire advisor to the U.S. government and a Soviet-trained planner would share common ground was the fact that there usually existed a developing country trying to follow a development plan influenced by both of their theories. Three examples illustrate both the unity and the diversity within the early "development" discourse.

First, in the early 1950s the Indian government requested that British Marxist Maurice Dobb report to them on the Soviet experience with central planning. Then the Indians grafted central planning upon their essentially capitalistic development program.(83)

In a second example, many Latin American nations continued to follow import substitution policies, condemning the powers of foreign extractive enterprises and promoting more equal income distribution with land reforms in the countryside while allowing individuals in that part of the industrial sector controlled by nationals to accumulate vast wealth. Paradoxically, the property-protecting, free enterprise Americans encouraged land redistribution in Latin America and in other parts of the third world.(84)

Finally, from the time of the first major public discussion of his development ideas Caribbean economist W. Arthur Lewis had a major impact on development planning, especially in Africa. He called for foreign investment and expropriation of the surpluses generated by farmers, all in order to assure industrialization.(85)

Needless to say, none of these would easily fit into the categories created by the "free enterprise" versus "planning" dicotomy. And the only elements these doctrines clearly share are their emphasis on industrialization and their compatibility with an actively managed international economic system dedicated to the extended principles of states' economic rights and duties.

In addition to the unity and diversity of third world development plans, one other factor unified early development economics: Much of it was invented within the United Nations. While economists working within the U.N. all shared an interest in identifying how international programs could aid third world development, the diversity of approaches advocated outside international organizations was replicated within. For example, while

Gunnar Myrdal of the Economic Commission for Europe shared Prebisch's interest in "structures" that could be historically linked to colonialism and which continued to impede development, he wrote about things like poor education, health, and transportation systems and domestic income inequalities rather than speaking of the unequal distribution around the globe of power over prices.(86) Myrdal pointed to a need for international aid programs like SUNFED. He did not point to a specific need for international pricing agreements. In contrast, W. W. Rostow, who also was connected with the European Commission when he wrote his first book on economic growth, linked poor education, transportation, and economic systems to "cultural impediments to development" -- opposition to science (including liberal economic science), technology, innovation, individual initiative, and even sexual sublimation.(87)

No NIEO advocates of the 1980s consider Rostow one of the U.N. economists of the fifties who influenced the emergence of the new order position, with good reason. Third world officials ignored Rostow's views from the beginning because they rested on an explanation of underdevelopment which challenged the principles under-lying the southern position. Rostow embodied American universalism. His arguments about cultural impediments to development implied that there was only one way to develop. While third world states shared one development goal -- industrialization -- throughout the fifties, they continued to affirm that many paths led to that end.

COMPLETING BRETTON WOODS AND MOVING ON TO DEVELOPMENT

The effects of Rostow's views, nonetheless, exem-plify the convergence between north and south that took place during the fifties. Views like Rostow's helped convince northern governments at the end of the decade to turn from the problems of creating the postwar system to the problems of providing the infrastructure for third world development. In the late fifties the north turned away from its own problems, which had triggered interest in creating the postwar system in the first place, to some of the third world problems that the postwar system had ignored from the beginning.

Histories of the Bretton Woods institutions rarely mention the third world concerns, such as creating the infrastructure for industrial development, when consid-ering the fifties. Third world issues did not have to be resolved in order for the IMF, World Bank, and GATT to become fully operational.

In the fifties only two things kept the World Bank from operating as it was supposed to, as the world's most significant source of funds for development. First, the unexpectedly high cost of European reconstruction had been borne outside the bank through the Marshall Plan. The bank only became significant in its own right as it accumulated capital from its members' annual contributions, which grew as western economies grew. Second, the bank needed to develop its own rationale for granting loans, its operational ideology.

Even while constrained by the fact that its loans had to be made for profitable projects, during the fifties the World Bank developed the ability to fund programs influenced by almost the entire spectrum of opinions on how economic growth could be triggered. Nonetheless, the bank continued to encourage potential borrowers to be open to foreign investment, to support liberal trade policies, and even to support the strategic interests of the DMCs. Yet, even while warning against "premature industrialization," the bank moved toward accepting industrialization as a central part of any development program.

Throughout the fifties the bank funded industrial infrastructure and industrial development projects because those were the sorts of projects designed by the states whose wealth and (relatively) liberal development doctrines appeared to promise that they would be able to repay loans, states like Australia, Italy, Japan, and the Nordic countries.(88) Somewhat unconsciously the World Bank developed a "public works" approach that it found hard to extend to the poorer states not recognized by the international financial community as good credit risks. Yet, by the end of the decade the bank wanted to do just that. By 1958 the bank had commissioned a study of the debt-servicing problems experienced by those poorer states that had tried to finance infrastructure projects with short term loans. As the decade closed, the bank began to solve the problem. It opened the IDA, the long term, low interest loan facility championed by the U.S. in lieu of SUNFED.(89) When it began to operate the way its founder's intended, the World Bank became, in part, the supporter of public works projects and industrialization in the "backward" countries that many who took part in the first U.N. debates had hoped it would become.

Unlike the World Bank, the IMF and GATT experienced more sudden breaks in their development. Those clear breaks assured that influential northern officials would have the opportunity to completely shift their attention from one set of global economic problems to another. That opportunity, in turn, made it possible for northern officials to focus on, and give some support to, the sorts of development policies the bank had come to back.

The IMF could only start working normally when most of its members had agreed to let their currencies be freely exchanged. Buttressed by their growth in the 1950s and relying, ultimately, on an American promise to convert dollars into gold at a fixed rate, most western European nations agreed to make their currencies

convertible at fixed rates in December of 1958. They
removed their national exchange restrictions and agreed
to live within the IMF rules, to maintain balanced
payments and support the relative values of their
currencies through short term borrowing and economic
policies monitored by the IMF.(90)

The GATT required more than the relative stability
and growth of the European economies before it could
become fully operational. The GATT's only enforcement
mechanisms involved requiring each of the contracting
parties to justify both specific trade restrictions and
their trade policy as a whole to the entire membership.
The membership could then approve or withhold approval of
specific restrictions. Prior to 1959 the GATT only heard
cases involving specific restrictions, without evaluating
whole national policies.(91)

Those precedent setting cases reflected the prag-
matic attitude taken by most members. They usually
placated the wealthier of two parties in a trade dispute.
More nations benefited from a wealthy nation's low
tariffs than from the low tariffs of a poor nation, and
the GATT's weak enforcement mechanisms could not induce
nations with diversified economies to comply. GATT
members could only remove trade preferences already
granted. For example, GATT ruled in favor of the U.S. in
a dispute with Czechoslovakia in 1951, establishing the
precedent that trade restrictions were justified for
reasons of national security. In approving the European
Coal and Steel Community in 1951 and in accepting that
West Germany could protect its agricultural sector in
1954, the GATT appeared to accept a principle that
regional economic development plans provided reason
enough for trade restrictions -- a principle that could
be justified under the emerging new order ideology, but
not under the ideology that designers of the postwar
system shared. Nonetheless, in the fifties, the GATT
granted few exceptions to third world countries who
claimed them to be justified by development principles.
Third world delegates, who remained a minority throughout
the decade, often commented on this apparent double
standard.(92)

Despite their complaints, third world members of
GATT did not withdraw. Some changes in the organization
through the decade clearly helped poorer countries. In
particular, the GATT amended its rules in 1956 so that
states whose exports competed with one another could
still demand negotiations to reduce import duties on the
product.(93) An even more significant, although inadvertent, concession to third world interests came in 1955
after it had become abundantly clear that the ITO would
never be formed. The chief author of the report, free
trade theorist Gottfried Haberler, noted that the GATT
had not promoted fully free trade. He condemned quantitative restrictions on third world agricultural products

imposed by DMCs in lieu of the tariffs they had reduced under the GATT.(94) When the report was adopted in 1958, at the same time the GATT became fully operational by adopting its procedures to review each member's complete trade policy, it appeared to promise increasing north-south cooperation.

Other equally positive portents for north-south cooperation appeared at the end of the fifties. Colonialism rapidly ended in all but a few nations; the practice that third world governments had identified as the cause of underdevelopment started to disappear. Prosperous European nations, who saw the convertibility of their currencies as a rite of passage into the membership in economic system on the same level as the United States, took up the call for the economic development of the poorer states. Another sign of that new equality was the abolition of the international organization which had coordinated European recovery and the creation of a successor organization, the Organization for Economic Cooperation and Development (OECD), that would include European nations and the U.S. as members with equal rights and responsibilities. In 1959 the Economist editorialized that the OECD should become something more than a symbol of the wealthy nations' new equality; it should become a real aid agency in recognition of the fact that the problems which led to the creation of the postwar economic institutions had been solved and that now, "the biggest fissure in the world at the moment is between rich and poor." To encourage debate on ways to meet the challenge, the Economist closed the fifties by serializing W. W. Rostow's new Stages of Growth.(95)

Other, less visible, portents contradicted the signs of increasing north-south cooperation perceived and reinforced by the Economist in 1959. We now can see that the maturation of the Bretton Woods institutions just signaled the end both of the first phase in the development of the south's new ideology and of the first phase in the postwar north-south conflict.

In one sense, Rostow's highly touted work (which became increasingly significant when he entered the American government with the Kennedy administration two years later) represented a significant concession to third world interests. Its call for aid and its implicit approval of industrialization rather than unending specialization in nonindustrial products reflected a significant shift in northern attitudes since the forties. Likewise, the reforms in the Bretton Woods system engineered in the fifties -- the IDA and IFC, and the new GATT rules -- along with the U.N.'s own development programs, equally conceded part of the third world opinion.

But official opinion in the third world had long since transformed what started as a simple interest in

industrialization and in using traditional trade policies
toward that end into something much more complex. Before
1960 the leaders of the third world had come to identify
themselves as those excluded from global economic
decision making, those whose economic need was the
greatest, and those who wanted to create a world where
the cultural integrity of each nation was the basis for,
and fostered by, international economic cooperation. New
ideologies give new identities. Even before 1960 the
seeds of the NIEO ideology defined a new international
identity for the governments of Asia, Africa, and Latin
America.

NOTES

(1)Molinari quoted in the Economist, Feb. 21, 1948,
p. 308. Wilcox from his A Charter for World Trade (New
York: Macmillan, 1949), p. 143.
(2)Michael Barrett-Brown, The Economics of
Imperialism (Baltimore: Penguin, 1974), p. 324-25.
(3)See the discussion of these concerns among
American policy makers in Fred C. Block, The Origins of
International Economic Disorder (Berkeley: Univ. of
Calif. Press, 1977).
(4)The most significant work along this line was
Albert O. Hirschman's National Power and the Structure of
Foreign Trade (Berkeley: Univ. of Calif. Press, 1945).
(5)John Maynard Keynes, The Economic Consequences of
the Peace (New York: Harcourt, Brace, and Howe, 1920). On
the impact of this study see Karin Kock, International
Trade and the GATT (Stockholm: Almquist and Wiksell,
1969), p. 4.
(6)See Lloyd C. Gardner, Economic Aspects of New
Deal Diplomacy (Boston: Beacon Press, 1971) and Kock, pp.
14-16.
(7)Phillip W. Bell, The Sterling Area in the
Post-War World (Oxford: Oxford Univ. Press, 1958), pp.
260-63; Bob Fitch and Mary Oppenheimer, Ghana: End of an
Illusion (New York: Monthly Review Press, 1966), p. 42.
(8)United States Department of State Bulletin
[hereafter: "DSOB"] May 3, 1941 and Gardner, p. 195.
(9)Kock, pp. 6-9.
(10)DSOB, May 3, 1941, p. 530.
(11)Kock, p. 6.
(12)DSOB, Oct. 10, 1942, p. 821.
(13)DSOB, May 24, 1941, p. 620.
(14)J. Keith Horsefield, The International Monetary
Fund 1945-1965 (Washington: IMF, 1969), p. 27.
(15)K. W. Rothschild, "The Small Nation in World
Trade," Economic Journal 54 (Apr. 1944): 26-27.
(16)Charles S. Maier, "The Politics of Productivity:
Foundations of American International Economic Policy
After World War Two," International Organization 31

53

(Autumn 1977): 609.
(17)Kock, pp. 32-33.
(18)Ibid., p. 10.
(19)Ibid., p. 11.
(20)On the limited anticyclical role of the IMF delineated in 1946 see William A. Brown, Jr., The United States and the Restoration of World Trade (Washington: Brookings, 1950), p. 83.
(21)Rothschild, p. 31.
(22)Brown, pp. 72-74; Wilcox, pp. 30-41.
(23)Kock, p. 67.
(24)Quoted in Horsefield, p. 123.
(25)Horsefield, pp. 95-96. Given the continuing consequences of the war's devastation and the lack of comparable statistics, the formula for deciding IMF quotas and votes involved many noneconomic consider-ations. It is thus more of an index of "effective power" than any simple economic ranking would be.
(26)Requiring reciprocal concessions based on the principle supplier rule gives bargaining advantages to nations with relatively more commodities to trade (a wider range of possible products from which to choose a concession) and disadvantages those nations that compete with many other nations in selling the same product because none is a "principal supplier" and thus able to claim reciprocal concessions from trading partners. See Kock, p. 63. GATT voting rules follow the one nation one vote principle agreed upon for the ITO in 1948, over the objections of the U.S., which wanted explicitly weighted voting. See Brown, pp. 145-46. Given the GATT's primary role as a tariff negotiation framework, the political principles embodied in its rules for negotiation are more important than those embodied in the contracting parties voting rights. The contracting parties cannot change the GATT rules by a majority vote because the tariff negotiating rules constitute the contract.
(27)Economist, Aug. 18, 1945, p. 221.
(28)Quoted in Kock, p. 4.
(29)Economist, Oct. 26, 1945, p. 652; Sept. 17, 1947, pp. 505-506; Nov. 22, 1947, p. 828.
(30)Economist, July 17, 1948, p. 90.
(31)Economist, Feb. 21, 1948, p. 308; Kock, p. 48.
(32)Brown, p. 98.
(33)World Bank, Annual Report (Washington: 1947), pp. 13-17.
(34)See Harry Price, The Marshall Plan and Its Meaning. (Ithaca: Cornell Univ. Press, 1955), p. 23 on Europeans choosing specific Marshall Plan goals; Brown, p. 136 on Latin American nations waiting for American aid pledges; and the Economist, May 8, 1948, p. 782 for Marshall's speech.
(35)Kock, pp. 41-52.
(36)Ibid.
(37)The best discussion of the demise of the ITO

remains that in Richard N. Gardner's Sterling-Dollar Diplomacy, expanded edition, (New York: Columbia Univ. Press, 1980), pp. 348-80.

(38)Alfred George Moss and Harry Winton, A New International Economic Order: Selected Documents, 1945-1975 (New York: UNITAR), p. 1. Hereafter references to this source will give the name and date of the actual document and its page number in the collection.

(39)Selected Documents, Charter of the United Nations, June 26, 1945, p. 1.

(40)UNRRA asked that all donor nations give two allotments of funds each equal to 1 percent of their national income in 1943. The figures below are from UNRRA, Report of the Director General to the Council (Washington: 1947), p. 55.

Country	Contributions	As % of 1943 Income
Total	$ 3,624,945,884	
Canada	138,738,739	2.00
U.S.A.	2,700,000,000	2.00
Australia	76,800,000	1.97
United Kingdom	624,650,000	1.97
New Zealand	16,640,000	1.96
Brazil	40,000,000	1.72
Iceland	1,435,208	1.71
Dominican Rep.	858,750	1.23
Panama	424,100	1.06
South Africa	18,112,500	1.00
Chile	3,074,516	.47
Nicaragua	120,750	.35
Costa Rica	115,511	.29
Mexico	3,938,223	.28
Paraguay	37,587	.20

(41)United Nations, Summary Record of the Meetings of the Second Committee of the General Assembly First Session, Second Part (Lake Success, NY: 1946), p. 51. Hereafter references to reports of Second Committee will include the session and subsession number, date of the actual debate, and page number in the English summary.

(42)Second, 1.2, Nov. 11, 1946, p. 51, and Dec. 12, p. 139.

(43)Second, 1.2, Nov. 11, 1946, p. 51.

(44)Ibid., p. 50, and see New York Times, Oct. 1, 1946, p. 10.

(45)Second, 1.2, Dec. 6, 1946, pp. 136-37.

(46)Second, 1.2, Dec. 5, 1946, p. 127.

(47)UNICEF, more than any other U.N. agency, follows the aid model La Guardia advocated.

(48)Second, 1.2, Nov. 20, 1946, p. 89. Earlier, Second, 1.1, Jan. 25, 1946, p. 12, Brazil claimed that its government had given 10 percent of its national income to UNRRA, a claim not challenged in the debate. See Cordell Hull, Memoirs (New York: Macmillan, 1948), p. 1678 for his view of Brazil at the time.

(49)See note 40 above.

(50)Second, 2, Oct. 10, 1947, p. 46, and see the discussion in Fitch and Oppenheimer, p. 42.

(51)John G. Hadwen and Johan Kaufman, How United Nations Decisions are Made, (Lyden: A. W. Sythoff, 1960), pp. 85-86.

(52)Second, 4, Oct. 1, 1949, p. 9.

(53)Second, 3, Nov. 2, 1948, pp. 168-69.

(54)Brazil, Second, 1.2, Nov. 20, 1946, p. 89; Argentina, Second, 1.1, Jan. 22, 1946, p. 8.

(55)Hadwen and Kaufman, pp. 95-100.

(56)Ibid., p. 110.

(57)Second, 4, Oct. 3, 1949, p. 17.

(58)United Nations Economic and Social Council, Commission on Human Rights, Official Records, May 2, 1952.

(59)Latin American states based their position on nineteenth century legal theorist Charles Calvo's doctrine that public property reflects the state and that the state has a right to make any private property, including that of foreigners, public in any way that best reflects the state. Prudence, Calvo says, dictates that foreign proprietors be paid for their property. See Edward M. Gallaudet's A Manual for International Law (New York: A. S. Barnes, 1879), an English language text based on Calvo's more extensive work. Especially compare pp. 79-80 to the Human Rights Commission position.

(60)Ada Bozeman, The Future of Law in a Multi-cultural World (Princeton: Princeton Univ. Press, 1971), pp. 6-7.

(61)Michael Brecher, India and World Politics: Krishna Menon's View of the World (New York: Praeger, 1968), p. 143.

(62)A brief comparison of the sections on general principles in the Selected Documents should suffice to prove this point. The Panch Shila appear in the Afro-Asian Conference Communique, April 24, 1955, p. 2, the Belgrade Declaration of the Non-Aligned Countries, Sept. 6, 1961, p. 9, and UNCTAD I: Final Act and Recommendations, June 15, 1964, p. 47-50, to mention a few significant places.

(63)Russell H. Fifield, The Diplomacy of South East Asia: 1945-1958 (New York: Harper, 1958), pp. 108-10.

(64)See La Guardia's acceptance speech, New York Times, March 30, 1946, p. 5.

(65)On Indonesia see Clifford Geertz, "Ideology as a Cultural System," in David E. Apter, ed., Ideology and Discontent (New York: Free Press, 1964), pp. 69-71.

(66)Robert A. Packenham, Liberal America and the Third World (Princeton: Princeton Univ. Press, 1973).

(67)Garry Wills, Nixon Agonistes (New York: New American Library, 1979), pp. 430-39. Two earlier uses of the term "universalism" are also interesting. In Sterling-Dollar Diplomacy, Gardner criticizes the Bretton Woods system for being "universalist" and means by that that the system payed too little attention to regional economic differences and that its framers did not consider the possibility of using regional organization more than the global, "universal" organization. Essentially, he uses the term to frame some Keynesian doubts about the system, suggesting it might not be equally good for everyone. See pp. 381-85 and his later partial revision, pp. xxi-xxii. Hans Morgenthau also talked about "universalism," the "universalism" of twentieth century nationalism. In this century, unlike in the last, nationalism has come to both encompass all other bonds of society and each nation has come to think of its own way of doing things as universally valid; in Politics Among Nations (New York: Alfred A. Knopf, 1948), pp. 267-69.

(68)Kock, p. 7, quoting an article written in 1941 by American free trade advocate, Percy Bidwell.

(69)World Bank, Annual Report (Washington: 1953), p. 9. See also the articles in Bert Hoselitz, The Progress of the Underdeveloped Countries (Chicago: Univ. of Chicago Press, 1952), especially Jacob Viner's "American Aims and the Progress of the Underdeveloped Countries," pp. 175-202.

(70)Nyerere on the Ivory Coast in Juluis K. Nyerere, Freedom and Development (London: Oxford Univ. Press), pp. 12-14; on the political system within Zanzibar, p. 276.

(71)Second, 1.2, Nov. 14, 1946, p. 73; Nov. 20, 1946, p. 89.

(72)Wilcox, p. 30.

(73)League of Nations, Industrialization and World Trade (Geneva: 1945), pp. 30 ff., 70.

(74)Kurt Mandelbaum, The Industrialisation of Backward Areas (Oxford: Institute of Statistics Monograph #2, 1945), pp. 1-4.

(75)Second, 3, Oct. 6, 1948, pp. 13-15.

(76)Colombia, Second, 3, Oct. 13, 1948, p. 60; United States, Oct. 29, 1948, p. 139.

(77)Raul Prebisch, The Economic Development of Latin America and Its Principal Problems (Lake Success: United Nations, 1950).

(78)Second, 5, Nov. 11, 1950, p. 138.

(79)Second, 6, Nov. 20, 1951, p. 19.

(80)World Bank, Annual Report (Washington: 1951), p. 19.

(81)In particular, Asian governments called the Bandung conference to respond to the failing British Colombo Plan, see Brecher, p. 52. Britain sharply limited funds for the plan in 1954 in order to send the bulk of funds to Malaysia where communist insurgents operated. The U.S. indicated it was willing to increase aid to Asia but wanted a specifically anti-communist pact to administer such aid. At first, most Asian nations opposed such a pact as a threat to sovereignty; see the Economist, Sept. 25, 1954, p. 957. Nonetheless, despite the aid issues that triggered the first Afro-Asian meeting, Menon says that the later idea of a nonaligned movement was not a response to economic development problems. See Brecher, p. 4.

(82)Ignancy Sachs, The Discovery of the Third World (Cambridge: MIT Press, 1976), p. xi.

(83)Maurice Dobb, Some Aspects of Economic Development (New Dehli: School of Economics, 1951), and see Gunnar Myrdal's comment on the Indian planning ideology in An Asian Drama, vol. 2, (New York: Twentieth Century Fund, 1971), Chap. 15.

(84)Fernando H. Cardoso, "The Originality of a Copy: CEPAL and the Idea of Development," CEPAL Review 22 (Second half of 1977): 24-29.

(85)W. Arthur Lewis, Aspects of Industrialization (Cairo: National Bank of Egypt, 1953), pp. 6-17.

(86)Gunnar Myrdal, Development and Underdevelopment (Cairo: National Bank of Egypt, 1956).

(87)W. W. Rostow, The Process of Economic Growth (London: Oxford Univ. Press, 1960, first ed. 1953), pp. 10-12.

(88)John H. Adler, "Development Theory and the Bank's Development Strategy," Finance and Development 14 (Oct. 1977): 32.

(89)World Bank, Annual Report (Washington: 1960), pp. 5-6. The early report on debt servicing is Dragoslav Arramovic and Ravi Gulhati, Debt Servicing Problems of Low Income Countries: 1956-1958 (Baltimore: Johns Hopkins Univ. Press, 1960).

(90)Brian Tew, The Evolution of the International Monetary System (New York: John Wiley, 1977), pp. 48-55.

(91)Kock, pp. 117-18.

(92)Ibid., pp. 168-69.

(93)Ibid., pp. 100-101

(94)Ibid., p. 174.

(95)Economist, Nov. 21, 1959, p. 63. Rostow's Stages of Growth appeared in Aug. 1959.

2
The "New" Ideology in the 1960s

[UNCTAD] will show whether the developed countries are capable of discharging the obligations imposed on them by their wealth. It will also require them to renounce their traditional policy of passively accepting the supremacy of market forces. Against blind respect for those forces and against the trade restrictions imposed by the strongest against the weakest ranges the new ideology which inspired the convening of the conference. That ideology . . . will constitute a new phase in the age old struggle for the liberation of peoples and respect for human dignity.

-- Alphonso Patino of Colombia, 1963

. . . the developing nations want change. They want a "new" international division of labor. They want and have a "new" trade forum. They want "new" trade principles. They want new and different techniques of aid, not necessarily at the sacrifice of the old but in addition to what is now being done.

-- Sidney Weintraub of the United States, 1964(1)

Even though the decade began with signs that the Bretton Woods system could be reformed in favor of third world interests, the sixties were marked by growing economic divisions between north and south. LDCs became more aware of how their interests clashed with those of the DMCs. From 1960 through 1965 evidence mounted that poorer nations received few of the benefits the liberal system had promised. Developed countries enjoyed most of the growth induced by trade. Trade favoritism among already industrialized states continued. Third world leaders saw such continuing abuses as proof that the postwar system merely continued prewar relations in a new

59

form. The LDCs, united under the ethic and analysis developed since the war, pushed for creation of a new international economic system dedicated to that new ideology.

In the first five years of the decade the ideology itself developed only along the lines already established in the 1950s. Third world economic analysis became more complex in response to new issues. Prebisch's framework allowed the south to apprehend and explain growing income and trade "gaps" between rich and poor nations. Third world governments proposed an array of new policies to increase their share of global trade. They suggested specific public aid targets, multicommodity pricing agreements, compensatory financing for trade income shortfalls, and special aid for the least developed LDCs (LLDCs), especially the new states in Africa. All of these new economic proposals attacked similar problems, consequences of the Bretton Woods system that no one who created the system had expected, or that none had expected would have such distressing effects on poorer nations.

By mid-decade the ideology had begun to change in fundamentally new ways. Adherents had developed a new self-awareness and self-confidence. They stopped calling for reforms and started calling for a new economic order. They had become aware of the ideology they shared and aware that the ideology outlined a plan for a new economic system. They knew that plan was not complete; for example, the ellipsis in Patino's comment stands in place of a long remark that the ideology had to be specified further. In the sixties, for the first time, third world officials began to pursue the development of their ideology consciously.

In the middle of the decade the ideology's adherents developed a specific political identity as the Group of 77. The agreement on a formal political identity triggered the alliance's development of its first political theory, explicit views about strategy and tactics which had not been part of the third world's shared position before. The southern allies insisted on using what they called "democratic means" to achieve their ends. They understood such means to include majority or consensual rule by national governments voting as equals, as well as the use of persuasion to influence legislative and public opinion in the wealthy states.

Later, third world leaders would learn from the failure of this initial strategy. As a result of their failures in the sixties, they would know how to exploit the DMCs' economic vulnerabilities in the early 1970s when the Bretton Woods system began to create problems even its key members felt.

In the 1960s, however, not only had the LDCs not yet agreed upon the political strategies needed to exploit

the vulnerabilities that would appear when the Bretton
Woods system started to break down; there were few hints
that such a breakdown would ever occur. The system was in
its heyday. It was brilliantly achieving the goals its
founders had set for it. The cover of the GATT's 1966
annual report makes the point well with its graphs of
indices of international trade and world production from
1956 to 1966.(2) Both rise dramatically, trade volumes
leading the way for production. The liberal system
assured the truly unprecedented global prosperity that
marked the sixties. For the wealthy market states, unlike
for the poorer ones, few unanticipated problems appeared
in the sixties to make them doubt the viability and value
of the system which had spurred the unprecedented growth.

One unanticipated development in the sixties,
indirectly connected to the system's success, created as
many opportunities for the third world alliance as it did
problems. But the new order ideology, as it existed then,
did not give the alliance the theoretical means of fully
resolving the problems while fully exploiting the
opportunities. The vast increase of new sovereign states
provided the alliance with many more members and thus
increased the political importance of the emerging
ideology. But the interests and frustrations of the new
states differed from those of states that had been
independent longer. Some of the new states said that rich
nations had duties to poor nations because colonizers had
historical duties to the colonized. This ethic based on
historical obligations clashed with earlier third world
notions about the permanent rights and duties of states.
This difference of opinion contributed to the failure of
the Group of 77's first political strategy by reducing
the impact of attempts to present a united front in order
to influence opinion in developed countries. This
disunity, however, left a fortuitous legacy for the
south: The unity of the third world behind the New
International Economic Order in the early seventies
caught many in the north by surprise.

The part of the story of the new order ideology told
in this chapter ends before the third world reaffirmed
its unity. It begins with the trade issues the founders
of Bretton Woods failed to anticipate and shows how those
emergent issues led to the first UNCTAD, the formation of
the Group of 77, and the first southern calls for a
completely "new" economic system. The second section
discusses the political analysis the group adopted in the
latter half of the decade. The third and final section
relates how other unanticipated consequences of the
system, first apparent in the sixties, led to the
developments in third world economic policy analysis at
the end of the decade. It also discusses the differences
in third world opinion that then were current, linking
them both to the different problems experienced by
different third world states as a result of the system's

operation and to the incomplete incorporation of the
newest states into the alliance.

FROM TRADE ISSUES TO THE GROUP OF 77

As would be expected of the international
organization most concerned with trade matters, the GATT
was the first institution to make the international
community aware of trade related global income "gaps." It
did so in 1960 by suggesting explanations for problems
others had previously identified but not explained. In
1958 Nehru had used postwar national income statistics to
demonstrate a widening income gap between rich and poor
nations.(3) By 1959 it had become commonplace for some
news magazines in worldwide circulation to identify the
north-south division of the globe as more critical than
the east-west division.(4) Nonetheless, in the late
fifties, when aid rather than trade issues still
dominated the north-south agenda, officials and
commentators rarely correlated the increasingly apparent
income gap with recent developments in international
trade. Of course, throughout the fifties third world
leaders recognized that higher returns from trade could
increase their national wealth; that is why they proposed
some new trade policies, then compensatory financing for
trade shortfalls, and finally even resurrection of the
entire ITO.(5) But actual figures on the third world's
declining proportion of both world trade and world income
first became available in 1960 through a report
circulated by the GATT.(6) The highly correlated figures
suggested that the third world's declining proportion of
world trade caused its declining proportion of world
income.
    GATT did not draw the causal connection from the
related trends. But third world leaders increasingly did
draw that connection by following, in part, the Prebisch
thesis. Most southern leaders first gave the implications
of the Prebisch argument serious consideration only when
the trade-related income gaps became apparent. Third
world representatives to the U.N. carefully discussed
different ways that nonmarket forces might be keeping the
prices of DMC manufactured goods relatively high. Some
called for establishing countervailing influences on the
world market in order to keep LDC prices high as well.
The poorer oil producing states formed OPEC and justified
it to the United Nations General Assembly as an
institution designed to keep oil prices high.(7)
(Ironically, they did not succeed in their stated purpose
until 1973.) In 1960 the Colombian delegate spoke to the
General Assembly's economic committee about establishing
"trade unions" of raw material producers.(8) As if to
capitalize on these developments, in 1961 ECLA
republished Prebisch's seminal study.(9)

Just as in the 1950s when some third world officials used parts of Prebisch's theory to understand and respond to trade problems created by cold war stockpiling policies, once again few third world officials completely adopted Prebisch's explanation of the trade and income gaps. Instead of focusing directly on the powers of the firms and unions in developed nations, most representatives of individual third world governments talked about the flaws in the postwar trade system that the Haberler report to the GATT outlined. Third world officials saw the relative decline in their income from trade as a reflection of the fact that wealthy market states had been able to mold the liberal system to their needs. The trade system, they noted, tended to allow DMCs to trade industrial products among themselves freely while forcing LDCs to pay tariffs on the same items. And the system allowed the north to erect protectionist barriers to southern imports.(10)

Only when the poorer nations turned to solutions to the apparent trade problems did they line up behind the Prebisch thesis rather than Haberler's. The LDCs never called for a return to the GATT's laissez faire principles; instead, the south continued to call for conscious adoption of global trade policies that would increase third world income, policies justified by their view of the rights and duties of states. As a Uruguayan official put it in 1960, in place of the GATT's "equal treatment" principle, which allowed richer nations greater power to influence economic relations than poorer nations (even before special concessions like those to the European Community had been made), there should be a principle of "equitable treatment," international policies aimed at fostering the trade relations appropriate to each nation's level of economic development and its development goals.(11) In particular, beginning in 1961 and following a set of proposals made by Africa's newly independent, most populous state, Nigeria, the third world demanded a system of generalized tariff preferences for third world goods.(12)

This new policy proposal did not fundamentally change the emerging third world economic ideology. Adherents simply added the new version of the trade issue and new proposed solution to other policy analyses already in the ideology. At the first conference of nonaligned countries in Belgrade in September of 1961 not only did the delegates condemn the postwar aid system for the way it linked cold war goals to development goals, they condemned the trade system as well. Delegates called on the developed nations to improve the terms of trade for LDC goods and to end restrictive trade practices that harmed poorer states.(13) At the same time, southern spokesmen in the U.N. reaffirmed their ethic and their central economic goal as keys to abolishing the trade and income gaps. As the Bolivian delegate put it, "Each

society has its own needs and its own means to satisfy
them. But if the underdeveloped countries wish to survive
they must industrialize."(14)

By 1961 even the GATT was calling for the industrialization of the third world as one means for dealing
with the poorer nations' declining share of world trade.
In a special study of trade and development for its
Annual Report, the GATT Secretariat analyzed possible
ways to ease the relative decline. It found little room
for expanding traditional exports and advocated
industrialization along the model of the Latin American
Free Trade Area instead. That model required that
national specialization in particular industrial lines
become an object of intergovernmental cooperation in each
of the developing regions. The GATT even raised the
possibility that intervention to raise the terms of trade
for traditional exports might prove worthwhile in the
short run, although it did not discuss specific ways to
accomplish such intervention.(15)

Continuing GATT interest in the declining relative
volume of third world trade reflected the fact that
liberal economists treated the problem as a real dilemma.
Most felt that in the long run terms of trade would swing
in favor of food and raw materials (rather than
manufactured goods) under the influence of diminishing
returns. Because raw materials exist only in limited
quantities, they should become scarcer, costlier to
extract, and, thus, relatively more costly as time goes
on.(16)

Liberal economists may still be right, in the long
run. But in the 1960s, predictions based on facile
analysis of the long run availability of raw materials
proved wrong. Instead of rising, the value of third world
raw material exports relative to northern manufactures
fell. That fact could be explained (without rejecting the
liberals' long run conclusions) by pointing to the
different manipulations of the world market by unequally
powerful states. The already rich benefited the most from
such manipulations. At least that was the conclusion both
the GATT and a significantly large group of third world
officials accepted. What to do about it was another
matter.

Just as the LDCs remained committed to their vision,
the GATT Secretariat remained committed to liberal trade.
The GATT's commitment precluded it from serving as a
framework for the sorts of policies third world governments preferred to use to combat the trade and income
gaps. In the early sixties they began to look for other
organizational frameworks.

In 1962 the Cairo Second Afro-Asian Conference
called for a United Nations trade conference to provide
an international forum outside GATT for proposals like
commodity pricing agreements, compensatory financing, and
a generalized system of tariff preferences. The U.N.

votes of the governments represented at the Afro-Asian conference, along with the votes of those Latin American states which had been invited observers and of socialist governments who wanted the U.N. conference to deal with ways to expand east-west trade, assured that the first United Nations Conference on Trade and Development (UNCTAD I) would be called quickly. The General Assembly scheduled the conference for late spring of 1964.(17)

In the months between the Cairo conference and UNCTAD third world frustrations over the effects of the postwar economic system coalesced. In addition to the problems of cold war-related aid policies and the GATT's obviously inadvertent function as an agency sanctioning DMC protectionist policies, other issues had been festering.

In the third world view, despite the creation of the IDA and the Special Fund, the World Bank and bilateral aid donors had consistently exacerbated the gap between rich and poor states by loaning only to the richest of the poor.(18) The IDA itself remained only a poor second-best alternative to SUNFED because the IDA adopted the World Bank's system of voting weighted in proportion to wealth, rather than the one nation, one vote system SUNFED would have followed. Dissatisfaction with the aid system even convinced the majority in General Assembly to set official targets for aid to third world countries, to define one of the duties of the wealthy states throughout the development decade more explicitly as the duty to give 1 percent of their GNPs to poorer states, a goal few wealthy states ever reached. The UNRRA goal for grants to needy nations, which some poorer states could say that they themselves had respected, provide the precedent for the 1 percent figure. Those unusual LDCs that had received significant aid since the second world war, such as India, complained about the burden that repaying those debts placed on an economy still trying to catch up with the wealthy states, the problem the IDA was supposed to solve.(19)

Even the Bretton Woods monetary system came under third world attack in the months leading up to UNCTAD I. According to the south, the wealthy countries controlling the monetary system were the only nations that could afford to make their currencies convertible. The major evidence LDCs offered for that assertion was the fact that it took nearly a decade and a half of interna- tionally supported postwar economic development before western European states wanted to make their money convertible. For those states that could afford them, convertible currencies made it easier trade, at least with other countries that had convertible currencies. The fact that LDCs could not yet afford convertibility meant that developed countries would be more likely to increase their trade with each other than they would be to increase their trade with LDCs. Given the LDCs' views about the rights and duties of states, they placed the blame for this situation on the postwar monetary system, which had enshrined the principle of convertibility, and not on themselves. The European precedent suggested, after all, that poorer nations should not be expected to live up to the monetary rules the postwar system demanded.

Despite this criticism, the postwar monetary system was the object of much less third world scorn in the early sixties than either the trade or aid systems. Third world spokesmen even praised the IMF in 1963 for establishing a system of short term loans that could be taken out by countries suffering losses in expected income due to sudden drops in the prices of commodities they exported. Still, the LDCs chastised the IMF for limiting this financing to an amount that would bring export earning up to a longer term trend, a trend that third world governments believed was declining for almost any commodity they exported.(20)

In light of these mounting grievances, when the Egyptian delegate began the General Assembly debate on economic matters directly after the Second Afro-Asian Conference had ended in Cairo, he summarized a history of frustrations going back to the Marshall Plan and UNRRA. He said that significant international systems for aid to DMCs, systems which took into account those countries' own definitions of their economic needs, had existed for years. Those systems, developed to aid postwar Europe, had never been copied in giving aid to Asian, African, and Latin American countries. Most significantly, similar consideration of third world nations' self-defined economic needs never took place.(21)

By June of 1963 the nations that would become the Group of 77 had formally outlined their UNCTAD positions through a series of regional meetings. At those regional conferences third world leaders turned their frustrations with the postwar economic system into a call for "a new international division of labor," a division that would no longer make the third world the world's "hewers of wood and drawers of water," the south said, using a Biblical phrase that already had long history in the literature on imperialism before 1963.(22) The "new international division of labor" simply meant that the third world should become industrialized.

In 1964 this call for a whole new international economic system was no doubt more symbolic than practical. Even if they had had the power to create a new economic order, third world governments still did not have the plan. The regional third world meetings came up with outlines of a new global system of production no more coherent or complete than any of the others the third world had presented since the war. The regional meetings simply reiterated the reform proposals that third world states had long supported. The call for a "new" world economy was more a way of symbolizing the increasing significance that third world governments attached to their proposals in the months before UNCTAD. Plans offered in the months before UNCTAD even differed a bit from region to region throughout the third world. The Latin American states emphasized that those nations that had benefited the most from the postwar economic institutions had the greatest duty to aid other nations. Latin America also placed solutions to debt servicing problems in one of the most prominant positions in its plan.(23) African states identified former colonies as the most needy states and gave special emphasis to calls for tariff preferences to be given to the least advantaged nations. While the Latin American resolution mentioned that proposal it placed it lower on the agenda simple because a smaller proportion of the Latin American states could be called "least advantaged" by any definition. The Africans also called for multi-commodity pricing agreements that would allow funds collected while protecting the ceiling price of one commodity (by selling from a buffer stock) to be used to defend the floor price of another commodity.(24) This was another policy discovered among the many never-enacted suggestions left by Lord Keynes.(25) Latin American and Asian delegates failed to consider it until the Africans brought it up at the joint meeting of the regions prior to UNCTAD.

Asians, Africans, and Latin Americans easily reconciled the differences in their draft proposals by invoking the principles they had developed in the forties. Both the debt problem, of special interest to the richest LDCs in Latin America and Asia, and the problems associated with stabilizing and increasing the prices of the weakest commodities traded, issues especially important to Africa, had to be included as issues to be addressed by the "new" world economic order. Each problem reflected a major impediment in the development paths particular sovereign states had chosen.

Third world unity behind shared principles increased in the months leading up to the first UNCTAD. Third world governments repeatedly emphasized the duty of each state to support the economic development programs chosen by other states. Third world spokesmen even asserted that this principle explained part of the value of their new ideology. They called the ideology a contribution to global economic development. Echoing Patino, who had made the statement at the head of this chapter the week before, a Libyan delegate explained to the General Assembly's economic committee in 1963 that third world states had discharged their development duties toward others by contributing a new, higher set of moral values to the development debate.(26) Along with Patino, the Libyan represented the general opinion of southern officials when he stated that the new ideology was an historically unique, valuable contribution to humanity.

At the first UNCTAD southern governments acted on the basis of their self-perceived moral leadership to have the conference approve their ethic and their analysis of the world economy. Before the meeting Raul Prebisch, who had been elevated from ECLA to be Secretary General of the UNCTAD in 1963, provided a ·new, more extensive gloss of his theories and a set of policy recommendations in a report entitled "Toward a New Trade Policy for Development." This report became the informal agenda for the conference.(27) The conference approved resolutions both restating the report's policy proposals and affirming bits of Prebisch's analysis. The resolutions called these proposals and assertions "trade principles" that would guide the "new and just world economic order" the conference intended to create.(28) All these principles had appeared earlier, outgrowths of the Havana Charter debates, the Panch Shila, assertions about the validity of Prebisch's analysis of trade, and the special demands that each third world region made directly before UNCTAD I.

Many governments rejected the third world's self-proclaimed moral leadership and the principles embodying it, but even at the first UNCTAD northern opponents to the south's call for a new order were divided. With fewer than three other partners, the United States voted against five of the third world's fifteen "general" principles. Those principles all affirmed parts of the third world view of the economic rights and duties of states -- the principle of the equality of states, the principles stating that trade and development were global concerns, and ones saying that every state had the right to choose its own economic system and control the natural resources within its boundaries. The U.S. was a minority of one opposing a principle that disarmament should be undertaken to free funds for development. Between four and nine other DMCs joined the U.S. when it opposed approving international commodity agreements, "equitable treatment," and development goals for the IMF. Britain and Australia alone opposed a principle that colonized nations should be given special development consideration.

No one opposed five other principles. Two referred to other special targets for development, the LLDCs and landlocked areas. Two more referred directly to the issues that triggered the calls for UNCTAD in the first place. DMCs agreed that their own moves toward economic integration, including the European Community, should not harm LDCs, and all states agreed that similar regional trade groups among LDCs should be allowed. The final principle approved without dissent was the abstract goal of the conference, movement toward a new international division of labor.(29)

These votes determined how the Group of 77 would

interpret the results of the conference. While many DMCs opposed the group's practical suggestions for increasing third world income from trade, the U.S. could be singled out as the major opponent to the even more fundamental third world principles. That meant there was little hope for the immediate future, in spite of all the bright talk about the "development decade" that had marked the end of the fifties. Immediately after UNCTAD I most third world spokesmen identified the U.S. as the primary author of the postwar system, the system's major beneficiary, and the major reason that fundamental reform of the system was impossible.

Such an assessment may have been too harsh. American opposition to some of the south's principles may only have reflected misunderstanding of the south's views. Sidney Weintraub, one of the American delegates, wrote after the conference that its "Final Act" (the document containing the fifteen principles) did not necessarily reflect what was in the minds of all those at the conference. That is certainly true. But the "Final Act" did reflect the ideology that Asian, African, and Latin American representatives to global economic meetings had been developing for twenty years; earlier third world positions provide a good guide to what was in the minds of southern delegates at UNCTAD. The history of the new order ideology suggests a slightly different understanding of "real" third world concerns than the one Weintraub offered.

Weintraub considered the third world proposals basically self-serving. He felt that the principles opposed by the U.S. were designed to let LDCs unfairly claim some of the current wealth some developed states had earned. To him the Group of 77's position appeared doubly unfair because it seemed to demand much less from the socialist states than from the DMCs.(30) Both judgements can be questioned even though they logically follow from American premises at the time.

One American premise was that the rules of international economic conduct had been long established and accepted by all nations. Yet in 1964 the the Bretton Woods system had only been operating as it had been intended to for five years and its rules had never been accepted by the majority of states at UNCTAD. The south still acted in 1964 the way the U.S. had in 1944, as if the best structure for international economic relations had yet to be discovered and agreed upon.

A second U.S. premise was that the LDCs goal of a "new" order was just a new way to express an old-fashioned state interest in aggrandizment at the expense of others. Yet the more complex third world goal remained as it had been in the 1940s; southern states wanted to establish an international economic system based on permanent national development rights and responsibilities. By 1964 the relative poverty of the

third world convinced its leaders that, under their own
principles, they were no longer required to materially
aid other states. Their responsibilities were limited to
things like promulgating their twenty-year-old "new"
moral values within the U.N., values that (while
self-serving in the short term) were considered a real
contribution by many in the south.(31) Southern aid and
trade proposals in 1964 no more envisioned reducing the
wealth of the DMCs than the U.S. UNRRA proposals in 1944
envisioned reducing the wealth of Latin American
contributors. Rather, both sets of proposals aimed at
assuring that a specific region of the globe would be
able to produce a greater proportion of the new wealth
constantly created by the world economy. The UNCTAD
proposals especially aimed at giving the third world more
of the globe's trade-induced growth, something the LDCs
seemed to have lost to the DMCs since the war.

In contrast, given American premises, the UNCTAD
proposals had to be seen as nothing other than a
challenge to the only legitimate order in the world
economy. They had to be understood as part of the LDCs'
strategy in a worldwide zero sum game in which their
economic gain was the DMCs' economic loss and in which
the DMCs' economic loss was the political gain of their
greatest rival, the communist bloc.

Given the nature of the south's grievances, which
predated the cold war, the American tendency to
understand the results of UNCTAD in east-west terms
disturbed most southern delegates. Nonetheless, at the
first UNCTAD the second and third worlds were clearly
allies. The socialist governments' goal at the meeting
was to, "air their grievances against import-export
restrictions and discriminatory cold war policies imposed
upon them by the developed countries."(32) Throughout the
conference socialist states seemed to accommodate third
world demands that they expand their trade with the
south, thus making it appear that the east-south
agreement could extend further than the conference
floor.(33)

The depth of the increasing ideological rift between
first and third worlds can be seen by comparing
Weintraub's image of the new system that third world
governments wanted to create to the image of the postwar
system held by the most radical third world governments.
The extreme northern (e.g., U.S.) and southern views had
come to resemble the "mirror images" that the superpowers
had of each others' aims. Like cold war mirror images,
the views of the extreme states in the north and south
assured ongoing misunderstanding.(34) The most radical
third world states viewed the postwar system as a
deliberately engineered mechanism for exploiting poorer
nations' property, just as the U.S. saw the proposed
system as a deliberately engineered mechanism for

exploiting developed nations' property. Both extremes
even understood the role of the socialist states in the
same way. While Weintraub viewed the Group of 77 as
unfairly excusing the socialist states from the group's
wealth-grabbing scheme, some third world leaders viewed
DMC moves in the sixties toward expanding east-west trade
as ways of integrating the socialist countries into the
unfair expanding trade system as equal partners and thus
leaving the third world, the only exploited region, with
an even smaller proportion of the world's trade.(35)
     Due in part to the fruitless ideological battle
between mirror images at UNCTAD, one of the more
interesting, deeper conflicts between the Group of 77 and
the United States hardly appeared: the conflict between
the assumed primacy of the rights of property owners that
underlies laissez faire doctrine and the assumed primacy
of national governments in defining property rights that
stands on the surface of the third world's interpretation
of the economic rights and duties of states found in the
U.N. Charter. Even in 1964 there may have been some
ground for compromise between north and south on this
fundamental point. In practice, northern states balanced
the claims of property owners against other national
interests as much as LDCs, in practice, balanced their
advocacy of the principle of sovereignty against their
other interests.(36) The UNCTAD debate forced neither
north nor south to consciously recognize that they
balanced their property principles with other concerns,
and did so in much the same way. The UNCTAD debate did
not even require them to discuss such fundamental,
substantive concerns.
     At the UNCTAD meeting the most fully and fruitfully
discussed conflicts between north and south occurred not
over principles but over specific trade policies and
trade theory. Unlike in the debate over principles, in
discussions of those topics most DMCs shared the same
views.
     At the level of practical trade policy north-south
differences had abated somewhat even before UNCTAD I, and
afterward they continued to abate throughout the decade.
The IMF's creation of a compensatory financing facility
illustrates the early move toward greater agreement.
Elevation of UNCTAD from a temporary conference to a
permanent institution of the United Nations created the
structure in which commodity agreements could be
negotiated. Nonetheless, the African proposal for
multicommodity agreements remained dormant throughout the
decade, although the IMF began to investigate ways that
its resources might be used to finance buffer stocks.(37)
In addition, the wealthier members of the GATT gradually
accepted the principle of granting tariff preferences to
developing nations. It took until the 1970s before many
states passed the legislation that would actually allow
such preferences to be awarded.(38)

None of these developments on the level of practical policy represented any widespread DMC acceptance of the empirical trade theory underlying the Group of 77's trade demands. The IMF's compensatory financing facility remained committed to the notion that long run trends in the world market represented fair prices. Rich states justified generalized tariff preferences as a new form of foreign aid, not as step required to increase third world trade income because it had been declining due to the powers of companies in DMCs to control world market prices. Even though the GATT Secretariat had provided evidence of the decline in the LDCs' proportion of world trade prior to the first UNCTAD, the GATT did not accept the theory that there was a trade-related "income gap" that prevented the LDCs from achieving their development aims. After the first UNCTAD, the GATT Secretariat reported that Prebisch's measure of this "gap" per se meant nothing because of the differences in export needs among LDCs. These differences made it impossible that any theory claiming to explain trade problems could be applied to the entire group of nations.(39)

On the surface, the GATT position on the trade gap seems to say nothing more than Weintraub's observation after the first UNCTAD that the trade gap was not necessarily a fact just because the majority of delegates at UNCTAD voted to say it was.(40) But the GATT position, unlike Weintraub's, can be linked directly to Gottfried Haberler's critique of Prebisch's theory. Haberler's 1958 GATT report condemning the DMC protectionist policies argued that such policies could cause the terms of trade for specific third world goods to decline, but he went on to argue that it was impossible to weigh the effects of extra-market interventions on world prices as a whole. The protectionist policies still employed by the LDCs might be counteracting the effects of DMC policies or the LDC policies might even be improving the terms of trade for some of their goods over the real, free market trend. Case by case analysis would be needed in order to determine the actual effects of these interventions. Until such analysis was undertaken, Haberler felt this aspect of Prebisch's argument should not be accepted as proven. Haberler also argued that it seemed paradoxical to expect that the terms of trade for so many diverse commodities as those sold by third world producers would all have the same trend at the same time; again he advocated more detailed study of individual cases than the Prebisch reports offered.(41)

The GATT was right that major differences among LDC economies existed in the sixties. The Group of 77 certainly recognized that, at least in its attempt to assure that each state's particular concerns become part of the alliance position. But the GATT implied that the differences among third world states provided sufficient reason for them to support the ultimate creation of a

world with no trade restrictions. The south rejected that
implication. At UNCTAD meetings and the international
conferences between them, third world governments
continued to view the terms of trade problem as one they
all shared and as one that could not be eliminated simply
by moving toward a more open trading system.

THE GROUP OF 77's POLITICS

After the first UNCTAD failed to lead to major
changes in global economic regimes, the Group of 77
emphasized political victories rather than ones in the
realm of economic policy. The group pointed to
accomplishments like the establishment of rules for
further north-south discussions and the creation of the
group itself. In fact, southern officials considered the
institutionalization of the third world alliance to be
the most important thing UNCTAD achieved.(42) In terms of
the history of the NIEO ideology that is certainly true.
The institutionalization of the Group of 77 marked the
beginning of the third period in the ideology's
development, the first period in which the third world
alliance developed its own political analysis.
UNCTAD I's hottest debate had made the group
extremely concerned with unity. DMC proposals that voting
in the conference be weighted according to trade wealth
caught Asian, African, and Latin American delegates off
guard. There was nothing new in this request. DMCs were
only reaffirming the political principles embodied in the
Bretton Woods system. Yet the demand surprised third
world delegates because they saw precedents for UNCTAD
not in the IMF and World Bank but in the General Assembly
and defunct ITO.(43) The group successfully countered the
DMC proposal and make UNCTAD adopt two decision-making
systems, both of which rejected weighted voting: decision
by consensus and decision by majority rule of states. But
the fact that the debate over decision-making rules could
take place at all taught members of the group two
lessons. They learned that the southern alliance had to
agree explicitly upon decision-making principles.
Moreover, they learned to consult among themselves about
strategy and tactics as well as goals in order to assure
that the south could use its majority effectively.(44)
In speeches at the first UNCTAD, southern officials
equated the political principles they wanted to see the
conference adopt with "democratic procedures."(45) This
equation suggested that the resolutions of UNCTAD and
similar meetings were "law" justified by popular
sovereignty.(46) If the south had been concerned, first
and foremost, with finding the shortest path to increased
north-south cooperation, the "democratic procedures"
slogan would have been a very poor choice. Many officials
from those DMCs where one person, one vote was more or

less the rule considered this third world concern with "democracy" to be a travesty. Few third world governments even attempted to approach democratic representation at home, and all shunned representing equal populations with one vote in international organizations.

However, if we ignore its immediate contribution to greater north-south misunderstanding and concentrate on its part in the development of the third world's mobilizing ideology, we can see the progressive role that the south's new concern with "democratic procedures" played. It made part of the south's unconsciously shared political views very conscious and very public. Arising at the time the Group of 77 itself was formed, the dispute over decision-making rules convinced group members that they needed to affirm a "political theory," a view of how decisions could and should be made. Developing such political ideas meant thinking about how the group's economic ideology could be made dominant. Even the little thought that went into quickly responding to the DMCs proposals with calls for more "democratic" means actually helped the south. Of course, majority votes in favor of third world proposals could hardly be expected to revolutionize the world economic system as long as the system's major supporters did not accept the legitimacy of majority rule. On the other hand, structured consensus formation could be used to reform the system fundamentally. DMCs would accept such procedures because the north retained its veto.

In promulgating new rules for "conciliation" at the first UNCTAD, the third world experimented with what turned out to be a successful means for making some of its views dominant.(47) More importantly, as a result of debate over political procedures, Group of 77 members, for the first time, became very aware that they really needed to test various political means and consciously repeat successfully employed ones, recognize the limits of their success, and consciously avoid repeating fruitless methods. By the end of the decade third world spokesmen knew that the systems of structured consensus building first attempted at UNCTAD I were an effective means of obtaining specific concessions from the developed nations but an ineffective means for achieving agreement on principles.(48)

In the years immediately following the first UNCTAD, the Group of 77 hardly built upon the political analysis it had so rapidly adopted in 1964. The group continued to work on the basis of "democratic" consensus formation with the major economic powers to come to agreements on specific concessions. The group tried to get decisions by majority rule when decision by consensus was impossible, but even by the second UNCTAD meeting in 1968 most LDC governments had started to distance themselves from the ineffective posturing that unenforceable majority rule decisions represented.(49)

Meanwhile, third world perceptions of the need to develop political links within the group convinced governments to make existing links more concrete. Between the first UNCTAD and the second, the group demonstrated the significance of its unity, and the fact that in certain contexts majority rule decisions could be effective, by its ability to unite U.N. aid programs and create the Industrial Development Organization (UNIDO) over the objection of DMC governments.(50) The Asian, African, and Latin American conferences of the Group of 77 prior to second UNCTAD resulted on unified regional positions. The group's meeting in Algiers prior to the conference easily resolved what differences there were in the regional plans. At UNCTAD II the group appointed designated spokesmen to argue their majority position.(51) Nonetheless, neither the majorities that the group bothered to muster behind its proposals, nor the consensus-making process, resulted in international agreement on fundamental issues.

After the second disappointing meeting of UNCTAD, the third world's political tactics became more complex. third world governments added to the notion of using "democratic means" to advance their position the idea that they should consciously attempt to influence elite and public opinion in the developed states. The group actually adopted this political tactic while under the influence of DMC elite opinion.

When former American defense secretary Robert McNamara began his presidency of the World Bank he called upon former Canadian prime minister Lester Pearson to form a commission and report to him on international development needs. Pearson chose Arthur Lewis and Roberto de Oliveria Campos along with five statesmen from the DMCs to join him. Their report, Partners in Development, ran through four popular printings in 1969 and 1970 after its first release in 1968.(52) The authors' proposals fundamentally agreed with the Group of 77's. The commission added a concern with establishing development related population programs that echoed proposals made by a number of group members but that had been rejected as part of the consensus of the group.(53) Likewise, the Pearson Commission expressed a concern for equalizing the distribution of wealth within developing nations. Governments of individual third world states had expressed such views, but the group had never collectively accepted them.(54) At the same time, the Pearson Commission affirmed a moral duty of the rich to aid the poor that was compatible with the third world views of states' economic rights and duties.

LDCs praised the Pearson Commission from the outset, although a number of governments demurred over the issue of birth control. Many third world U.N. representatives immediately adopted the simple political analysis the Pearson Commission report offered for the failure of previous international development efforts; they represented failures of "political will" on the part of governments, especially DMC governments.(55) The delegate from Cameroon expressed the southern view well when he argued that "political will" had created the Marshall Plan and "political will" could still create effective international cooperation for economic development.(56)

To energize DMC political will in 1968, the third world suggested mounting a campaign to influence DMC public opinion.(57) In 1969 Tanzania proposed that legislators from the Group of 77 attempt to influence fellow parliamentarians in developed countries to change their governments' foreign policies.(58) The General Assembly's extensive Declaration on Social Progress and Development of 1969 reflect both proposals. In addition, as part of the campaign to change northern opinion, the General Assembly charged the Secretary General with disseminating the declaration as widely as possible.(59)

Events since 1969 may make us think the third world was naive to believe that public opinion in the north mattered. No theory which considered public opinion important appears to have guided the one set of third world actions that actually made the most people in the north aware of southern views -- i.e., the unpopular OPEC price increases. Yet in the U.N. debates of 1968 and 1969 only one member of the group, Sudan, argued that an emphasis on influencing DMC public opinion was misguided.(60)

Events in 1968 made the third world belief in the effectiveness of public and legislative opinion very reasonable. An American president had refused to run for another term when it became clear to him that the public and Congress would no longer support his foreign policy approach. Mass demonstrations almost toppled the French government. Moreover, the liberal western political theories that a majority of third world leaders had learned and still accepted, in theory if not in practice, identified the opinions and goals of mass publics and their representatives as the proper source of foreign policy, and, much more importantly, as the actual source of foreign policy in those states with active liberal political institutions, the DMCs.(61)

Despite these good reasons for attempting to influence DMC opinion, third world attempts to energize northern political will remained small operations throughout the sixties. The only resources committed to the effort were those of the U.N. agencies, the Secretary General's office and UNCTAD in particular. Yet this small-scale expression of concern with influencing DMC opinion had effects on the emerging DMC ideology beyond the simple fact that it happened to be one of the earliest bits of political theory the Group of 77 collectively and consciously adopted. Like moves toward strengthening the alliance itself, attempting to influence the attitudes of people within DMCs required LDC supporters to present their opinions about the world economy in a more unified and coherent, and thus more convincing, form. It required third world leaders to make their ideology even more explicit and distinct.

MORE NEW ECONOMIC ISSUES FOR THE SOUTH

However, the real diversity of interests within the third world mitigated against the development of a more explicit, coherent, and convincing ideology in the late sixties. That diversity had been made greater by new economic issues. The Bretton Woods system's heyday of income and trade growth affected different third world states in different ways. While the Group of 77 was able to respond to the new issues by creating hypothetical programs that would have provided some benefits to every third world state if they were enacted, the group had trouble finding ways to logically link all the new programs they proposed in a single, coherent economic policy analysis. The group could easily blame some of the new problems on the Bretton Woods system; analysis of those problems could be easily integrated into the ideology. Those problems that could not be so easily blamed on the system were much harder to coherently link to the rest of the ideology.

The increasing lack of coherence in the ideology's policy analysis became all the more problematic because the south's solidarity behind a single interpretation of the economic rights and duties of states began to break. In the late sixties had enlarged the third world alliance to included governments that defined the economic duties of wealthy states as responsibilities incumbent upon them because of their past or current colonialism. Potentially, this opinion could have wrecked the ideological foundation of the third world alliance by opening up ethical questions which had be closed for years. Instead, members of the group simply stopped reiterating one part of the ethical foundation of their analysis. They continued to discuss the the economic rights of states in general terms as well as the specific duties of wealthy states, including a duty they newly agreed was incumbent upon colonizers, like Portugal and South Africa, to compensate for their colonialism. But, in the late 1960s the south ignore its older argument that the general, permanent duty of every state to unique economic development of other states provided the major reason why material aid could be demanded from the wealthy.

While members of the Group of 77 never publically confronted each other with demands to debate their different moral codes the disagreement over principles reinforced newly developing conflicts of interest within the alliance. Poorer LDCs supported one ethic; richer LDCs supported another. Without a unifying view of the economic rights and duties of states it became hard for LDCs to argue that all the new problems separate states experienced in the 1960s should be with under the same agenda. This reassured those supporters of the existing economic system who believed that third world calls for a "new" economic system were inherently incoherent. Even if, as the third world argued, there were some unfortunate unintended consequences resulting from the operation of the Bretton Woods system, those problems appeared to be localized ones that in no way changed the evaluation of the Bretton Woods system offered by its strongest advocates: Under the system world trade and economic growth had expanded like they never had before, and they had done so at the expense of no nation.

Of course, third world states measured the costs of the Bretton Woods system not against systems that had gone before but against the expected costs of the reformed system they wanted to see created. In those terms, they could argue that the actual system had unexpected costs that only some states had borne.

Throughout the sixties third world governments linked their analyses of the disadvantages of the IMF and World Bank. Functionally, both institutions seemed the same to many hard-pressed governments. Both provided loans that could be used to meet government expenses. Likewise, third world leaders thought of the bilateral aid systems in the same terms. The bilateral aid systems functioned as part of the world economic order, the Bretton Woods system broadly understood. In the sixties four new effects of the postwar aid and monetary order came to bother third world governments.

As we have seen, those less industrialized countries that actually did receive loans for development in the fifties had trouble repaying their debts, especially when that had taking out short term loans to finance the sort of infrastructure projects the south most demanded in the fifties. Such projects showed no immediate profit and mounting debt became even more difficult to pay back since third world trade remained stagnant.(62)

At the opposite end of the spectrum of wealth, the poorest LDCs felt the aid system led to the increasing relative impoverishment of the LLDCs relative to other states. LLDCs received a small proportion of available aid. The World Bank's understandable concern with its own financial health meant that prior to the creation of the IDA it loaned mostly to states that could easily pay their debts, states that were relatively wealthy already.(63)

Third world governments identified a similar problem associated with world liquidity. Because the U.S. dollar had been the world's most accepted currency since the war the U.S. could expand global liquidity accumulating trade

deficits for goods Americans purchased abroad.
Consequently, the initial benefits of expanding the
amount of money in global circulation went to the United
States, the wealthiest state; and because the U.S.'s most
important trade partners were DMCs, the multiplier
effects of increasingly global liquidity were extended
almost exclusively to the DMCs, thus, in the third world
view, increasing the relative poverty of the LDCs.(64)
When the IMF moved toward creating an internationally
managed means for expanding global liquidity in the
latter half of the decade -- through IMF Special Drawing
Rights (SDRs) -- IMF member allocated those funds on the
basis of the IMF quotas used to compute voting weights.
This system had almost the same effect as the pure dollar
standard. It gave most of the initial advantages of
increasing the global money supply to the already wealthy
regions.(65)

Third world states first raised one final, related
issue in the sixties. Those third world states that had
taken advantage of bilateral aid began to draw attention
to the economic strings attached to economic aid in the
same way that they first had brought attention to
political strings in the 1950s. Requirements that aid be
used to purchase goods from donor countries -- goods that
could often be purchased at lower prices elsewhere --
especially bothered them. Beyond the simple economic
disadvantages of these arrangements when compared to the
multilateral aid systems the south had advocated since
the forties, the economic strings attached to bilateral
aid increased the recipient economy's dependence on that
of the donor.

As we have seen, the third world's solutions to the
new aid problems they discovered in the sixties were
similar to the solutions they offered to similar problems
in the fifties. Because they blamed those aid problems on
the Bretton Woods system, they simply used their existing
principles and plans for an alternative system in order
to understand and suggest solutions to the new problems.
Under their long standing principles, the south
emphasized the special responsibility of all states to
aid the LLDCs and defined the minimal material
responsibility of the developed nations with the aid
target of 1 percent of GNP. In addition, the south acted
to assure that the U.N.'s Special Fund and technical
assistance programs would be coordinated and directed
toward third world industrialization, thus creating a
model for the multilateral aid system the south desired.

To third world leaders, inadequacies in the existing
system also explained the new monetary problems they
experienced. In again blaming Bretton Woods third world
leaders, sought solutions to the new monetary problems in
slight amendments to their own emerging vision of an
alternative system. They talked about expanding the IMF
so that it became, in part, an aid agency. They proposed

that any new international liquidity created by the IMF be allocated to states on the basis of some measure of economic need.(66) This proposal went back to ideas on the subject advanced in the 1950s by Maxwell Stamp, the British director of the IMF, and from there back to Lord Keynes's bag of hypothetical economic tricks and to the alternative vision of the postwar system which had been the basis for the third world's own policy analysis.(67) The south justified the proposed "Link" in the same way they justified other aid programs, as a way for wealthy states to fufill their duty to materially aid the economic development plans chosen by those less advantaged.

Supporters of the Bretton Woods system never denied that the system in part "caused" the four new aid and monetary problems that third world states experienced in the sixties. Supporters did deny that the things that "caused" the problems were problems in themselves. Instead, they saw them as necessary elements in any truly workable aid and money regimes. The problems experienced by the richest and poorest LDCs were unfortunate, but, Bretton Woods system advocates argued, no state or private investor would give development loans if they did not expect them to be repaid. True, supporters argued, the unique role of the U.S. in expanding world liquidity had never been carefully planned, but the fact that it (somewhat surprisingly) worked was reason enough to maintain the principle it embodied of expanding liquidity to nations on the basis of their economic might. Likewise, many leaders saw tying aid to repurchase agreements as a small domestic political price that rich countries had to pay in order to offer any aid at all. To supporters of Bretton Woods, these were less problems than facts, and certainly they were not the basis for new grievances with the existing order.

Third world spokesmen in the sixties did not try to respond to northern doubts about the reality of the new aid and money problems the south faced. They might have been able to do so by explaining how the emerging hypothetical alternative to Bretton Woods would insure things like investor confidence and popular support for aid from within DMCs, but it had been hard enough to integrate these new issues into the third world's own prior understanding. Yet these aid and money issues were easier to integrate into the southern consensus than another set of problems third world states experienced in the sixties, ones that could not be blamed so easily on the Bretton Woods system. Had third world officials been more willing to grant the Bretton Woods system its successes they might have been able to see this final set of new problems as like their new aid and money problems: unintended byproducts of the postwar system's operation.

The increasingly liberal trade system that the postwar regimes advanced provided opportunities for large

firms to invest abroad with greater ease than ever
before. Of course, individually, almost every country
around the world also encouraged such investment. By the
end of the sixties, nevertheless, most third world states
expressed some dissatisfactions with their relationships
to what the U.N. Secretariat had dubbed in mid-decade
"transnational corporations," TNCs.(68) Third world
representatives complained of profits being repatriated
in excess of the funds brought into the country by
foreign firms, and of the difficulties in assuring that
foreign investors followed the guidelines set out in
national development plans.(69) While third world
spokesmen did not try to explain the rise of TNCs, the
southern ethic suggested where solutions to their
problems with TNCs might be found. It pointed toward
finding the means to assure that the self-defined
interests of states remained sovereign in relations with
foreign firms. But the 1960s closed not only before the
south developed a shared analysis of the rise of TNCs but
also before they even came to share views about how to
combat the problems foreign investment created. The south
turned over the problem of developing such analysis to
the United Nations secretariats.(70)

A somewhat similar problem, "the brain drain," also
became a third world issue in the sixties. The successes
of the liberal international system helped make it
possible for highly skilled people from poorer countries
to find and move to jobs in the richest parts of the
world. In the sixties third world governments saw the
brain drain as a problem, but the Group of 77 offered no
analysis of its origins or specific programs for
eliminating it or its effects.(71)

A sort of obverse of the brain drain became a new
issue in the sixties as well. Skilled people left poorer
countries to go to wealthier ones, but that transfer was
not balanced by the transfer of skills and technology
from the rich to the poor. The postwar international
economic system treated technological innovations like
any other property. Governments of poorer countries could
have access to new technology only through the market, by
buying patent rights or encouraging the owners of those
rights to invest in the poor country. In the sixties,
however, before the role of the Bretton Woods system as a
protector of existing property rights had been openly and
loudly debated, the third world raised their concerns
about increasing "technology transfers" without linking
those concerns to specific condemnations of existing
regimes. Rather, third world governments proposed the
existence of a new "right to the fruits of technology," a
proposal to treat know-how as a common good, a collective
resource that no individual could claim an ultimate
property right to control.(72) In later years discussion
of this view would open up the north-south debate over

limits on the roles of international economic management
organizations that was never opened at the UNCTAD
conferences or at other meetings in the sixties. In the
sixties, beyond the simple affirmation that this new
right -- an extension of the rights and duties of states
-- existed, the third world had little more to say about
easing the transfer of technology.

The TNC, brain drain, and technology transfer issues
would have contributed little to the increasing
incoherence of the third world's "new" ideology had the
Group of 77 been able to remain solidly behind the view
of states economic rights and duties they had long
shared, the ideas that justified the first southern views
on these new issues. But the Group of 77 did not remain
solidly behind its oldest principles at the end of the
1960s. Paradoxically, decolonization, which increased the
number of states in the third world, proved the greatest
threat to the alliance's unity. Unity could only be
restored, in the short run, by deemphasizing the older
principles.

Governments of the newer states, mostly African,
explained the duties of developed states to make extra
efforts on behalf of the globe's poor in a markedly
different way than older members of the third world
alliance explained the same duty. The more radical
African governments in the early sixties, following those
of Guinea and Ghana, consistently spoke of duties imposed
on wealthy states by the fact that they had once
exploited their colonies.(73) The former colonizers owed
a debt to the colonized. Africans suggested many
historical precedents for such notions, including the
compensation paid by the American government to former
slaves, the more significant twentieth century precedent
of the war debts paid by those who lost the world wars,
and the debts paid by the Federal Republic of Germany to
Jewish citizens and to the state of Israel.(74) Franz
Fanon's The Wretched of the Earth, published in the early
sixties, expressed this view well:

> When we hear the head of a European state declare
> with his hand on his heart that he must come to the
> aid of poor underdeveloped people we do not tremble
> with gratitude. Quite the contrary; we say to
> ourselves: "It's a just reparation which will be
> paid to us."(75)

During the sixties this theme was taken up by
representatives of many new states both within and
outside of Africa in such a way that latent divisions
among third world states became apparent.

If this ethic of reparations were to be accepted in
lieu of the notion of permanent states' economic rights
and duties, then either many of the early members of the
third world movement, including the Latin American

states, would have no claim to aid from wealthy
countries, or else the relevant historical period for
assessing debts would have to be pushed back to the
beginning of the modern world economy. In the later case
the analytical distinction in the third world ideology
that colonialism was the basic early cause of
underdevelopment would be given moral force as well. Few
nations accepted this particular resolution of the
differences between newer and older members of the
alliance in the sixties. Latin American delegates to
international meetings, in particular, almost never used
the historical argument from colonialism as a
justification for the duties of wealthy states.(76)

In peculiar contrast, some wealthy states used the
restitution ethic to justify their lack of action in
support of the LDCs. By the 1968 second UNCTAD the
socialist states of eastern Europe, which had appeared to
be so cooperative to the third world at UNCTAD I, had
adopted the restitution ethic. They said that their
duties differed from those of the DMCs because as
socialist states they neither had been colonizers nor had
they exploited poorer countries through the instruments
of neocolonialism.(77) Neocolonialism, after all, had
been linked only to capitalism by the popularizer of the
concept, Kwame Nkrumah.(78)

After they learned the position that the socialists
would take, Group of 77 members reunited behind at least
that part of their old ethic that said all rich states
had duties to poor ones. The Charter of Algiers, agreed
to before UNCTAD II, reflected that part of the earlier
stand without ever mentioning reparations for
colonialism.(79)

This charter makes specific demands upon the
socialist states. Nonetheless, it devotes no space to
outlining the general ethic for international economic
relations. In one sense, this lack of the usual
restatement of the general ethic could be interpreted as
just reflecting a recognition that the principles of the
new economic order had already been stated at the first
UNCTAD and voting on them again at the second would just
be an example of a fruitless use of the Group of 77's
majority. Now was the time to "move away from the stage
of deliberation to the plane of practical action."(80)
But, by not explicitly restating the older understanding
of the economic rights and duties of states and saying
that they were the only fundamental principles for the
new order, the Group of 77 left room for some of its
members to argue for aid on the basis of the restitution
ethic.

Two factors continued to assure that the dispute
over the restitution ethic would generate further
developments in the south's ideology. First, most of the
LDCs to which the ethic appealed were also LLDCs, those
that were the most dependent on exports of commodities

that sold in what they believed to be particularly wild,
fluctuating markets, and those that received the least
foreign aid. This was the group of countries some
scholars in the north started to call the "fourth world,"
the poorest nations whose economic interests differed
from those of the wealthier third world states. The
restitution ethic symbolized the particularly severe
problems of the least advantaged. Second, the ideological
predilictions of many of those people sympathetic to the
LDCs in rich countries made them more sympathetic to the
restitution argument than to the one based upon assumed
permanent rights and duties of states. Jean Paul Sartre
exemplifies this northern view in his preface to The
Wretched of the Earth where he argues that the shame
Europeans feel when confronted with knowledge of the
worst horrors of colonialism would make them accept
Fanon's view that restitution was essential.(81)

Yet at the end of the sixties, when third world
states first mounted an effort to influence public and
elite opinion in the north, they did not rely on the
powerful restitution ethic because not all third world
states shared it. The 1969 Declaration on Social Progress
and Development, which was supposed to be so widely
distributed, exemplifies the moral compromises the
alliance had to reach at the end of the decade.(82) Its
second and third articles lay out the by then traditional
rights of states. Its first, fourth, fifth, sixth, and
seventh articles lay out specific egalitarian rights of
individuals and families. The bulk of the rest of the
document lays out only specific duties of governments,
some of governments in developed countries, some of
governments in developing countries. Article 26 specifies
that restitution for aggression and illegal occupation
must be paid by the aggressor state. But this article
does not say that back payments for colonialism that had
ended was necessary. All the specific UNCTAD principles
of 1964 are included as specific duties. What is missing
in this program, as in the Charter of Algiers, is an
overarching article explaining all these duties of
developed states under a single justification -- either
as specific instances of a duty to aid the unique
economic development of the neediest or as specific
instances of a duty to provide reparations for
colonialism.

In some ways, of course, this loose definition of
the duties of developed states, this lack of an
overarching article, contributed to the later success of
the ideology in attracting supporters in the developed
world. Third world silence on the ultimate moral ground
of northern duties under their new economic order allowed
northern supporters to choose their own justification.
Like Sartre, they could emphasize a duty based on
historical rights violated during colonialism. Like
Pearson, they could emphasize a general, ahistorical duty

of wealthy states. Nevertheless, the person in the developed countries who was not yet sympathetic to the plight of the LDCs could find as many contradictions in the late-1960s version of the third world position as sympathizers could find justifications for creating a new economic order.

This incoherence in the third world view at the end of the decade made it difficult for those who first observed global economic meetings then to see the "third world" as a reality. Identifying a "third world ideology" from a single meeting at the end of the sixties would be just as difficult. Just as the new order ideology had been temporarily lost in the cooperative north-south dialogue at the beginning of the "development decade," the disagreements within the south at decade's end made statements of their common position increasingly vague, abstract, and indistinct. Observation of the common third world position at any point in the decade other than its very beginning and end would yield an entirely different picture. The new order ideology remained distinct throughout most of the sixties.

It passed through two separate stages of growth just as significant as the first stage it had passed through while the Bretton Woods system was forming. The second and third stages, like the first one, were characterized by fundamentally new issues that members of the third world alliance were learning to apprehend in the same way. During the whole decade southern adherents to the new order ideology reiterated their consensus about the economic problems that the Bretton Woods system left unresolved and added to it an analysis of what to do about new problems that the operation of the Bretton Woods system helped create. In the first half of the decade, the second stage in the development of the ideology, only these new problems related to the system's operation served to trigger ideological innovation.

The second half of the decade, the third stage in the ideology's development, was more eventful. Adherents consciously defined their collective political identity, made the further specification of their shared views a conscious goal, and began to develop strategies to make their views dominant. Of course the third world had a collective identity by 1959, but conscious reflection on that identity, which was needed before further specification of shared views could be made a conscious goal, only came with the formation of the Group of 77 and the subsequent development of political strategy which marked the third stage.

The fact that reflection upon their collective identity had become commonplace for group members by the end of the decade made it possible for them to consciously redefine that identity in order to assure group unity. When the ideological conflicts between the richer and poorer developing states appeared at the end

of the decade members of the group could make their
shared views more amorphous to accommodate the
conflicting views. That made the group's ideology look
less coherent. But a more significant commitment to
consciously developing a shared position remained the
foundation for the group's stated views, even at the end
of the sixties. Reinforced by strategic commitment to
group unity that developed as a conscious political
tactic in the late sixties, the ability to reflect upon
and redefine what it meant to be "the third world"
allowed the alliance to rapidly turn their position,
which was temporarily amorphous at the end of the
sixties, into the much more coherent and concrete calls
for a New International Economic Order that dominated the
seventies.

NOTES

(1)Patino speaking at Second, 18, Oct. 4, 1963, p.
27; Sidney Weintraub, "After the U.N. Trade Conference:
Lessons and Portents," Foreign Affairs 43 (Oct. 1964):
46.
(2)GATT, International Trade 1966 (Geneva: 1967).
(3)Quoted by the Indian delegate at Second, 13, Oct.
18, 1958, p. 45.
(4)See e.g. the Economist's editorials cited in
chapter 1, note 95.
(5)This was a Bolivian suggestion, Second, 12, Oct.
27, 1958, p. 87.
(6)GATT, International Trade 1960 (Geneva: 1961),
pp. 7-10. See also Undersecretary de Seynes's report on
trade, Second, 15, Oct. 12, 1960, pp. 7-9.
(7)Saudi Arabia, Second, 15, Oct. 18, 1960, p. 100.
(8)Colombia, Second, 15, Oct. 28, 1960, p. 114.
(9)Raul Prebisch, "The Economic Development of Latin
America and Its Principal Problems," Economic Bulletin
for Latin America 7 (Feb. 1962): 1-22.
(10)On the third world view see Mexico, Second, 15,
Oct. 28, 1960, p. 110 and Turkey, Second, 15, Nov. 1,
1960, p. 123.
(11)See the appeal by Uruguay to U.N. members to live
up to Charter duties by instituting "equitable
treatment," Second, 15, Oct. 27, 1960, p. 87.
(12)G. Aforka Nwekwe, Harmonization of African
Foreign Policies 195-1975: The Political Economy of
African Diplomacy (Boston: Boston Univ. African Studies
Center), p. 94-107.
(13)Selected Documents, Belgrade Declaration of
Non-Aligned Countries, Sept. 6, 1961, p. 9.
(14)Second, 16, Oct. 20, 1961, p. 76.
(15)GATT, International Trade 1961 (Geneva: 1962),
pp. 20-28.
(16)John A. Pincus, Trade, Aid, and Development (New

York: Council on Foreign Relations, 1967), pp. 126-27.
    (17)Branislav Gosovic, UNCTAD: Conflict and Compromise (Leiden: A. W. Sijthoff, 1972), pp. 15-21.
    (18)E.g., Tunisia, Second 15, Nov. 1, 1960.
    (19)Second, 17, Oct. 17, 1962, p. 72. This was first suggested in the U.N. by Krishna Menon, Second, 15, Nov. 11, 1960, p. 195.
    (20)See e.g., Chile, Second, 18, Oct. 16, 1963, p. 106.
    (21)Second, 17, Oct. 4, 1962, pp. 19-20.
    (22)Joshua, 9:21.
    (23)Selected Documents, Charter of Alta Gracia, Mar. 7, 1964, pp. 29-31.
    (24)Selected Documents, Niamey Resolution on the U.N. Conference on Trade and Development, Dec. 13, 1963, pp. 20-21.
    (25)See the short intellectual history in the annex to the group of experts report on the structure of the United Nations system, A New United Nations Structure for Global Economic Cooperation (New York: United Nations, 1975), pp. 61-69.
    (26)Second, 18, Oct. 8, 1963, p. 57.
    (27)Raul Prebisch, Towards a New Trade Policy for Development (New York: UNCTAD, 1964); on the report as the conference agenda see A. D. Friedeberg, The United Nations Conference on Trade and Development: The Theory of the Peripheral Economy at the Centre of International Discussions (Rotterdam: Rotterdam Univ. Press, 1969), pp. 70-84.
    (28)Compare Friedeberg's discussion above with the UNCTAD principles in Selected Documents, UNCTAD I: Final Act and Recommendations, June 15, 1964, pp. 43-50.
    (29)Selected Documents, UNCTAD I: Final Act and Recommendations, June 15, 1964, pp. 43-47.
    (30)Weintraub, p. 52.
    (31)Hence Patino's remark quoted at the head of the chapter.
    (32)Gosovic, p. 164.
    (33)Ibid., p. 165.
    (34)Urie Bronfenbrenner, "The Mirror Image in Soviet-American Relations: A Social Psychologist's Report," Journal of Social Issues 17, no. 3 (1961):45-56.
    (35)Gosovic, p. 166, note 42.
    (36)See, for example, the general argument about the United States in Stephen D. Krasner, Defending the National Interest (Princeton: Princeton Univ. Press, 1978).
    (37)Margaret Garritsen de Vries, The IMF 1966-71: The System Under Stress, vol. 1 (Washington: IMF, 1976), pp. 269-76.
    (38)Explicit GATT acceptance of this notion was quite straightforward by the mid-1970s. See Selected Documents, Tokyo Declaration, Sept. 14, 1973, pp. 444-49.
    (39)GATT, International Trade 1965 (Geneva: 1966), p.

19.

(40)Weintraub, p. 48.

(41)Friedeberg summarizes Haberler's criticisms, pp. 53-56.

(42)Selected Documents, Joint Declaration of the Group of 77 at UNCTAD I, June 15, 1964, p. 33.

(43)Gosovic, pp. 52-57.

(44)See the penultimate paragraph of the Joint Declaration, Selected Documents, p. 34.

(45)See the affirmation in Selected Documents, Cairo Declaration of the Non-Aligned Countries, Oct. 10, 1964, p. 94.

(46)See Gosovic's analysis, p. 57.

(47)On the creation of these consensus or "conciliation" procedures see Gosovic, pp. 56-57, and see pp. 171-72 on concessions the south obtained.

(48)Ibid., p. 172.

(49)Consider, e.g., the Nigerian statement in the Second Committee during planning for UNCTAD II. Instead of calling for new principles, the way Nigerian's had when they helped lead the call for UNCTAD in the early part of the decade, he emphasized conciliation procedures and demanded that the UNCTAD agenda be very specific, Second, 22, Oct. 4, 1967, p. 16.

(50)Selected Documents, General Assembly Resolution 2152: United Nations Industrial Development Program, Nov. 17, 1966, p. 843. UNIDO coordinates policy with the U.N. Development Program and the U.N. Capital Development fund which provides multilateral aid through voluntary contributions by U.N. members. The capital development fund was created at the same time as UNIDO.

(51)Selected Documents, Charter of Algiers, Oct. 24, 1967, pp. 135-45, c.f. the Nigerian speech, Second, 22, Oct. 4, 1967, p. 16.

(52)Lester Pearson, ed., Partners in Development (New York: Praeger, 1969).

(53)Ibid., pp. 56-57.

(54)Ibid., pp. 7-10.

(55)Ibid., pp. 3-32.

(56)Second, 23, Oct. 14, 1968, p. 7.

(57)Indonesia, Second, 23, Oct. 11, 1968, p. 2.

(58)Second, 24, Oct. 16, 1969, p. 30.

(59)Selected Documents, General Assembly Resolution 2543: Implementation of the Declaration on Social Progress and Development, Dec. 11, 1969, p. 855.

(60)Second, 24, Oct. 15, 1969, p. 19.

(61)See Chinweizu's emotional account of these beliefs among members of Africa's elite in the independence generation, "The Cult of Liberal Democracy," The West and the Rest of Us (New York: Random House, 1975), pp. 234-46.

(62)At the 1966 meeting of the Second Committee India forecast that debt servicing payments for the third world would be greater than incoming aid in less than fifteen years. Second, Oct. 13, 1966, p. 20.

(63)See chapter 1, note 91.

(64)The early discussions in the U.N. along these lines took place in 1966. See the Syrian speech, Second, 21, Oct. 14, 1966, p. 69.

(65)See the Algerian speech, Second, 24, Oct. 20, 1969, p. 61.

(66)This proposal was contained in an IMF report discussed by the delegate from Sudan, Second, 21, Oct. 17, 1966, p. 85.

(67)An Economist editorial of July 27, 1963 issue (p. 34), suggests increasing global liquidity simply by giving needed aid to poorer states. The editors distinguish this proposal slightly from Stamp's. Stamp would have the actual level of international trade determine the level of increased liquidity in the system, although an aid element would be introduced by giving much of that new liquidity to poorer states.

(68)By Undersecretary de Seynes reporting to the Second Committee, Second, 20, Oct. 5, 1965, p. 7.

(69)Cuba had raised these issues at the beginning of the decade, Second, 15, Oct. 27, 1960, p. 94, but few other states mentioned TNCs in the U.N. until the late sixties.

(70)In 1968 the Asian Regional Conference of the International Labor Organization urged the organization's staff to address questions of TNCs. In the same year U.S. members of the organization urged a similar study. Thus that organization studied the relationship between TNCs and social policy before UNCTAD or the Economic and Social Council did. The later began their work in 1972. U.N. Department of Social and Economic Affairs, Multinational Corporations in World Development (New York: United Nations, 1973), pp. 116-17.

(71)The first U.N. discussion of the brain drain was triggered by Iran, Second, 22, Oct. 15, 1967, p. 50.

(72)Oscar Schacter, Sharing the World's Resources (New York: Columbia Univ. Press, 1977), pp. 105-24. Schacter's primary concern is with the broader legal and ethical questions suggested by the issue.

(73)Ibid., pp. 20-21.

(74)Ghana, Second, 15, Oct. 20, 1960, p. 35; Guinea, Second, 16, Oct. 18, 1961, p. 49.

(75)Franz Fanon, The Wretched of the Earth (New York: Grove Press, 1968), p. 102.

(76)Latin American delegates rarely use the argument that wealthy nations were obligated to repay for colonialism. They do argue that a history of colonialism is a cause of underdevelopment and that the wealth of the developed states obligates the developed states to aid the underdeveloped.

(77)See Gosovic, p. 166, and the strong statement of this position in Selected Documents, Joint Statement of the Socialist Countries on the Second Development Decade and Social Progress, Sept. 21, 1970, pp. 204-207.

(78)Kwame Nkrumah, Neocolonialism, The Last Stage of Imperialism (London: Nelson, 1965).

(79)The Charter of Algiers eschewed the moral justifications found in previous third world statements and replaced them with a discussion of third world poverty and the failure of previous international efforts to reduce it.

(80)Selected Documents, Charter of Algiers, Oct. 24, 1967, p. 136.

(81)Jean Paul Sartre, Preface to Fanon's The Wretched of the Earth, pp. 7-34.

(82)Selected Documents, General Assembly Resolution 2542: Declaration on Social Progress and Development, Dec. 11, 1969, pp. 850-54.

3
1970–1974: Cracks in the Old Order and Calls for the New

> If listeners to the lengthy speeches and readers of the flow of documents acquired a slight sensation of having heard much of the debate before, a rapid perusal of earlier documents will show their suspicions to be justified. "What I tell you three times is true," is, of course, very largely the case in relation to the developing world's problems.
>
> -- Barbara Ward, 1974

> The Present Declaration on the Establishment of a New International Economic Order shall be one of the most important bases for relations between all peoples and nations.
>
> -- The General Assembly, 1974(1)

If anything, Barbara Ward's sympathy for the third world makes her overestimate the originality of the 1974 New International Economic Order texts. Only the notion that the third world policy analysis was sophisticated enough to actually govern global economic relations was new. The 1974 documents repeated old views, yet they were more consistent and comprehensive than any previous set of new order texts. In 1974 the newly named "NIEO" ideology provided a more coherent basis for an alternative to Bretton Woods than it ever had before.

Nonetheless, in retrospect the language of the 1974 texts has even more of an Alice in Wonderland quality than Barbara Ward detected. But when they wrote the 1974 texts, new order advocates shared a new hope that the old order was falling. They believed that restating their views could be something more than ritual. Third world officials knew as well as Barbara Ward did that no genie with magic words, or even the wiliest sympathizers with the U.N., would be able to convince all governments of the truth of the third world position. But changes in

American economic policy beginning in 1971 appeared to signal the end of the postwar economic system. The system's operation had begun to have unanticipated consequences unacceptable to its major supporters. By 1974 all national governments recognized a need to change the international economic order. The LDCs thought they had a chance to influence the change that was bound to take place.

To be able to present the coherent new order proposals they presented, third world governments had to engage in unprecedented, complex international politics between 1970 and 1974. Four types of third world actions influenced the coherence and content of the NIEO ideology by the time the proposals it framed had become major issues on the international agenda.

First, in uniting to react to the increased trade restrictions imposed by the U.S. and the decreased value of all aid as a result of American actions taken in 1971 third world officials reaffirmed that the unity of their alliance was fundamental and that it was based on common grievances with the present global economic order. They reaffirmed that the present order operated to the equal detriment of all third world states.

Second, to help cement the renewed unity that these new grievances established, third world leaders -- both government officials and scholars -- began to adopt the intellectual framework provided by the dependency and neocolonialism theories that had been worked out by independent third world thinkers since the mid-1960s. That framework provided a more coherent way to understand the most recent problems experienced by third world countries, the problems associated with TNCs and existing impediments to the transfer of technology. The framework served to minimize new research on economic differences among third world regions, differences which had caused the cracks in the LDC alliance in the late sixties. And analyses of dependency and neocolonialism convinced some of the leaders of older third world states in Latin America and Asia to accept that developed states had historical duties to LDCs; thus the dependency framework contributed to a resolution of the conflict over ethics between richer and poorer third world states.

The dependency framework also justified a greater sense of grievance with developed nations because it suggested that LDCs had suffered from ideological as well as political domination. The sense of grievance helped legitimate more aggressive actions to improve the economic position of the south -- including the OPEC price increases -- while it called into question the ability of developed states to negotiate major changes in the economic order without prodding. Third world political action more militant than the employment of "democratic means" thus became more acceptable to the alliance as a whole. In addition, the dependency framework suggested that fundamental change in the international system could remove dependence. Third world leaders had to argue for revolutionary change.

While doing so they resolved the roles of their, still contradictory views of the responsibility of developed nations. The restitution ethic became the basis for the north's moral duty to negotiate a new order. The notion of permanent states rights and duties to aid the unique economic development of every other state remained the single ethic that would guide action in the world economic system that would then be created.

A third aspect of the inter-LDC politics that created the 1974 new order demands is leadership. Leadership of the alliance as a whole was much more evident and important in the early 1970s than it had been ever before. Leaders tended to select themselves rather than be selected; nonetheless, in the early seventies some national governments and individuals organized the entire alliance to anticipate and employ the newly experienced economic vulnerabilities of the postwar system's supporters.

Finally, third world governments united to anticipate and react to the new economic policies that developed states suggested in international meetings as proposed solutions to the system's crises. Some policies advocated by the north, creating international means for dealing with environmental degradation and controlling population, were responses to the unanticipated "resource limits to growth" revealed by the vast expansion of the world economy since the war. Similarly, northern proposals for controlling the international energy trade were indirectly responses to limits to growth problems, although much more directly to the unanticipated development of a powerful bloc of third world oil producers. The responses of third world leaders to these problems had consequences for their NIEO ideology. Southern ideologists argued the oil price increases were legitimate but changed their views on some other issues in response to the north's concerns.

This chapter begins with a review of the divisions within the southern alliance in 1970. Then it discusses the causes of each of the four types of political action outlined above, their consequences for the new order ideology, and the sources of new elements added to the ideology as the result of each type of action.

THE THIRD WORLD DIVIDED

In 1970 observers could see two camps in the third world. Each had a different approach to international and domestic economic problems. Those differences can be exemplified by contrasts between the resolutions of the nonaligned states, which met that year in Lusaka, and the resolutions on the Second Development Decade that the General Assembly adopted a few months later.(2) The first program was much more radical than the second.

Both theoretical and tactical differences separated the two blocs within the third world. The nonaligned states, predominantly nations that had obtained their independence since the second world war, predominantly from Africa, and predominantly very poor, emphasized colonialism and neocolonialism as the forces impeding global economic change. The General Assembly where the Latin American states played a major role (and, of course, where the developed states had a voice) concentrated on more specific barriers to economic change, things that had long been identified by supporters of the new order ideology -- low levels of international aid and trade restrictions imposed on third world products, for example. The General Assembly did not mention neocolonialism. It limited its political discussion to reiteration of specific economic duties of states and closed by calling on national governments, particularly in developed states, to influence public opinion and convince the wealthy of their duties. The nonaligned states, in contrast, spoke of "democratic means" only in terms of "democratization of international relations," that is, "the right of all countries to participate in international relations on an equal footing."(3) In addition, the nonaligned states emphasized economic duties of developing states toward one another by focusing on a newly named strategy, "collective self-reliance."(4)

In 1970 collective self-reliance was still more of a symbol than a program. It referred to no one policy. Aid to the least developed states, autarky, and receiving aid from China were all included under this rubric.

The notion of collective self-reliance grew out of the frustrations felt by the poorest developing nations with their unsuccessful attempts in the sixties to find solutions to their economic problems through changes in the global system. The states most concerned with collective self-reliance were the ones that first raised the issue of aid to the least developed in the 1960s. The principle had been affirmed by the U.N. but in 1970 it still had no influence on the policies of aid agencies, including the U.N. programs.(5) In response to international aid that they felt was meager relative to their needs, some LLDC governments began to consider their own national resources to be the only sure basis upon which they could make development plans. "Self-reliance" symbolized that recognition without pointing to any particular policy. "Collective self-reliance" of third world states suggested that inter-third world aid and cooperation was essential. The nonaligned states committed themselves to that aid without specifying programs except to reiterate that all third world states should unite behind efforts to aid the least developed.(6)

The General Assembly as a whole, in contrast, included all of the relatively wealthy third world states. By 1970 some of those states, especially in Latin America, had already become a sort of global "middle class," a semiperiphery capable of making some economic advances within the postwar system. They did not suffer the specific frustrations the LLDCs knew. To most Latin American states the idea of opting out of the present system, which seemed to be what "self-reliance" meant, was absurd.

Of course, opting out of the international system was just as absurd to most nonaligned members. They had no such choice. Their international affirmation of self-reliance reflected little desire to leave the system. Instead, it reflected their growing realization that most developed states were not going to expand their aid commitments no matter how poorer states tried to convince northern elites of the moral duties incumbent upon the wealthy or upon former colonizers. The nonaligned adopted the view presented by the Sudanese in the U.N. two years earlier: Developed states gave aid for their own reasons. The poorest states were forced to be self reliant, or, at least, reliant upon the collec- tive help that developing states could offer one another.(7)

In affirming collective self-reliance the more radical nonaligned states moved away from the position that the duties of former colonizers to aid former colonies could be an effective ethic in the international economy. The duties of third world states under "collective self-reliance" reflected the duties the nonaligned had said every state had at Bandung and earlier. The nonaligned states thus proved a 1970s version of the Indo-Sino Panch Shila. In fact, the resolutions of the Lusaka conference linked this duty of collective self-reliance to the dictates of the U.N. Charter, interpreted as it had been by the third world since 1946.(8) In this sense "collective self-reliance" represented a step toward unifying the positions on ethics taken by different third world states in the sixties. The poorest third world states moved back toward the long-standing new order position.

Yet "collective self-reliance" did little to resolve the ideological differences among third world nations, at first. The roots of the notion, the models of collective self-reliance praised both by third world officials and by scholars in 1970, hardly appealed to nonsocialist third world states or to those with outward-oriented economic policies. The nonaligned states took China and Yugoslavia to be examples of nations that had achieved self-reliant development.(9) "Self-reliance" had been given a stronger ideological form in the democratic socialist program of Tanzania, the Arusha Declaration, which proposed a Spartan sort of development centered around self-reliant village collectives.(10) The single most cited example of international, collective self-reliance in 1970 was the railroad connecting Zambia and Tanzania. It was built not with the expensive technical assistance and vast capital outlays of a northern bilateral aid program or of a U.N. project, but with the aid of Chinese work teams living in Africa in a style little better than that of their African hosts.(11) From the point of view of a development planner in (say) Brazil or Iran in 1970, collective self-reliance looked like an inward turning, autarkic program compatible, at best, with the minimal requirements of a barely developing national economy. Indeed when Tanzania's Julius Nyerere stated his nation's development ideology he emphasized that his country could not become a mass-consumption industrial society in the forseeable future, a view that the leaders of wealthier third world states rarely offered in an analysis of their own countries.(12)

In 1970 the fundamental differences in economic interests perceived by the more- and less-wealthy third world states remained. The notion of collective self-reliance would only come to help bridge the ideological rift when wealthier third world states started to push for aid to the least developed.

THE THIRD WORLD REUNITED

During the 1971 autumn session of the General Assembly the wealthier southern states did push for a more direct identification of the LLDCs. The General Assembly ordered all U.N. agencies to come up with special plans for aiding those states, plans that were to be "comprehensive" and "action oriented."(13) This turned out to be just one example of the increasing third world unity during that session.

The long-term dynamics of the global economic system established at the end of the second world war assured that third world governments would have reason to reconstruct their unity. The system generated problems that made the U.S. government adopt a new economic policy in August of 1971. The problems that southern nations believed the policy would create for them generated the south's renewed unity.

Ostensively, the American decisions had nothing to do with third world issues. American policy makers were trying to improve the position of their economy relative to economies of other developed market states. The most dramatic, if not the most substantive, part of the new U.S. policy involved severing the last link between the value of the dollar and gold. That was enough to make even the popular press see a transformation of the

international economic system.(14) Nevertheless, the new
policy was not designed to usher in a new international
economic order. In fact, it was enacted when it was in
order to save the economic system from greater
crisis.(15)

The immediate problem the Americans faced in 1971
was a massive trade deficit, primarily to western Europe.
The trade deficit added to the long-standing payments
deficit the U.S. had with its developed partners.
Earlier, American imports from developed countries and
American export of capital to them had facilitated
economic growth in Europe and Japan. Likewise, American
payments deficits were, in a sense, integral to the
system because they assured that the international
currency, dollars, was available in the volume needed for
trade. Dollars could be used to be used to buy goods from
any state. Foreign holders of dollars could safely refuse
to spend them immediately on goods that could be
purchased only in the U.S. because currencies remained
convertible. In fact, if need be, foreign holders of
dollars could convert them into gold through the U.S.
government.

At the very beginning of the Bretton Woods system's
regular operation, in the late fifties, the convertibility of dollars into gold was an especially important
part of what made the system work. It meant that the
dollar, and each of the currencies that could be
converted into the dollar, was backed by a relatively
stable measure of value. Merchants from all countries
could feel secure while engaging in international trade
because the money they had a money they could trust.
Trade expanded and triggered economic growth that
benefited many nations. Not the least of the benefits
went to the U.S., whose trade expanded to provide the
capital equipment needed for the economic recovery of the
formerly-developed states.(16)

After the Japanese and western European economies
reached the same mass production levels as the U.S.
economy, the benefits of this system to the U.S. started
to diminish. Western European and Japanese interest in
purchasing American goods failed to grow as quickly as
before. Foreign markets for American goods could have
expanded had the U.S.'s major trading partners revalued
their currencies upward against the dollar, making
American goods relatively cheaper. Markets also could
have expanded had the U.S. devalued the dollar. But the
Bretton Woods institutions provided no easy means for
forcing the relevant governments to adopt either of these
policies. The IMF could recommend that (say) the Germans
or the Japanese revalue their currencies, but the IMF had
no power to enforce the recommendation. Nations with
strong currencies hardly needed the balance of payments
loans the IMF provided. The IMF was equally powerless
relative to the U.S. It could not force the U.S. to

devalue the dollar the same way it could "force" any other debtor state, by offering loans with devaluation as part of the quid pro quo. The "values" of various currencies the IMF actually could attempt to devalue were stated, in large part, in U.S. dollars. The Bretton Woods system itself had to change if there were to be a U.S. devaluation because the American currency was not merely a national currency with a value that could be freely changed against an international standard; it was the international standard, as much as the gold it was convertible into. The American Treasury's valuation of dollars relative to other currencies thus served two functions. It not only defined the value of the currency that could be used to buy American goods, it provided the international standard of value for all currencies.

By 1971 the American government had come to see these two goals as contradictory. Domestic economic interest, in reducing the trade deficit, demanded that the U.S. devalue the dollar. International economic stability seemed to depend on the U.S. accepting an overvalued dollar. This contradiction assured that some aspect of the postwar system would change. The Nixon administration did not decide to scrap the Bretton Woods system in 1971; that would have been the much greater crisis that the government wanted to avoid. Nonetheless, the administration attempted, successfully, to force other DMCs to renegotiate some of the fundamental principles of Bretton Woods.

The unilateral U.S. action was designed to do one of the things the IMF could not do to ease the U.S. trade deficit. The U.S. decisions were not aimed at removing the dollar as an international standard of value, which would have been one way to approach the problem. Rather, the U.S. aim was to force new exchange rates between the dollar and the currencies of America's major trading partners, to make U.S. goods less expensive abroad.(17) Removing the convertibility of the dollar to gold forced those holding dollars abroad to seek another way of being sure their dollars continued to hold value. The easiest way was to let the value of the U.S. dollar relative to other convertible currencies be more freely determined by international money markets and by new financial agreements among the DMCs. Because there was an impetus to value the dollar accurately relative to other currencies, the dollar was effectively devalued.

In order to encourage the adjustments in the trade and money policies of other DMCs that the effective devaluation of the dollar would require, the United States took some actions that, inadvertently, affected the LDCs as well. In addition to suspending dollar-gold convertibility, the U.S. government announced across the board tariff increases of 10 percent on goods coming into the U.S.(18) Third world products became more expensive to Americans; third world income from trade was bound to

fall.
    And the effective devaluation of the dollar, itself,
hurt third world economies. Dollars that the LDCs
received from the multilateral aid agencies and the IMF
were devalued so that, in real terms, aid decreased
rapidly. By mid-1972, dollars purchased significantly
less in all DMCs other than the U.S. than they had a year
before.(19) It took significantly more of the dollars
from a World Bank loan for Senegalese fishermen to buy
Norwegian tackle. It took significantly more of the
dollars from an IMF drawing for the Ivorian government to
settle a debt in Marks to the West Germans. Of course, no
increase in U.S. aid alleviated this problem of the
decreased value of multilateral aid denominated in
dollars. The point of the overall U.S. program was to
make foreigners more interested in buying goods produced
in the U.S. where the dollar in 1972 could still purchase
most of what it could in 1971. In fact, rather than
increasing U.S. aid in 1972, the government decreased it
even in the "real" terms of its purchasing power in the
U.S. alone.(20)
    The third world reaction to the new American
economic policy was swift and negative. In 1970 third
world delegates had dispensed with the general debate on
economic matters at the fall U.N. session because the
debates were so repetitive. Positions were known. There
was nothing new to say.(21) But the third world
vigorously reentered the debate in September 1971.
    During the fall 1971 General Assembly session
southern delegates never contradicted each other's
analysis of the economic decisions the American
government had made in August. The third world argument
can be separated into four parts, discussions of (1) the
reasons for the American decision, (2) the role of the
third world in alleviating American economic problems,
(3) the regrettable consequences of the U.S. action that
the south would have to suffer, and (4) the actions that
should be taken in light of the American decisions.
    Third world delegates argued that the ultimate
reasons for the American decisions could be found in
flaws in the Bretton Woods system, flaws that existed
only because southern interests were not consulted when
the system was created.(22) This view justified
increasing third world input into the decisions to
restructure the IMF that would have to be made in wake of
the American decisions. But the historical assertion was
never backed by analysis of how the Bretton Woods system
could have been any less flawed with third world input.
    The Libyan and Iraqi delegates identified the more
immediate cause of the American actions as the American
payments deficit. The deficit had grown throughout the
Indo-China War, they argued. It was caused by the war and
by the vast cost of the U.S. military bases in
Europe.(23) The Libyans concluded that southern states

were not responsible for the economic problems of a developed nation when those problems were caused by such "foreign adventurism."(24)

Complementing this analysis of the reasons for the American decisions, the Peruvians noted that southern states had, in fact, contributed to the American economy. Most third world states had trade deficits to the United States similar to the deficits the U.S. had to its developed trading partners. In addition, the south contributed through profits repatriated to American TNCs operating in third world countries, profits that, he argued, exceeded the new U.S. investment in the south.(25) Egypt and Mexico reiterated this point about TNC profits flowing into the U.S.(26) The Mexican delegate went so far as to illustrate that the U.S. was profiting from its developed trading partners in Europe in the same way. These three delegations described the United States as governed by people who would irrationally and unfairly make nations that had contributed to American economic vigor suffer for American economic setbacks, setbacks that had been caused by the "adventurism" discussed by Libya and Iraq.

Third world delegates saved their most vehement denunciation of the U.S. for predictions about the consequences of U.S. action. In light of the reduction of real American aid to the third world, the Philippine delegate predicted the immediate failure of the U.N.'s Second Development Decade.(27) Most LDC spokesmen noted that American tariff surcharges would reduce the south's income from trade. The Nigerian delegate charged that as a result, African states would join Latin American states and some of the large nations of Asia as victims of high debt-servicing requirements, becoming debtors with loans they could never hope to pay unless development programs were reduced or halted.(28) The Sudanese representative suggested another consequence of the American decision: Productivity was the key to development. Political instability assured lower productivity. And reductions in third world trade income assured political instability.(29) In sum, the south held that the new American economic policy assured an abrupt slow-down in LDC development, and that was a global crisis.

To alleviate the problems they expected to arise because of the American policy, most third world ambassadors just reiterated old formulas. For Upper Volta, one of the world's poorest states by any economic measure, direct financial assistance from the U.S. to compensate for the trade lost due to American tariff increases was a practical and moral necessity.(30) The Mexican ambassador, in contrast, said that Mexico would not make claims for damages to the Mexican economy that would occur because of decisions already made. Rather, Mexico demanded creation of a global monetary system that would prevent nations from getting into the economic straits that the U.S. had found itself in in the first place.(31) While the Mexican delegate continued the tradition of the more conservative, older third world states and refused to argue for restitution the way African states did, he did so only in order to frame a more radical demand for restructuring the monetary order. Following the Mexican theme, the Egyptian delegate argued that, of course, the new monetary order would include the Link between international provisions of liquidity and foreign aid.(32)

In contrast to the long-standing third world programs offered by other states, Libya suggested a new departure. The Libyan government argued that it was time that the third world used its dormant capacity to influence raw material prices in order to change the world economy. This was a notion that the third world had long approved in theory, but that few governments practiced.(33)

Throughout 1970 and 1971 Libya had moved to nationalize all stages of domestic oil exploration and production. The government then used its power over traditional consumers of Libyan oil to raise its price.(34) At the U.N. Libya merely suggested that its example be followed by other third world states. After all, DMCs seemed not to realize the continuing contribution of LDCs to DMC wealth. DMC governments failed to consider how the repatriated profits of TNCs helped the north. And the north failed to recognize the role played by the decline of DMC raw material prices relative to those of manufactured goods from the developed countries. According to Libya, southern states had every reason to follow its example, to nationalize those firms they had the power to nationalize and to raise the commodity prices they had the power to raise.

In sum, the American decisions provided an impetus for recreating third world unity and, ultimately, for reestablishing a unified third world ideology. For all practical purposes the unity of the Group of 77 was reestablished by the end of the General Assembly's 1971 session when the group made the assembly pass concrete proposals for providing U.N. aid to the LLDCs. But the ideological basis of that unity remained a bit tenuous.

A rapid progression of international conferences on economic matters, called long before the American decisions, maintained the impetus toward greater unity and built momentum from late 1971 through 1974. In October 1971, while the U.N. debates about the global economy continued in New York, meetings of the Group of 77's regional subgroups covered the same topics in Addis Ababa, Bangkok, and Lima. At each conference delegates upbraided the U.S. for its decisions. In the African view the U.S. was trying to force the south to solve northern economic problems.(35) At Lima the Latin American states agreed upon new extensions of the old notions of states'

economic rights and duties. Henceforth the economic
rights of states included a state's right to demand
removal of obstacles to its development when those
obstacles were imposed by other states. The Lima
conference considered American tariff surcharges examples
of such obstacles. The Latin Americans extended the
duties of states to include a specific duty of wealthy
states to solve their payments problems without hurting
the economies of poorer states.(36)

When the Group of 77 met together in November, the
Latin American position on new economic rights and duties
became the view of the group as a whole. This added a new
element to the shared ideology, the notion of a nation's
"right to develop." In practical terms the LDCs used the
"right to develop" as an overarching justification for
all the conflicting positions about the wealthy nations'
"duties to aid." The new right implied that states
seeking a self-reliant development path had the right to
expect that developed states would not oppose actions
taken toward that end -- nationalizations and
restrictions on trade and investment.(37) The south also
used the right to develop to demand that developed states
anticipate and facilitate the movement of some
industries, including textile and clothing manufacturing,
to the LDCs. This later policy was first proposed at the
Asian states' meeting at Bangkok.(38) Finally, this new
principle, like the earlier versions of the third world
ethic for international economic relations, implied a
right of all nations to live under a world economic
system that did not impede their specific national
development plans. Thus, not surprisingly, although this
notion had first been raised to frame grievances with the
specific problems that the breakdown of the Bretton Woods
system caused for Latin America, only a month after the
idea was first raised the Group of 77 used it to justify
fundamentally new policies, simply because those policies
were integral to the development plans of a few nations
that were part of the group.

Surprisingly, though, despite third world resentment
of the new American economic policy and despite the
Libyan precedent, the Group of 77 joint meeting placed
little emphasis on exploiting DMC economic vulnerabilities in order to achieve LDC goals. The group's position
on tactics remained the commitment to influence public
and elite opinion in the DMCs.(39) Nonetheless, by the
end of 1971 many group members had made their
dissatisfaction with this approach very clear. At the end
of the three regional meetings only the Asians went on
record supporting the tactic.(40) During the U.N. debate
in October only Uruguay made proposals along these lines,
urging UNESCO to mobilize public opinion to support
developing states.(41)

At the third UNCTAD meeting in the spring of 1972
the group supported stronger affirmations of the right of

individual states to control natural resources.(42) But the south did not stop trying to convince the elites and publics of developed states to accept responsibilities toward poorer states. Nonetheless, the one resolution passed on the subject did little more than praise the press briefing given by UNCTAD officials before the conference.(43)

In part the new, more militant tone of the group at UNCTAD III can be explained by the conference's location. Some observers from the DMCs have suggested that Santiago, the capital of Salvador Allende's newly elected Marxist government, attracted the most radical staff members from third world economic ministries, people interested in observing the experiment in social change going on in Chile.(44) Since global economic meetings were so frequent in the early seventies, younger, more radical staffers could easily have won the right to go to Santiago. For that reason northern delegates took the debates in Santiago with a grain of salt. Yet, UNCTAD III's resolutions came to be a model for later third world positions rather than a more militant exception.

No doubt Santiago, with its Marxist government, influenced the south's position at least indirectly. Throughout March and April of 1972 the world press reported stories of the earlier unsuccessful attempts of the American C.I.A. and the American transnational corporation I.T.T. to prevent Allende's election. Stories about continuing attempts to destabilize his regime appeared as well, implicating other corporations, other branches of the U.S. government, and even the World Bank.(45) Had UNCTAD III been held at another time or on the other side of the globe, few third world officials would have had reason to reflect on the Chilean experience. In Santiago they did reflect on the power transnationals in cooperation with their home governments wielded over third world states. Perhaps the new third world emphasis on using their own power to control transnational firms and raw materials can be explained by that reflection.

By the end of 1972 even the more conservative Latin American states were making more radical statements about the world economy than they ever had before. The catchphrase of that autumn's U.N. debate was "collective economic security." Uruguay called for "collective economic security" to be the fundamental principle of the new, post-Bretton Woods economic system that the United Nations should create.(46) "Collective economic security" implied that third world states had to unite their powers to assure that their "right to develop" was respected. In that sense, "collective economic security" started as a Latin American version of "collective self-reliance." The 1972 General Assembly economic debate had only two major themes, "collective economic security" and the "new economic order" it implied.

Throughout the debate third world states praised themselves for working to achieve collective economic security. Peru noted that almost all members of the Group of 77 granted tariff preferences to the LLDCs. The Peruvian delegate praised the formation of the Andean Pact for the same reason. The pact created a south American alliance aimed at more stringent monitoring and control of foreign investment.(47) The spokesman for the United Arab Emirates affirmed that the oil producing states shared the same problems that other raw material producers faced. For that reason, he said, the oil producers would continue to aid poorer third world nations.(48) Many governments assured each other that it had been the unity of the third world that had forced the north to accept what the south identified as the only significant reform in the IMF since the U.S. decisions in 1971 had certified the beginning of the end of Bretton Woods. The developed nations allowed their caucus in the IMF, the Group of 10, to be expanded to "the Group of 20," including ten third world members, in inner councils where substantive reform of the monetary system was discussed.(49)

At the same time, in 1972 the LDCs continued to discuss what a new economic order dedicated to "collective security" and earlier versions of their principles would look like. Most of the south's proposals had been heard before, and the few innovations followed directly from what had been proposed before. Chile argued that the global economic system should truly be made global by including eastern Europe and China.(50) The Mexican delegate reiterated this position, using the opportunity to stress that the Soviet Union's economic duties to poorer states were very similar to those of the United States. Finally, the Mexican ambassador closed by extending the global aid doctrine that had been proposed by La Guardia in 1946. Mexico called for a global progressive income tax on nations. The duties of wealthy nations to poorer nations would be specified and vary with per capita wealth. And the relative financial needs of poorer states would be pinpointed the same way.(51)

By the end of 1972 official pronouncements indicated as great a conscious unity among the LDCs as had existed in the mid-1960s. Yet many divisions remained below the surface. Unity had been achieved at the expense of advancing tactics beyond what they had been in 1967. "Collective economic security" symbolized a radicalization of the position taken by the more conservative third world states, but when translated into practical proposals for changing the international system "collective economic security" provided no more significant new policy directions for the Group of 77 as a whole than "collective self-reliance" had for the nonaligned states. Even though third world leaders discussed the creation of a global economic system that would periodically redistribute wealth to poorer states, their proposals to achieve that goal had existed for years. The redistribution could happen through commodity agreements, increased aid, or the proposed Link, as well as through a global income tax on nations. But the third world position still lacked a coherent strategy for making any of these proposals a reality. Developing such a strategy would be difficult. Despite professions of third world unity and the new reasons for that unity stemming from American economic policy, differences in economic interest from region to region in the third world remained. Each of the differing interests had to be satisfied, at least in part, during any transition to a new order so that third world unity would not be shattered by the process of transition itself. That is what made inventing such strategies so difficult.

THEORY AS A SOURCE OF UNITY

Before 1970, outside the international conferences on economic matters and more isolated from the requirements of day-to-day foreign economic policy making, groups of third world scholars had developed economic analyses that would expand the range of tactics available to the south and help cement the ideological basis for third world unity during the crucial period in the early seventies. Theories of dependency and neocolonialism appeared in every third world region in the late sixties. These theories stressed similarities among third world states rather than differences. They helped LDCs understand the rise of transnational firms and and the existence of impediments to the transfer of technology, the major new economic problems experienced by the third world in Bretton Woods system's heyday. At the same time, the new theories arose from and remained compatible with the analysis of global trade problems and of the promise of industrialization which the south had long accepted.

Third world scholars developed neocolonialism and dependency theories as a challenge to the "modernization" framework developed in the north.(52) Modernization theorists look to the examples of the European states, the Soviet Union, the United States, and Japan to prove that economic development is similar everywhere. They ask, "What should people in underdeveloped countries do to develop quickly?" Dependency theorists, in contrast, hold that the wealth of developed nations and the poverty of underdeveloped nations are both results of the same global process, an ongoing process that continues to produce development in some regions of the world and underdevelopment in others.

The dependency framework actually existed in the third world before the modernization framework was developed. In the 1950s scholars in the newly independent states confronted a conventional wisdom which said that any local economic development would have to be structured by the export requirements and political whims of the colonial powers.(53) Likewise, Prebisch's early analysis of development in Latin America emphasized the greater power of the developed center to control the global production system, which restricted Latin American development.

Nonetheless, in the 1950s and 1960s few third world governments would accept a development policy analysis emphasizing dependency alone. The most prominent third world scholars shared the official view that the south had some control over its development. Prebisch's ECLA in Latin America and influential economists from the new states, such as Caribbean economist W. Arthur Lewis, emphasized possibilities for autonomous development through their advocacy of import-substitution policies and, later, of regional economic integration.(54) In Africa decolonization theorists, including Fanon and Memmi as well as the many national independence leaders who were scholars in their own right, concentrated upon gaining political independence and called it the key to economic independence. Fanon and Memmi even said that intellectuals who concentrated too much on economic dependence were raising psychological barriers to national development.(55)

The emergent intellectual prominence of the dependency school in Latin America and the Caribbean and of studies of neocolonialism in Africa and other third world regions represented the legitimation of the dependency framework. In the late sixties dependency theorists became involved in the more official discourse on economic development, the discussion that went on in third world universities and United Nations research organizations.

In Africa the relegitimation of the dependency framework was relatively simple. Unlike Latin America states, few African governments developed a stake in defending the theories of economic modernization that deemphasized international structural constraints upon development. After decolonization African governments continued to emphasize the economic decisions made abroad that restricted African economic development -- decisions made by (1) foreign consumers of African raw materials, (2) states and international agencies granting aid to the continent, and (3) potential foreign investors. Kwame Nkrumah's Neocolonialism, published in 1965, said that attempts to foster economic development through an open, outwardly-directed policy of encouraging foreign investment and exports was doomed. Nkrumah argued that the economies of developed capitalist states required exploitative world economic relations akin to colonialism to be continued after independence. Thus he appeared to repudiate the statement he had so often made before, a

sentiment shared by many other African independence
leaders, that all else would follow once Africans had
"seized the political kingdom."(56) By 1970 the United
Nations economic research unit in Africa, the Institute
for Economic Planning and Development in Dakar, was
promulgating the same thesis in the views of its Egyptian
director, Marxist economist Samir Amin.(57)
    In Latin America and the Caribbean the official
emphasis both of national governments and the U.N.
research arm, ECLA, was more on finding economic
modernization policies available to governments rather
than on searching for all forms of independence. While
questions associated with the dependency framework tended
to be ignored in the western hemisphere until the
mid-sixties, Prebisch's analysis of trade dependency
continued to be a foundation of later ECLA views.(58)
    Further development of dependency ideas in Latin
America began, according to dependency theorist Fernando
Cardoso, when the failure of the modernization programs
ECLA had advocated became clear. Import substitution and
regional integration did not result in the type of
development enjoyed by the societies that were the models
of modernization.(59) By 1965 ECLA economists were
looking for new analyses of Latin American economies and,
although the states that ECLA served did not support the
development of dependency theory, the organization itself
supported independent dependency scholars. In their view,
histories of Latin American "dependency" could explain
the failures of policies ECLA had advocated.
    Norman Girvan and other Caribbean dependency
theorists explain the relegitimation of their framework
in their own region in the same way. Development policies
influenced by the modernization framework had failed.
Elements of the particular modernization theories that
had been developed by local economists, especially Lewis,
implied that dependency was real. Thus dependency ideas
could easily be adopted by scholars in Caribbean
universities and research institutes where research was
officially directed toward solving development
problems.(60)
    With the increasing legitimacy of the dependency
framework came increasing legitimacy for specific
historical explanations that many dependency theorists
advocated. This analysis, in turn, entered the New
International Economic Order ideology.
    Between 1968 and 1970 dependency theorists in both
Latin America and the Caribbean published analyses of the
forms dependency had taken since the second world
war.(61) They emphasized the increasing significance of
transnational firms. Such firms just represented the
latest way that economies of developing states were
transformed to serve the developed world. Dependency
scholars unraveled the strings of dependency tied by
TNCs. They distinguished the effects of profits

repatriated to TNC home countries from the effects of
TNCs' monopolies of industrial technology and from the
ways TNCs strengthened certain elites in developing
countries. In sum, the dependency theorists argued that
because TNCs had industrial monopolies, third world
elites had to pay monopoly rents in order to get the
technology needed for development. If a southern nation's
elite encouraged development through TNC direct
investment, the tendency of TNCs to repatriate would take
away the development advantages. If the elite tried to
buy industrial technologies, they would have to maintain
the traditional export sector in order to obtain the
large amount of foreign exchange needed to buy capital
goods from TNCs abroad. Neither policy allowed real
development, that is, the ability to leave a dependent
position in the world economy.(62)

After the American actions in 1971 -- which by 1972
the U.N. Secretariat had directly linked to increased
payments deficits in most LDCs -- many third world
officials adopted some of the dependency analysis of
TNCs. They linked this analysis of TNCs to the problem of
development programs becoming highly dependent on an
increasingly difficult-to-maintain positive balance of
payments. Third world states had to have payments
surpluses in order to afford more capital goods from
abroad. Southern officials placed this analysis under the
moral rubric of states' duties to aid the economic
development of other states. The 1972 Peruvian and
Chilean U.N. delegates argued that corporations should be
required to live under a code of conduct that would limit
repatriated profits.(63) The delegate from Uruguay argued
that DMC governments should facilitate the direct
transfer of technology and bypass TNCs.(64) The U.N.
Economic and Social Council adopted a resolution in June
1972 that triggered most of the U.N.'s subsequent
investigations of TNCs and the transfer of technology.
Subsequent U.N. studies reflected dependency analysis.
They presented the rise of TNCs as a logical consequence
of the postwar international economy. Poorer states that
had few powers to control firms became victims, unlike
the wealthier states (where most TNC investment actually
occurs). In response, the U.N. proposed providing
alternative sources of modern technology and improving
the negotiating skills of third world officials who dealt
with TNCs.

Dependency theory contributed much more to the new
order ideology than an analysis of TNCs and the transfer
of technology. More significant was the dependency
theorists' concentration on global structures that
affected all third world nations to the exclusion of
analysis of regional differences in the third world. That
emphasis contributed to third world unity.

The effectiveness of dependency theories in this
regard is again related to their increasing legitimacy.

By 1970 dependency and neocolonialism theorists held prestigious jobs in universities in all third world regions as well as in the African and Latin American U.N. research arms.(65) They used the resources of their professional positions to increase their contacts with those who shared the same perspective in other parts of the third world and in developed countries through individual meetings and conferences. In 1968, for example, Andre Gunder Frank, whose dependency ideas affected Latin America, met with Samir Amin.(66) One conference among dependency scholars in 1972 resulted in a sort of textbook of dependency analysis, an issue of the West Indian journal Social and Economic Studies. All of the articles appeared in English, what Cardoso calls the "Latin" of contemporary world scholarship.(67)

The international spread of dependency theory extended beyond the southern regions on either side of the Atlantic. Asian scholars and government officials, like their Atlantic counterparts, became disgruntled with modernization ideas of the 1960s. One of the foremost Asian policy analysts who changed his mind was Mahbub ul Haq, once planning minister of Pakistan and later World Bank vice president. His 1976 study, The Poverty Curtain, contains a compelling personal account of how he came to reject the modernization theories which had guided his unsuccessful planning.(68)

Ul Haq personally contributed to the conscious unity of third world scholars behind the new order ideology. By 1972 he, like the Latin American dependency theorists, felt that adherence to northern models of modernization by third world planners was a form of ideological dependence. He summarizes his thoughts then:

> Should we [third world scholars] not establish our own institutions of intellectual self-reliance . . . which would give form and substance to our aimless search for appropriate development strategies at home and our disorganized efforts to coordinate our negotiating positions abroad?(69)

With a group of other third world scholars in U.N. positions including Gamani Corea (Secretary General of UNCTAD), Enrique Inglesias, (Executive Secretary of ECLA), and Samir Amin, ul Haq created the Third World Forum in 1973, a group dedicated to "intellectual self-reliance."

The forum never became a major source of new dependency ideas: it simply supports the efforts of the south to gain the New International Economic Order. It never speaks out against the ruling elite of any developing state. It does not analyze class struggles within LDCs, although shifting class relations are the characteristics of dependency and neocolonialism that most interest those dependency theorists with fewer government ties now, a decade after the forum was created.(70)

The creation of the forum, nonetheless, brought part of the dependency framework into a significant position in the international debate. By agreeing to the forum's first statement in 1973, the directors of UNCTAD, ECLA, the U.N. Institute in Africa, and the most prominent Asian economist in the international organization system went on record affirming that all third world states shared the same international structural impediments to development.(71) None of those agencies or individuals could have been expected to conduct or disseminate research that emphasized contradictory regional economic interests from that point forward.

In addition to providing a further basis for treating the LDCs' economic problems as a unit, dependency theorists directly helped to resolve the tactical dilemma faced by third world governments when they tried to find ways to change the international system. Positing strong systemic, rather than domestic, sources of development and underdevelopment reinforced the view that only fundamental changes in the international system would work. In the dependency theorists' view, the fact that some people in developed states actually benefited from the underdevelopment of other regions made it naive to expect DMC leaders to change the system in response to rational, moral arguments alone. In fact, some third world intellectuals such as Nigerian social-historian Chinweizu concluded that the south's concern with democratic procedures indicated ideological dependence on northern political theory as great as the ideological dependence that many southern economists had on northern modernization theory.(72) As a result, by 1973 more aggressive approaches to convincing northern nations to change the global economic system became commonplaces of third world rhetoric. The resolutions of the September 1973 meeting of the nonaligned states in Algiers illustrate the trend. They decried "dependence and neocolonialism" arguing that ". . . the developing counties in general are still subject directly or indirectly to imperialist domination." The nonaligned states attacked "ideological domination" by the developed states and called for collective economic security measures. They even demanded that the scope of United Nations concerns with security should be expanded to include economic matters.(73)

Surprisingly, the same views that contributed to this aggressive tone also indirectly provided third world officials with a stronger basis from which they could negotiate a new order with the north. The dependency theorists' concentration on finding impediments to development still affecting all third world states allowed third world leaders to resolve the differences between the few radical states that still affirmed the

restitution ethic and the other states that based their
argument upon the permanent rights and duties of states.
Under the dependency framework governments of states
which had long been independent could argue for
restitution for current "exploitation," say by
transnational firms, as easily as new states could. Older
states could even link those claims to a colonialism that
was long dead. Only the form of dependence, not its
substance, had changed. When ul Haq was in the process of
changing his views about development, he wrote one of the
more entertaining explanations of this view as comment on
Partners in Development requested by Barbara Ward. He
noted that India had long been a "partner in development"
with Britain. Throughout Britain's colonial rule India
provided her with capital. Based on rough figures, with
low interest rates, Britain "owed" India about half a
trillion dollars in 1970. Of course, he said, Britain
would be in no position to pay that, and India, concerned
with stability in the world economy, would not want
Britain to go broke trying to do so. Nonetheless, ul Haq
had an imaginary northern friend who did not believe in
renegotiating debts and would insist that Britain pay
now. In contrast, ul Haq argued that the debt just
indicated why Britain should take part in negotiating a
more stable and fairer international economic order for
the future.
Employing a more conventional dependency analysis,
other leaders of older third world states adopted the
same position. The Mexican government of Luis Echeverria
used the "restitution duty" in 1971 and 1972 as an
argument that northern states should approve the creation
of an international Charter of Economic Rights and Duties
of States.(75) The working group that was to write the
charter was approved by UNCTAD III in Santiago. The group
was to derive the charter from prior principles -- the
UNCTAD trade principles of 1964, the 1968 Charter of
Algiers, and the ideas about the right of every nation to
develop agreed upon by the Group of 77 immediately before
UNCTAD III.(76) All of these principles pointed to an
economic order bounded by the rights and duties of states
first proposed in the 1940s. The actual charter reflected
that ethic rather than the restitution ethic used to
explain why the north should agree to the creation of the
charter in the first place.(77) The charter debates thus
illustrate the place that was found for the restitution
ethic in the new order ideology before 1974. It became
just one reason why colonial and neocolonial northern
states should negotiate toward the new order.
Thus, the reason ideas about dependency and
neocolonialism were so rapidly included in the new order
ideology in the early seventies was very simple. In one
sense a dependency framework had always been the
structure of the economic analysis proposed by third
world governments in international meetings. Since the

forties, Asian, African, and Latin American delegates had said that optimal third world development was impeded by global economic structures neither created nor controlled by the third world itself. The adoption of the particular structural analysis of transnational firms and of the problems of technology transfer was facilitated by the fact that these were relatively new, relatively unstudied issues which bothered many third world states. Dependency theory provided a readily available explanation of these new problems without contradicting any other third world assumptions. The real frustrations that third world economic planners felt with northern models of development encouraged them to adopt the dependency framework as well. So did the felt need for the continued political unity of the third world, which could only be achieved by deemphasizing the economic differences among southern states and by finding a position for the different third world views about ethics in a unified ideology.

Dependency theory by itself did not convince southern policy makers to abandon northern economic models or reunify the principles underlying new order policy analysis. Active leadership had to turn the potential provided by dependency ideas into actual contributions to the third world alliance and its ideology. Ul Haq and other third world scholars, Echeverria and his government, and others all convinced members of the alliance to emphasize southern unity. The leaders used compelling arguments from the dependency framework: Third world intellectual life was ideologically dependent on the north. All third world states had experienced colonial dependence in the past and continued to experience neocolonial dependence today. These arguments, in turn, became part of the new order ideology.

LEADERSHIP AND THE 1974 NIEO PROGRAM

Intellectual and political leaders of the third world had further major effects on the emerging ideology in early 1970s. The most dramatic example of effective third world leadership was Egypt's organization of Arab OPEC members to use the "oil weapon" as part of the Egyptian strategy in the October 1973 war against Israel.(78) While the preconditions for this successful strategy -- the existence of petroleum-dependent developed nations -- were created in part by the success of the expanding global liberal economy, the direct target of the strategy was hardly the postwar economic system itself. The "oil weapon" was a tactic designed not to create the New International Economic Order, but to aid Egypt in its rapid strike against Israel. Nonetheless, the decision made by all OPEC members --

including Iran, a supporter of Israel -- to raise the world price of oil soon after the Arab OPEC members had stopped oil sales to Israel's developed allies was reinforced by the Arab boycott. And the decision to raise prices was aimed at changing the world economy. As a result of the price increases and the disruption in the global system for allocating oil caused by the boycott, DMC governments became eager to to engage in discussions about "resource interdependence." To put it another way, DMCs were interested in discussing reform of some aspects of the postwar trade system because they themselves had experienced problems the system could not cope with and even helped generate. Self-selected leaders of the third world, in particular the governments of Algeria and Iran, seized the chance presented by the OPEC price increases to catalyze the Group of 77 to organize and present its long-standing demands in the most coherent and comprehensive way possible.

In January 1974 Honari Boumedienne, the president of Algeria, called upon the Secretary General of the United Nations to organize a special session of the General Assembly to discuss matters of raw material production, trade, and development.(79) Boumedienne found himself in an unusually strong position to make such a request. He was president of one of the more radical Arab oil states and thus the target of DMC requests that the oil issue be discussed internationally. He was also the official, temporary leader of the nonaligned states. Leadership passed to the local head of government in the country where the group's last meeting had taken place. In 1974 the Algerians took an unusual step by employing some of the power inherent in what was meant to be a purely routine position by making their request in the name of the nonaligned movement.

The request for a General Assembly session found immediate support not only from the nonaligned states but from all other members of the Group of 77 as well as the DMC governments. The U.N. Secretary General was ready to call the session immediately. He delayed only because the Group of 77 asked that it be postponed until the group could meet and prepare a more detailed positions.(80)

The story of the group's consultations between February and April 1974 has yet to be told in detail. It will probably be a very dull one. Yet the result was something that appeared to be fundamentally new -- a defiant call for international trade, finance, and monetary systems that would amend or replace those that were already existing. In substance, though, all the proposals for the NIEO, all the economic analysis offered by the Group of 77 at the Sixth Special Session of the General Assembly, and all the principles underlying that analysis were quite old. The two months between the time the Secretary General wanted to meet and the time the conference actually began was a little less than the time

usually needed to conduct the regional meetings and full
Group of 77 meeting before the more routine UNCTADs. Few
new issues could have encumbered the group's
deliberations.

One that certainly did was the adverse effects that
the OPEC price hikes were bound to have in the third
world. As one U.N. official puts it "anti-imperialism"
assured that the third world supported the OPEC
action.(81) And if that was not enough, members of the
group could rely upon an Iranian proposal that the OPEC
states manifest the duty incumbent upon them with their
new wealth by aiding the states most seriously affected
by the price increases.(82)

What was new at the Sixth Special Session was the
discipline Group of 77 members showed in their support of
the NIEO "Declaration and Programme of Action." A few
group members, particularly Iran and Algeria, guided the
debate. The Iranian delegation made many of both the
substantive and procedural motions and, more than any
other single delegation, responded to northern objections
to the new order program.

The Sixth Special Session did not turn out to be the
substantive debate on the oil question that the DMCs
wanted. In a limited sense, it was quite the opposite.
The meeting served to legitimate OPEC price actions by
having them approved by the assembly as a whole. That, no
doubt, was one of the Algerian and Iranian goals. More
significantly, for the first time the General Assembly
approved a massive resolution covering all of the
economic issues the third world had raised since the
second world war. The resolution touched on sovereignty
over national resources, improving terms of trade through
international regulation of trade based on equitable
treatment, reforming the global monetary system to
include an aid component, expanding concessionary
multilateral aid, providing debt relief, controlling
TNCs, promoting international support for
industrialization, and reforming the United Nations
system to give third world governments greater control
over international economic decisions. When presented
together, the proposals outlined a very different order
than the one that existed in 1974.

Despite the fact that the new order proposals of
spring 1974 were internally coherent and covered all
third world issues, they could hardly become "one of the
most important bases for relations between all peoples
and nations" as they claimed they would. The proposals
did not include sympathetic responses to the specific DMC
concerns with monetary problems and resource
vulnerabilities which had been exposed so recently.
Rather, leaders of the third world had simply used the
opportunity given by the growing DMC concern with its
resource dependence -- the willingness of DMC governments
to hold a special session on resource matters -- in order

to reiterate the south's position and make it more widely known.
Likewise, at the regular General Assembly session in the fall of 1974 leaders of the third world continued to use their limited powers to assure that the south's position was fully, coherently presented. General Assembly routine gave Algeria the presidency that year. Daniel Patrick Moynihan argues that the Algerians used the chair to railroad the Charter of Economic Rights and Duties of States over DMC objections, again eschewing substantive debate on the sort of new international economic system that was possible.(83) The charter, the result of Echeverria's initiative in 1972, was the most explicit and comprehensive statement of new order principles in a decade. It completed the statement of the new order program begun with the NIEO declaration in the spring.
The leaders of the third world who helped bring about these statements -- Boumedienne, Echeverria and their governments, other OPEC governments, and some Arab states -- did so for their own reasons. Personal, domestic, and regional interests played as much a role for them as the goals of the third world alliance. What Yoram Shapira says of Echeverria can be applied equally well to the others. Echeverria came to the U.N. in 1971 to publicize attacks on the trade restrictions imposed by the new American economic policy, and he argued for the charter in Santiago because, as Shapira says, Echeverria

. . . perceived a radical transformation of the international system as necessary for furnishing a solution to domestic problems and a national malaise.(84)

The leaders of the third world retained more specific allegiances to their own nations. They organized third world reaction to the signs of breakdown in the Bretton Woods system -- the U.S. decisions in 1971, the DMCs' oil vulnerabilities -- in order to advance international changes they considered important to their national interests. Third world leaders in the early seventies were not selected by some sort of competitive politics within the alliance because of their special commitment to alliance goals. They selected themselves. The leaders were those governments that took the opportunities offered by the evolving politics of international economic relations to create leadership roles for themselves. Those opportunities occurred both because the third world alliance itself had evolved so that, for example, the apparent leader of the nonaligned movement had some clout, and because unintended consequences of the expanding postwar global economy had created some specific ways in which the north was vulnerable to third world power.

RESPONSES TO NORTHERN INITIATIVES

Some DMC scholars and policy makers linked those unintended consequences of postwar growth that they first felt in the early seventies to global issues broader than the inadequacy of the gold-dollar based monetary system or the vulnerability of mass-production economies that used foreign oil. In the early seventies northern scholars rediscovered "resource limits to growth" and logically and emotionally linked them to the subsequent oil shortages created by the oil weapon and the OPEC price increases.(85) Northerners brought problems associated with these "limits" to international conferences as early as the U.N. conference on the environment held at Stockholm in 1972. Northern spokesmen argued strongly that environmental pollution coming from increasing industrialization was a global problem. Later, directly after the Sixth Special Session, a U.N. conference on population met. There, northern spokesmen linked rapid population growth to an increasingly rapid approach to global resource limits.

The immediate implications of both of these arguments were detrimental to the south's new order position. Even so, many of the original limits-to-growth scholars had advocated redistribution of the world's wealth.(86) But the existence of environmental limits to growth could imply that new industrialization in the unindustrialized third world should be stopped. And when the population problem was seen as a global issue it implied that population control rather than industrialization should be the first priority of third world development.

In response to these issues third world scholars promulgated analyses of world society suggesting that the environmental consequences of third world development and the south's population problem were minor. In doing so these scholars expanded the new order ideology to include answers to problems that had first been relevant only to developed states. While the initial southern answers were not all that sympathetic to northern concerns, for the first time the new order ideology was dealing with "global" problems first perceived by the north as such in addition to the "global" problems that only the ideology's southern adherents felt.

Environmental degradation appeared as a "limits to growth" problem of the seventies before the population question did. In fact, ul Haq's experiment in "intellectual self-reliance," the Third World Forum, began as a response to northern concerns with environmental limits to growth, to the exclusion of development, at Stockholm.(87) But the LDC view rapidly moved closer to the northern position taken there. In

1972 the nonaligned states took the position that
environmental control was not a problem relevant to third
world states except to the degree that environmental
controls might imply ". . . additional costs of
development . . . for developing countries."(88) By 1973
the south was stating this concern as an incidence of
states' economic rights and duties:

> The heads of State or Government of nonaligned
> countries stress that environmental measures adopted
> by one state should not adversely affect the
> environment of other states, or zones outside their
> jurisdiction.(89)

This peculiar article repeated the language of the demand
more frequently heard in the north that one country's
pollution should not be allowed to adversely affect other
countries. Apparently the cost of cleaning up pollution
remained the nonaligned· states' major concern.
Nonetheless at the same conference the nonaligned states
affirmed:

> Any infringement of the right of effective control
> by any state over its national resources and their
> exploitation by means suited to its own situation,
> having respect for the ecological balance, is
> contrary to the aims and principles of the United
> Nations Charter and hampers the development of
> international cooperation . . . [emphasis added]

In responding to a northern issue, the issue itself,
international principles to maintain the environment,
became part of the NIEO ideology. Ultimately, the issue
was reflected in Charter of Economic Rights and Duties of
States as its final operative article (#30):

> The protection, preservation, and enhancement of the
> environment for the present and future generations
> is the responsibility of all States. All States
> shall endeavor to establish their own environmental
> and development policies in conformity with such
> responsibility . . . All states should cooperate in
> evolving international norms and regulations in the
> field of the environment.(90)

This article contains the only principles of states'
economic rights and duties not found previously in the
1964 UNCTAD principles, the 1968 Charter of Algiers, or
the principles advocated by the Group of 77 immediately
before UNCTAD III. It is a "northern" principle
integrated into the south's ethic.
    The story of the population issue is quite
different. The northern concern with limiting population

growth in order to slow the rush toward global economic
limits was rejected by third world governments as a
whole, just as the previous emphasis on population
control in the Pearson Report had been. The 1974
population conference approved a "World Population Plan
of Action" dedicated to economic development, not to
population control. As the plan's objectives state:

> Population policies are constituent elements of
> socio-economic development policies, never
> substitutes for them.(91)

Third world intellectual leaders, joined by northern
supporters, turned the emphasis on population control
aside more directly. "The Cocoyoc Declaration" of a U.N.
conference called in Mexico under the direction of
Barbara Ward and including forum members Amin, Corea, and
ul Haq concluded:

> A North American child or European child, on
> average, consumes outrageously more than his Indian
> or African counterpart -- a fact which makes it
> specious to attribute pressure on world resources
> entirely to the growth of Third World
> population.(92)

Thus, the concern for population control never became
part of the new order ideology.

Perhaps the contrasting ways the LDCs reacted to
these two northern issues in the early 1970s can be
explained by the intellectual merits of the northern
arguments alone. There is certainly little basis for the
assumption that population growth in the LDCs will cause
us to quickly approach resource limits to growth, at
least as long as the global distribution of wealth
remains as it is now. One the other hand, there is little
reason to expect that third world industrialization will
contribute much to world pollution unless the pace of
industrialization increases markedly. And third world
population growth would make us rapidly approach resource
limits if it continued after a new, more equitable world
order was realized.

The real explanation for the different ways new
order advocates handled these northern issues involves
more than the relative merits of the the arguments. It
has to do with the compatibility of each issue with prior
third world opinions. Environmental regulation could be
seen as a duty of resource owners under the third world
ethic. Population control, perhaps, might have been seen
as a similar duty of states. But the north had previously
proposed population control as a universally valid
development policy. That represented a violation of the
general principle of a state's right to choose its own
development path. Population control for development can

never become a third world position as long as some
individual third world states have cultural or religious
opposition to contraception, because each state has a
right to such opposition according to the south views of
the rights and duties of states.

Despite the LDC rejection of the population issue,
the major story of emergent NIEO ideology in the first
half of the seventies was still one of "northern" issues
-- the economic problems of developed states, the
reactions of their governments to those problems, and the
reaction of the south to northern actions.

In the short-term there is no doubt that the most
dramatic action taken by any of the developing states in
the early seventies, the oil price increases, only made
northern problems worse, just as the price increases made
the immediate economic problems for most southern states
much worse. And the NIEO program itself offered nothing
to solve the monetary and trade problems the north
experienced. Nonetheless, if only with the environmental
issue, third world governments did demonstrate the
ability to accept some northern issues as their own. This
was an especially important development. If the new order
program was to have anything approaching the significance
that the south expected in 1974, it would have to deal
with northern problems as well as southern ones. Despite
the grand rhetoric at the Sixth Special Session, a
working new order would have to be supported by the
developed nations.

NOTES

(1)Barbara Ward, Economist, May 18, 1974, p. 65.
Selected Documents, General Assembly Resolution 3201:
Declaration on the Establishment of a New International
Economic Order, May 1, 1974, p. 893.
    (2)Selected Documents, Lusaka Declarations, Sept.
10, 1970, pp. 194-203; General Assembly Resolution 2626:
International Development Strategy for the Second
Development Decade, Oct. 24, 1970, pp. 856-65.
    (3)Lusaka Declaration, p. 197.
    (4)Ibid., p. 199.
    (5)The "least developed" category was accepted by
UNCTAD in 1964. The first U.N. list identifying those
states, a list needed before any policy could be
implemented, proposed in early 1971, Selected Documents,
Report of the Committee for Development Policy, Apr. 1,
1971, p. 869. The list included sixteen states in Africa,
eight in Asia and Oceania, and one in Latin America. It
was not until the autumn 1971 session that the General
Assembly approved the list.
    (6)Lusaka Declarations, p. 203.
    (7)Ibid., p. 199.
    (8)Ibid., p. 195.

(9)See Tanzanian President Julius Nyerere's comments on Yugoslavia and China made in 1970, Freedom and Development (London: Oxford Univ. Press, 1973), pp.147-49, 237.

(10)Henry Bienen, Tanzania: Party Transformation and Economic Development (Princeton: Princeton Univ. Press, 1970), pp. 403-47.

(11)Nyerere, pp. 232-39.

(12)See Nyerere's biography by William E. Smith, We Must Run While They Walk (New York: Random House, 1971), p. 3.

(13)Selected Documents, General Assembly Resolution 2768: Identification of the Least Developed Among the Less Developed Countries, " Nov. 18, 1971, p. 868.

(14)Fred L. Block, The Origins of International Economic Disorder (Berkeley: Univ. of Calif. Press, 1977), p. 197.

(15)Ibid., p. 198.

(16)Ibid., pp. 70-108.

(17)Ibid., p. 197.

(18)Block calls the action ". . . a blatant violation of rules governing international trade." p. 203.

(19)OECD, Development Cooperation: 1973 Review (Paris: OECD, 1973), p. 14.

(20)See the summary of the report by the U.N. Secretariat, Second, 27, Sept. 25, 1972, p. 7.

(21)Second, 25, Sept. 18, 1970, p. 4.

(22)Second, 26, Oct. 6, 1971, p. 31; Oct. 8, 1971, p. 72.

(23)Second, 26, Oct. 12, 1971, p. 84; Oct. 5, 1971, p. 35.

(24)Second, 26, Oct. 12, 1971, p. 84.

(25)Second, 26, Oct. 6, 1971, p. 31.

(26)Second, 26, Oct. 11, 1971, p. 79; Oct. 12., 1971, p. 98.

(27)Second, 26, Oct. 5, 1971, p. 62.

(28)Second, 26, Oct. 8, 1971, p. 53.

(29)Second, 26, Oct. 12, 1971, p. 91.

(30)Second, 26, Oct. 7, 1971, p. 53.

(31)Second, 26, Oct. 1, 1971. p. 79.

(32)Second, 26, Oct. 12, 1971, p. 98.

(33)Regional pacts of producers acting to increase prices were discussed within the United Nations in the 1940s. Cocoa producing nations restricted supplies to raise prices, without success, in the early 1960s.

(34)Second, 26, Oct. 12, 1971, p. 84.

(35)Selected Documents, African Ministerial Meeting Preparatory to UNCTAD III, Oct. 14, 1971, p. 243.

(36)Selected Documents, Consensus of Lima, Oct. 13, 1971.

(37)Selected Documents, Lima Declaration and Programme of Action, Nov. 7, 1971, p. 278.

(38)Selected Documents, Declaration of Ministerial Meeting of the Asian Group of 77, Oct. 7, 1971, p. 213.

(39)Lima Declaration, p. 276.
(40)The Declaration of Ministerial Meeting of the Asian Group of 77 says, "[We]. . . consequently believe that the unified expression of shared hopes and aspirations by Ministers representing the overwhelming majority of mankind would go a long way in evoking favorable responses from the international community in particular from the Peoples and Governments of the developed states." p. 215.
(41)Second, 26, Oct. 12, 1971, p. 99.
(42)Selected Documents, UNCTAD III: Resolution and Other Decisions, May 12, 1972, pp. 346-47, 352-53.
(43)Ibid., pp. 320-21.
(44)Daniel Patrick Moynihan, A Dangerous Place (Boston: Little Brown, 1978), p. 50.
(45)The articles were triggered by a series of revelations in Jack Anderson's political column beginning on March 21.
(46)Second, 27, Oct. 10, 1972, pp. 77-78. Robert F. Meagher identifies "collective economic security" as a Brazilian idea. An International Redistribution of Wealth and Power: A Study of the Charter of Economic Rights and Duties of States (New York: Pergamon Press, 1979), p. 47.
(47)Second, 27, Oct. 3, 1972, pp. 33-34.
(48)Second, 27, Oct. 9, 1972, p. 89.
(49)Chile, Second, 27, Sept. 29, 1972, p. 20; Peru, Oct. 3, 1972, p. 33.
(50)Second, 27, Sept. 29, 1972, p. 17.
(51)Second, 27, Oct. 5, 1972, p. 50.
(52)Fernando H. Cardoso, "The Originality of a Copy: CEPAL and the Idea of Development," CEPAL Review 22 (Second Half of 1977): 33-36.
(53)G. E. Cumper, "Dependence, Development, and the Sociology of Economic Theory," Social and Economic Studies 23 (Sept. 1974): 466.
(54)Norman Girvan, "The Development of Dependency Economics," Social and Economic Studies 22 (Mar. 1973): p. 2
(55)Franz Fanon, The Wretched of the Earth (New York: Grove Press, 1963); Albert Memmi, The Colonizer and the Colonized (New York: Orion Press, 1965).
(56)Kwame Nkrumah, Neocolonialism: The Last Stage of Imperialism (London: Nelson, 1965).
(57)C. C. Stewart, "Center-Periphery and Unequal Exchange: Origins and Growth of Economic Doctrine," Presented at the joint annual meeting of the African Studies Association and the Latin American Studies Association, Houston, Nov. 1977, p. 7.
(58)Cardoso, "Originality of a Copy," p. 14.
(59)Ibid., p. 35.
(60)Girvan, pp. 11-18.
(61)See the summary of works from the early seventies in Fernando H. Cardoso, "The Consumption of Dependency Theory in the United States," Latin American Research

122

<u>Review</u> 7 (Fall 1977): 18-21.

(62)Theotonio Dos Santos, "Dependency and Underdevelopment," <u>American Economic Review</u> 60, no. 2 (1970): 231-36.

(63)<u>Second</u>, 27, Sept. 29, 1972, p. 17; Oct. 3, 1972, p. 33.

(64)<u>Second</u>, Oct. 10, 1972, p. 79.

(65)See Girvan, and see Cardoso, "The Consumption of Dependency Theory."

(66)Stewart, p. 7.

(67)<u>Social and Economic Studies</u>, 22 (Mar. 1973); Cardoso, "The Consumption of Dependency Theory," p. 8.

(68)Mahbub ul Haq, <u>The Poverty Curtain</u> (New York: Columbia Univ. Press, 1976).

(69)<u>Ibid.</u>, p. 84.

(70)Analysis of social stratification within the third world has always been a theme of dependency writers and has become more prominent as time goes on. For example, see Fernando H. Cardoso and Enzo Faletto, <u>Dependency and Development in Latin America</u> (Berkeley: Univ. of Calif Press, 1979), a translation and reprinting of an earlier work. The preface discusses the role of class analysis in dependency studies.

(71)Ul Haq, p. 84.

(72)Chinweizu, <u>The West and the Rest of Us</u> (New York: Random House, 1975), pp. 234-46.

(73)<u>Selected Documents</u>, Fourth Summit of Non-Aligned Countries, Sept. 9, 1973, pp. 423-26.

(74)Ul Haq, pp. 140-41.

(75)<u>Second</u>, 26, Oct. 11, 1971, p. 79; <u>Second</u>, 27, Oct. 5, 1972, p. 49.

(76) <u>Selected Documents</u>, UNCTAD III: Resolutions and Other Decisions, May 12, 1972, pp. 58-59.

(77)<u>Selected Documents</u>, General Assembly Resolution 3281: Charter of Economic Rights and Duties of States, Dec. 12, 1974, pp. 901-906. Only one of the thirty-four articles, article 16, refers to restitution required of states continuing colonialism, aggression, neocolonialism, racial discrimination, and apartheid.

(78)Heikal, Mohamed, <u>The Road to Ramadam</u> (London: Collins, 1975), pp. 268-74.

(79)<u>Official Records of the General Assembly Sixth Special Session</u>, Plenary Meetings (New York: United Nations, 1976), p. vii.

(80)Ibid.

(81)J. Singh, <u>A New International Economic Order</u> (New York: Praeger, 1977), p. 4.

(82)Ultimately the proposal resulted in U.N. action aiding the "most seriously affected countries," <u>Selected Documents</u>, pp. 920-22.

(83)Moynihan, p. 151.

(84)Yoram Shapira, "Mexico's Foreign Policy Under Echeverria: A Retrospect," <u>InterAmerican Economic Affairs</u> 31 (Spring 1978): 30.

(85)Donella Meadows et. al, The Limits to Growth (Washington: Potomac Associates, 1972). See Moynihan's comment on the significance of limits to growth ideas, p. 51.

(86) Advocates of economic theories that take into account limits to growth tend to desire greater regional and personal economic equality.

(87)Ul Haq, p. 84.

(88)Selected Documents, Georgetown Declaration and Programme of Action, Aug. 12, 1972, p. 390.

(89)Selected Documents, Fourth Summit of the Non-Aligned Countries, Sept. 9, 1973, p. 417.

(90)Charter of Economic Rights and Duties of States, p. 906.

(91)Selected Documents, World Population Conference, Aug. 30, 1974, p. 475.

(92)Selected Documents, Cocoyoc Declaration, Oct. 12, 1975, p. 500.

4
The Debate Since 1974

If history is to be our guide, I believe that we may be on the threshold of a historical turning point. On the national level such a turning point was reached in the United States in the 1930s when the New Deal elevated the working class to partners in development and accepted them as an essential part of the consuming society. On the international level we have still not arrived at the philosophical breakthrough when the development of the poor nations is considered an essential element in the sustained development of the rich nations and their interests are regarded as complementary and compatible, not conflicting and irreconcilable. And yet we may be nearing that philosophical bridge.

-- Mahbub ul Haq, 1975

The world economic system of the last three decades has ceased to work effectively. We all believe it needs urgent and major reforms and restructuring.

-- Willy Brandt, 1979(1)

Substantive north-south debate over how to restructure the international economic order could begin only after the kind of turning point ul Haq expected in 1975. Only then would both north and south worry about convincing the other side, yet be interested enough in agreement to remain open to being convinced themselves. That is the attitude needed in any substantive debate.(2)

The development of both northern and southern views after 1974 should show if the turning point has been reached. Parties in a substantive political debate change their views in response to each other's concerns. If ul Haq is right, sometime after 1974 we would expect to see changes in the NIEO ideology resulting from both the south's serious consideration of the north's views and the south's responses to the north's serious consideration of its own views.

To use David Apter's ideas about mobilizing ideologies, ul Haq's turning point would occur when the north recognized that the south would have to be involved in order for global economic regimes to be reformed in the way the north itself wanted. The north's acceptance of the south as a partner would give the south reason to reevaluate its own views.

In fact, few north-south disagreements have disappeared since 1974. Little substantive, intergovernmental debate on north-south matters has occurred. Yet the south's ideology has changed, if only a little, in response to northern concerns.

Was ul Haq wrong, then, when he said that a turning point was about to occur in 1975? Would it be wrong to apply Apter's theory and say that a fifth and final period in the development of the south's ideology began in 1975 because the north crossed ul Haq's philosophical bridge and started to consider the third world necessary partners in world development?

Not completely. A new degree of mutual under-standing between north and south appeared in 1975, and it continues, even if agreement remains far away. The south's views became the agenda for all multilateral discussion of north-south relations, and substantive north-south debate began to occur, even if rarely in intergovernmental forums.

Few governments thought such debate was important. After 1974 northern European states simply adopted much of the NIEO ideology as their own; little remained for them to convince the south of, or for the south to convince them of. The Warsaw Pact states and France defined themselves as in agreement with the south and had little interest in substantive debate that would show how different the third world's position and theirs really were. The United States and the important northern states that tend to follow the U.S. lead -- West Germany, Britain, and Japan -- stepped in and out of the north-south dialogue. Sometimes they supported rapid resolution of outstanding north-south conflicts. Sometimes they did not. At no time did they support substantive political debate on north-south issues. American policy makers held that on fundamentals northern and southern views were incompatible. The most powerful northern states only wanted to exchange concessions with the south; they did not want to debate until both north and south had a single view of their common interests.(3) Futhermore, the south never pushed for substantive debate, although the Group of 77's political analysis shifted more and more in that direction.

Nonetheless, some substantive north-south debate has taken place since 1974, and, as a result, the LDCs have changed some of their views. Yet northern governments have rarely been direct sources of those changes. Instead, nongovernmental leaders have. Northern European officials were not the only ones to cross ul Haq's philosophical bridge. After 1974 many northern opinion leaders outside government, people like Willy Brandt, began to push for resolution of the north-south conflict. In the process they adopted some new order views and began to debate others. In response, the south increased its consideration of what northerners wanted international economic regimes to accomplish. In addition, the south adopted much of its new political analysis, its analysis of how to make the NIEO a reality, directly from the nongovernmental organizations through which northern opinion leaders expressed their support of some southern goals.

To illustrate these changes, this chapter is divided into four parts. The first section is a narrative of the north-south intergovernmental dialogue from 1975 through 1982. The second part discusses those northern goals that the NIEO ideology began to include after 1974. The third section looks at the policy proposals that the south has dropped since 1974. The final section discusses the experiments in tactics the LDCs have employed and illustrates why the south may decide that substantive intergovernmental debate is needed.

THE NORTH-SOUTH DIALOGUE SINCE 1974

Nineteen seventy-four was the year of NIEO demands. The Declaration and Programme of Action passed by the General Assembly's Sixth Special Session and the Charter of Economic Rights and Duties of States, adopted by the General Assembly in its regular fall session, contained nothing more or less than the south's position. Adoption of those resolutions involved little attempt to debate, or even to consider, alternative views.

Within two months after the adoption of the charter the most high-profile parts of the north-south dialogue had drastically changed. In February at Lome, the capital of Togo, the European Community and a group of third world nations from all southern regions except Latin America agreed upon a long-negotiated treaty. It provided European development financing and financing for third world trade income shortfalls while taking into account European needs for assured access to third world raw materials and markets.(4) A few months later twenty-two nations began to meet in what was called the "Conference on International Economic Cooperation" (CIEC) in Paris. The conference's agenda included oil and the related resource issues that the north had thought would be on the agenda of the Sixth Special Session. The north insisted that participation in the CIEC be limited in order to assure it did not become a repeat of the 1974

General Assembly sessions. At the same time the British Commonwealth met and approved a detailed, constructive analysis of the north-south problems that really represented a consensus of both its wealthy and poor members. Nineteen seventy-five also saw a cooperative meeting of UNIDO(5) and another United Nations special session called for the month before the beginning of the U.N.'s regular fall meetings.

The first four speeches to the General Assembly's Seventh Special Session exemplify the whole session and the rest of the north-south dialogue since then. Delegates were more cooperative than in 1974, but suggested little prospect for substantive north-south agreement. Despite many professions of sympathy by north to south and south to north, a great deal of misunderstanding remained.

Brazil spoke first. On most topics, the Brazilian delegate said, he was offering the Group of 77's opinion. He held two, somewhat contradictory, views of the prospects for the north-south dialogue: Because most northern states still had no national interest in the development of the south, realism suggested that the prospects for the north-south dialogue were dim. Yet, a bargain could be struck between north and south in which the north would gain a right to secure supplies of southern raw materials -- that is, no more OPEC surprises -- in exchange for accepting southern principles.(6) The proposed bargain actually contradicted those principles since they included the sovereign right of states to control their own natural resources. Perhaps Brazil was proposing to give up that fundamental right in order to get northern agreement on other southern principles. Or perhaps it expected the north to agree to some statement of third world principles before the LDCs agreed to some treaty giving the north assured access; at that point the south could turn right around and say that agreeing to such a treaty would violate the principles the north had just affirmed. The Brazilian speech suggested that any hope the south had for a north-south settlement was misguided.

Daniel Patrick Moynihan followed the Brazilian, reading a message prepared for U.S. Secretary of State Henry Kissinger, who had decided to continue his shuttle diplomacy in the Middle East rather than attend the conference. Nonetheless, the fact that Kissinger had even momentarily thought about attending the meeting represented a major shift in U.S. policy, a shift apparent throughout the speech Moynihan read. The speech announced the reversal of the general U.S. opposition to commodity agreements and proposed a number of major new U.S. aid initiatives.(7) These involved improving third world agriculture, something no third world state opposed, yet something that was hardly an NIEO priority given the long-standing southern focus on industrialization. Nonetheless, even though the Kissinger speech concentrated on things that were somewhat beside the main point of the NIEO program, the speech did represent a major shift in U.S. policy toward the third world position. Southern states recognized that shift throughout the conference and since.

Italy, representing the European Community, spoke after the United States. Self-satisfied, the Italian delgate praised the Lome agreements and suggested that the European Community had long been in the forefront of developed country efforts on behalf of the third world.(8) Later in the conference European Community members received some confirmation of their view of themselves. Tunisia singled out France as the only major DMC that really pushed for third world industrialization,(9) and Yugoslavia praised the British government's cooperative policy toward the NIEO.(10)

Finally Norway, not a European Community member but one of the northern European countries that have always been sympathetic to the south, took the podium. The Norwegian spoke more briefly than the others, but much more directly about what developed countries had to do if they supported the NIEO. Norway recognized that such an order would mean industrialization and diversification of third world economies, which, in turn, would mean the end of some industries in the north. In order that no one in Norway would have to suffer from the government's policy of encouraging the NIEO, the Norwegian government had adopted adjustment assistance policies, becoming one of the earliest of the few governments that compensate workers whose industrial jobs are lost to competition from poorer nations abroad.(11)

In ul Haq's terms, the Norwegian statement demonstrated that Norway had crossed the philosophical bridge. The Norwegian government recognized that for its own economy to advance the economies of third world nations had to advance as well, and it even based its domestic economic policy on that assumption. Most Norwegians shared their government's view of how their development and that of third world are linked. For them economic development was more than growth. By 1975, Norwegians, and other northern Europeans, unlike most people from DMCs, tended to agree when pollsters ask if the wealth of people in developed countries is somehow diminished by the poverty of people in other parts of the world.(12)

It could be argued that the European Community's Lome policy represented a similar crossing of the philosophical bridge. At the very least, European Community members wanted to secure markets and sources of raw materials in the third world and would encourage third world development in order to do so.

It could not be argued that the same concerns motivated the American change of heart evident at the

Seventh Special Session. That in no way implies that Kissinger's speech was not significant or sincere. But as Catherine Gwin argues, the main reason the U.S. changed its policy toward the NIEO was because its previous policy of trying to divide the south, pitting the poorest nations against the oil states, simply had not worked.(13) The policy failed both because the third world took a united stand and because the U.S. never really decided whether it wanted to ally with the poorer states against OPEC or with OPEC against the NIEO demands. Kissinger recognized that a more cooperative strategy for achieving U.S. interests was essential. U.S. interests involved secure supplies of oil for itself and its wealthy allies, but they did not include third world development. If anything, the United States was interested in limiting its material commitment to southern development in 1975. Recession following a period of high inflation made the U.S. government cautious about new financial commitments. Rather than saying that third world development was essential for U.S. development, Kissinger's speech said that U.S. growth was essential for third world growth. The first thing he thought the developed countries should do to help the third world was to get their own economies in order.(14)

Since 1975, inflation and recession, along with the threat of inflation and recession, have dominated the developed economies unlike in any decade since the twenties and the thirties. Consequently, the Americans have constantly reiterated their view that the best thing northern governments could do for the third world is to establish stable continuous growth in their own, northern economies. Third world spokesmen have always said that this argument misses the point of the third world's NIEO demands.(15) Most recently the UNCTAD Secretariat's preparatory document for the 1983 UNCTAD VI meeting argued that recovery of the world economy required deliberate policies to encourage recovery in the developing nations.(16) Nonetheless, many northern governments and even many U.N. officials affirm what has been the U.S. position since 1975, that southern economies depend on northern economies but not vice versa.

Only one year after the Seventh Special Session the U.N. Secretariat reported to the General Assembly that the greatest hope for third world development that could be found in the events of 1976 was the recovery in developed nations. Nonetheless, the Secretariat made a point of saying that its interest in northern recovery should not be misconstrued as affirming the "drop-by-drop" theory of development. The north should do more to aid the third world than the little bit it could do after solving all northern economic problems.(17)

The Secretariat's views should be read as saying

that very little happened in 1976 to make third world
governments hopeful. Despite the change in northern tone,
the Seventh Special Session resulted in no substantive
agreements. 1976's fourth session of UNCTAD resulted in
nothing but agreement that some issues surrounding a
proposed integrated program of commodity pricing
agreements, to be funded by a common fund for buffer
stocks, should be discussed later. Some northern
governments wanted them discussed only at the CIEC, which
continued to languish in Paris without agreement. The
best that the Group of 77 could say about the UNCTAD IV
meeting was that in response to its substantive failure
members of the group had agreed to coordinate their own
efforts even more.(18) For example, from 1977 onward the
foreign ministries of each country in the group approved
a united statement on current economic matters before
each autumn's U.N. session.(19)

The few portents of possible north-south agreement
came from the actions of intergovernmental and
nongovernmental organizations, not from government to
government talks. At the fall U.N. session Jamaica's Don
Mills spoke for many Group of 77 members when he praised
a new attitude apparent in the World Bank.(20) While the
bank had not responded to the General Assembly's 1974
demand that all specialized agencies develop action plans
for the NIEO, it had significantly changed its policies
since the beginning of the decade. Bank President Robert
McNamara replaced his earlier insistence upon population
control as a panacea for development with a more
sophisticated understanding of the local and global
structural constraints. The bank began to emphasize
education and health programs designed to break local
cycles of poverty. In addition the bank substantially
increased low-interest aid through the IDA. The World
Bank also began to support a policy initially championed
in the U.N.'s specialized agencies by the International
Labor Organization, using development policy to eliminate
poverty around the world by focusing aid on "basic
needs."

The Group of 77's position on "basic needs" began
and remained somewhat ambivalent. Too great a
concentration of international effort on supporting basic
needs would take emphasis away from the group's
fundamental development goal, industrialization. In that
way, basic needs programs supported by the north looked a
lot like other northern efforts aimed at deflecting the
north-south dialogue from what the LDCs felt was its
proper course -- northern concerns with population
control, resource limits to growth, agricultural
development, and northern economic recovery. An Indian
U.N. delegate in 1978, for example, affirmed the
importance of fufilling basic needs but argued that
concerns for social justice should not divert attention
from the need to change the global economic system.(21)

On the other hand, "basic needs" development began as something of a third world idea. The International Labor Organization and the World Bank picked it up from a group of Latin American scholars who used it to criticize the philosophy underlying the original limits to growth studies of the early seventies. Rather than deriving policy conclusions based on assumptions about what would happen if present trends were allowed to continue without policy changes, the way the northern limits to growth scholars had, the Latin American group argued that goals for global development should be set first and any efforts at modeling the world system should discover how best to achieve those goals. The Latin American group simply chose eliminating poverty worldwide as one of the goals that the world system should strive to achieve.(22)

Somewhat ironically, in 1976 the south began to take the advice of a much more direct successor of the original northern limits to growth study. The original limits to growth study had been financed by the Club of Rome, a primarily western European and North American group of business people, government officials, and academics interested in global problems. In response to the criticism generated by the first report the club commissioned more studies. The third, Reshaping International Order, appeared in 1976 and argued for most of the third world's NIEO proposals as well as for proposals to deal with environmental limits to growth and global security problems.(23) Partially in response to this Club of Rome report's recommendations, Peru proposed adding to the NIEO program the demand that nations move toward disarmament and that the money saved by reduced military budgets be directed to development.(24)

The report had further effects on the LDCs' position. The report outlined both a long term plan for achieving the new order as well as plans for immediate change. The long term plan specified the time needed to enact the major changes it envisioned much more carefully than the 1974 NIEO plans had, making it clear that a completely transformed international order was not really feasible for a generation, even with constant effort. At the beginning of the 1976 General Assembly debate on economic matters the Secretariat reiterated the same time frame, arguing that subsequent debate should consider the NIEO as something to be achieved between then and the end of the century.(25)

Ideas found in the Club of Rome report had an even more significant effect on the south's views the next year. Again it was the Peruvians who brought the views into the intergovernmental debate. Nineteen sevety-seven was a year of great disappointment for the south. CIEC ended without substantive agreement on the third world program. Contradicting the north's explanation of the failure of the 1974 General Assembly meetings as the result of having too many nations involved, the south explained the failure of CIEC as a result of having so few states represented. Mexico led off the fall General Assembly debate by saying that the assembly's major concern in 1977 should be to prevent such unrepresentative meetings from taking place again.(26) Peru followed up with a much more detailed discussion of the CIEC, ending with the proposal that even if specific NIEO negotiations were to be conducted by small groups of states, all those negotiations should be carried out within a framework previously negotiated by all nations.(27) This proposed structure of negotiations was almost identical to the one proposed by the Club of Rome.

Other LDCs immediately adopted the Peruvian position. Brazil had the Peruvian speech reprinted and distributed widely during the General Assembly meeting.(28) The Group of 77 has maintained the Peruvian view of how north-south negotiations should be conducted ever since.

The original Peruvian speech noted that the one really positive thing that came out of the CIEC discussion was something that should come out of any substantive political debate, a real exchange of ideas. The Peruvian delegate felt that northern governments, especially the then new Carter administration in the U.S., had learned something about the south's views and had been convinced by some of them.(29) Unfortunately, he still noted a great deal of the northern attitude that, according to Gwin, had motivated the original American change of heart toward the NIEO in 1975. Some northern states still considered the purpose of north-south negotiations to be "palliative or philanthropic."(30)

The same debate illustrated much continuity in the American attitude. As evidence of the seriousness with which Carter took the U.N. debate, as U.S. representative he had sent Richard Cooper, a highly respected economist, probably the most qualified representative the U.S. had ever sent to U.N. economic meetings. Cooper reiterated the American view that the most important thing the U.S. could do for southern development was to keep its own economic house in order. When he commented on additional policies, he only emphasized things like basic needs that the south felt were somewhat beside the main point. He did not invite the south to be involved in transforming international economic regimes.(31)

Cooper's attitude represented something of the "Trilateral" position that characterized the early Carter administration. European, North American, and Japanese government officials, corporate leaders, and policy makers created the Trilateral Commission as a response to the economic problems of the early seventies. Trilateral members emphasized reestablishing the postwar free trade system on a stronger footing.(32) Trilateral reports proposed that the consensus needed to rebuild global economic regimes should be built in two parts, with the

"Trilateral countries," the United States, Japan, and the European Community (or at least its leading member, West Germany) agreeing among themselves and then dictating to, or "inviting the consensus of," the rest of the world. A 1977 report even proposed this as the way to gain global consensus on means to solve third world development problems.(33) President Carter built his administration around fellow Trilateral members. Consequently, despite the increasing sympathy with the south that Peru had noted, the U.S. remained opposed to the Group of 77's strategy for negotiating a new order.

The north-south dialogue changed little throughout the rest of the Carter years. The General Assembly responded to the Peruvian proposal to have framework negotiations involving all states by having "committee of the whole" meetings on economic matters at each fall session. In 1979 Jamaica's Don Mills pointed out that such meetings had accomplished nothing.(34) No one disagreed. The UNCTAD V meeting in 1979 resulted in little further progress on the integrated commodity program.(35) A United Nations Conference on Science and Technology for Development met in September 1979, but achieved no substantive agreement on technology transfer. An uneventful meeting of UNIDO took place in 1980. Finally, the General Assembly met in another special session on the NIEO in 1980. The meeting did nothing more than prior meetings of the committee of the whole. The U.N. came up with a plan for the 1980s as a development decade, but that plan contained no framework treaty for NIEO negotiations.

The only thing that made the south hopeful at the 1980 special session was a speech by United States Secretary of State Muskie. Muskie referred to his government's recently completed Global 2000 Report, which outlined reasons why U.S. development would become increasingly dependent on growth in other parts of the world. The report noted the disarray of the postwar economic system and the need for reform.(36) Muskie's speech affirmed an American move away from Trilateralism that had been developing for some time. In May 1979 American security advisor Brzezinski had spoken of ". . . widening our primary relationships to encompass countries in Latin America, Africa, and Asia," and of developing a new "genuinely global" American foreign policy.(37) Muskie's speech a year later implied that the U.S. had crossed the philosophical bridge and recognized the south as partners in development who would have to be part of the initial consensus on any restructured international economic order.

Nevertheless, the U.S. remained opposed to the ways in which the south proposed negotiating the NIEO, even when those proposed means had significant northern support. The Carter administration attitude toward a north-south summit on development exemplified that attitude.

The idea for such a summit came out of the first report of the Brandt Commission,(38) another nongovernmental group created in the seventies. This independent commission on development topics organized had been organized by Willy Brandt, former German prime minister and head of the world social democratic movement. The commission's aim was to produce a sort of ten year update of the Pearson Commission report. Brandt, therefore, chose his commissioners from policy makers and business people around the world, especially those from the north. Overall, the Brandt commissioners began with more conservative leanings than the members of the Pearson Commission. The Brandt Commission included Edward Heath, former head of the British Conservative Party, and Peter Peterson, Nixon's Commerce Secretary, both more conservative figures than the British and American politicians chosen by Pearson. Nonetheless, in comparison to the Pearson Commission's conclusions, the Brandt Commission's were more radical and more compatible with the NIEO ideology.

The Brandt Commission proposed to spark languishing north-south negotiations by a summit meeting of a limited number of heads of government from both developed and developing countries who would discuss and debate north-south matters.(39) The press throughout the north quickly backed the 1980 Brandt summit proposal. But the U.S. government, involved in a presidential election and a foreign affairs crisis in Iran, did not.

Immediately after the 1980 U.S. presidential election, Mexico's president, Lopez Portillo, who along with Austrian socialist leader, Prime Minister Bruno Kreisky, had agreed to host the Brandt summit, visited with the new American president-elect. To the surprise of many in the south who knew Reagan as the man who rejected the Global 2000 Report out of hand and had never expressed the slightest belief that the LDCs were essential to the development of the north, Portillo convinced the new U.S. president to attend the summit held at Cancun, a Mexican resort.

As the Mexican Foreign Ministry's report of the Cancun summit makes clear, the vast majority of those represented -- third world nations along with Austria, Canada, and Sweden -- spent their time trying to convince the representatives of three nations -- Reagan, British Prime Minister Margaret Thatcher, and West German Foreign Minister Hans Dietrich Genscher -- to support an updated version of the Peruvian proposal of a way to negotiate a new order.(40)

The new proposal called for a three phase series of "global negotiations." Negotiations would begin with establishing a framework within the General Assembly. Then bargaining over reforms of specific parts of the U.N. system would be conducted within the agency that would be most affected -- e.g., development finance negotiations in the World Bank, trade negotiations under the auspices of the GATT and UNCTAD. Finally, the whole package of new order agreements would be discussed again by the General Assembly, which would iron out disagreements among proposed reforms and ratify the entire package.

Reagan's government found the proposal for global negotiations particularly problematic, and not just because it was to begin with the sort of huge General Assembly meeting that the U.S. had always considered pointless. The proposal had first been made by Algeria in 1979 after the failure of the General Assembly committee of the whole. Algeria made the proposal at the nonaligned summit in Havana, a meeting that had been particularly hostile to the U.S. (In fact, Reagan made it a condition of his acceptance of the Cancun invitation that titular nonaligned leader, Fidel Castro, not be included.) The nonaligned proposal for global negotiations had gone to the General Assembly. For over a year informal negotiations had continued in New York about how such negotiations should be conducted. But one of the first things the new Reagan U.N. representatives did was to withdraw from those discussions. They feared that global negotiations could go on for years and result in a treaty similar to the Law of the Sea Treaty being negotiated then. The Reagan government felt it could not support that treaty but feared not signing it after the U.S. had taken part in negotiations for so long.(41)

Because of the Reagan administration's hesitancy, Cancun ended without substantive agreement on starting global negotiations. Nonetheless, the Mexican Foreign Ministry concluded that the Cancun summit was a success simply because it facilitated agreement on global negotiations. All states, including the U.S. and its two close allies, affirmed the need for those negotiations and accepted the General Assembly as their first venue and the specialized agencies as their second.(42) The U.S. rejoined the informal meetings in New York aimed at resolving further differences.

Despite the Cancun agreement, at the end of 1982 the north-south dialogue had not advanced. Law of the Sea negotiations ended in April with the U.S. rejecting the pro-third world treaty and the U.S.'s major northern allies abstaining. Global negotiations remained stymied because of a disagreement that Britain, West Germany, and the U.S. had with the other members of the General Assembly. Those three states demanded that the assembly not be empowered to change any agreements reached in the specialized agencies. The third round of global negotiations would only be able to ratify those agreements when global negotiations return to the assembly in their final stage.(43)

The stalemate over global negotiations assured that

the south's views did not change in 1982. Third world
speeches during the autumn General Assembly debate that
year contained only one thing new: Even while reiterating
calls for global negotiations to transform the global
economic order, for the first time in eight years
southern officials rarely used the phrase "New
International Economic Order."

THE DEBATE AND NIEO GOALS

No matter how southern rhetoric has changed, third
world NIEO goals have changed no more after 1974 than
they did in the thirty years before. After 1974 the south
adopted new goals suggested by its northern supporters
only when those goals could be made subordinant to the
third world primary goal, industrialization. The south
rejected attempts by its northern supporters to make
"fulfilling basic needs" as important as
industrialization, but in the process the LDCs added
something similar as a secondary goal. The third world
completely rejected an attempt by some of its northern
nongovernmental supporters to oppose further
industrialization. And the LDCs did nothing to expand
their NIEO goals to include those that DMC governments
think are central to any international economic system.
The goals the LDCs adopted from their northern
European allies include those in the Peruvian proposal
for global disarmament to finance development. This
proposal had been made at the first UNCTAD in 1964 and
then ignored by the south for more than ten years.
Disarmament had long been a distant goal of some of the
south's strongest northern supporters, including
Sweden.(44) As long as disarmament was tied to
development, LDCs were happy to create a U.N. majority in
favor of a special General Assembly session on the
topic.(45) An element of opportunism contributed to the
south's adoption of this goal. The most consistent
champions of Peru's disarmament for development proposal
have not been LDC governments; they have been
nongovernmental commissions like Willy Brandt's and the
disarmament commission later formed by Brandt Commission
member, Swedish Prime Minister Olof Palme. In fact,
Brandt's report points out that since 1974 most third
world nations have been accelerating arms purchases even
more than most developed nations.(46)
Another new third world goal adopted in a similar
way began with a proposal made by Austrian Prime Minister
Kreisky. Kreisky suggested a Marshall-like plan for
infrastructure development in Africa in order to
stimulate European economies.(47) Third world officials
extended his idea to a call for a new Marshall Plan for
the entire third world, one that would stimulate
economies throughout the north.(48) This was one of the

rare cases when the LDCs expressed concern with northern growth.

The only other example concerns trade and protectionism among northern countries. Just as northern concern about the slow and uneven recoveries after each of the recessions since 1974 motivated Kreisky's proposal, the same concern made many northern governments worry about protectionism that might follow if the rapid cycles of recession and weak recovery continued. The south adopted this concern with maintaining the liberal trade system among developed states. But the general issue of northern protectionism became important to the south only when attached to the older NIEO issue of unfair tariffs on LDC goods.

In 1979 the Tokyo Round of GATT negotiations ended with agreements on significant tariff and nontariff barriers to trade among DMCs. Fears of mounting protectionism and continuing recession, which had been voiced by some northern scholars for almost a decade, eased. The New York Times even cautiously suggested that the postwar economic system had survived its greatest trial intact.(49) Nonetheless, all the LDCs in GATT except Argentina boycotted the trade pact ceremonies protesting that duties on exports from LDCs had been reduced significantly less than those on DMC exports. Moreover, DMCs continued to protect national industries with which the LDCs could best compete.(50) At the fifth UNCTAD meeting the following month the DMCs insisted that they had done what they could for the LDCs under GATT rules. They did not want to violate those rules because, as European Community delegate Sir Roy Denman put it, without the pact the west would have to return to ". . . the economic blizzards of the 1930s, the hunger, fear, and political extremism experienced then."(51)

The DMCs refused to reopen tariff negotiations, and the LDCs then adopted northern rhetoric about the global results of protectionism in order to argue more convincingly for greater access to developed markets.(52) Third world attacks on protectionism among northern states as well as on northern protection against LDC goods continue to appear, even if they appear somewhat uncomfortably alongside third world proposals for international approval of development-oriented national restrictions on trade.

The south reacted more consistently and vigorously to northern concerns with development for "basic needs," concerns that became so important after 1974. Those concerns commanded greater attention in the south because many northern democratic socialists and liberals who support the third world consider development for basic needs to be fundamental.(53) Northern concern with basic needs can be traced back to sixties' critiques of aid, including the Pearson Commission report, which emphasized that the bulk of foreign aid given for humanitarian purposes never improved the lives of the world's poor. It was used for the political and economic aggrandizement of particular third world elites, often the real goal of northern donors.(54)

Despite the fact that early suggestions for basic needs development came from northerners sympathetic to the south and even from southern scholars, many LDC leaders saw such strategies as attacks on their ideas. Third world officials viewed basic needs strategies supported by the U.S. government under Carter and by the World Bank as northern attempts to change the focus of global debate by proposing that domestic equity be a condition for receiving further aid. If northern officials had been successful, so the argument goes, they would have escaped responsibilities to provide aid. That was the real aim of "basic needs" proposals. Don Mills outlines these objections and concludes:

> There is a great need, therefore, for the concept of basic needs to be brought into a realistic relationship with the facts of political and economic organization and development so that its intrinsic value can be preserved without it becoming a philosophy of development, or the ultimate aim of the development process.(55)

Even if the basic needs notion has been used by some northern governments as a simplistic justification for inaction, the idea underlying it has always been part of the position of most northerners who sympathize with the south and are interested in something more than castigating third world elites. Gunnar Myrdal's economic theories, for example, demand increasing economic equality throughout the world, well beyond assuring that each person's basic economic needs are met, as a goal of economic development and as a means for both providing incentives to save and assuring the ability to produce. Nonetheless, Myrdal argues that the structural constraints in many developing states make it impossible for them to institute programs encouraging domestic economic equality until greater national wealth has been created.(56) Likewise, the intuitive notion of international economic justice expressed by La Guardia in the forties rested upon globally meeting basic human economic needs, but La Guardia felt it was wrong to blame governments for saying that other economic goals were more important. Each nation's primary economic development goals would probably be unique. Nonetheless, meeting basic economic needs was, for La Guardia, a global responsibility to achieve a goal that was the same everywhere. Meeting basic economic needs would allow nations to more easily pursue their unique economic development.

The social democratic perspective exemplified by

Myrdal's ideas and the type of liberalism La Guardia expressed can bridge the gap between the Group of 77 and those northerners who ignore southern demands. In fact, northern European states have become go-betweens in the north-south conflict in part because of their insistence that the NIEO be amended to meet basic economic needs.(57) Likewise, private individuals who share such perspectives have been able to do the most to organize support for the NIEO in developed countries, in part because they have demonstrated their own support for meeting basic needs development. Michael Harrington, the head of the American democratic socialists, makes this explicit in his The Vast Majority, published in 1977. He argues the merits of the south's position and appeals to the charitable "best side" of the American people, their sympathy with the poor, the attitudes which motivated the development of basic needs strategies in the first place.(58) The popularity in the north of even the Brandt Commission's report, which deliberately avoids appeals to charity, certainly comes in part from its concern with the plight of the world's poorest people rather than with the plight of the governments of the world's poorest nations.

The importance of basic needs notions to the south's strongest northern allies assured that the third world, itself, would adopt something akin to this goal. Beginning with the General Assembly's Declaration on Social Progress and Development in 1969, NIEO documents describe economic justice for individuals as a defining characteristic of development. After the Sixth Special Session in 1974, third world spokesmen began to link economic justice for individuals more directly to the central NIEO goal of industrialization. For example, the Latin American industrialization conference:

> . . . stressed that domestic industrialization policies must take into account the need for an adequate distribution of income to make possible the expansion of domestic markets. In that way industrial growth can be conducive to the attainment of the objective of raising the standard of living and eliminating unemployment.(59)

The more flowery language of the UNIDO conference in 1975 put the point this way:

> All states should recognize that, in any industrial development process, social justice must be the irreplaceable means, in the spiritual, economic, and social aspects, to obtain the objective of a just society pervaded by a spirit of solidarity.(60)

The point is to advocate justice for individuals as a secondary goal, a means to achieving the more significant

NIEO goals of industrialization and national unity. This statement illustrates one way third world NIEO advocates propose to resolve their debate with their northern supporters over basic needs policies. Meeting basic needs will become a necessary, but secondary, new order goal.

Yet the debate remains open. The third world alliance could decide to treat domestic economic justice the same way it threats population control, as one possible, but not necessary, means to achieve more important development goals, a means that individual third world governments should be free to choose or not to choose. Meeting basic needs could hardly be a consistent part of the third world ideology as long as many LDCs do little to meet them, as long as some southern leaders can be forced by the facts to make statements like the one Raul Prebisch made at UNCTAD V in 1979 when he concluded that:

. . . callous elites in the developing countries were ruining the chances of the people to raise living standards through trade. They had turned their countries into "privileged consumption societies."(61)

Prebisch proposed that national development programs be more strictly monitored by international agencies to assure that public welfare is improved, a view perfectly consistent with proposals like those of the Brandt Commission and the 1976 Club of Rome study. Southern governments have not adopted Prebisch's view on this subject as their own. While the debate over basic needs may have made meeting them an NIEO goal, the new order ideology still considers it up to national governments to decide whether or not the goal has been achieved.

The late-seventies nongovernmental debate on a reformed international economic order brought up one other goal that the south more firmly rejected. In the early seventies, under the influence of limits to growth ideas, praise of industrialization waned in the developed nations. This had an effect on the third world. Almost any LDC contains a small class of people who will find anti-industrialism appealing. V. S. Naipaul, a novelist who is far from sympathetic to the goals of third world governments, nonetheless shows how weak an anti-industrial philosophy will be in a nation like India where the landed elite might look for the integrity of a dimly remembered preindustrial past. Such concerns can easily be directed by government policy into programs for "appropriate" or "intermediate" technologies, alongside but not replacing more traditional means of industrialization.(62) Nonetheless, in the seventies many northern sympathizers expressed hope that the south would have a future, if not without industry, at least free from the horrors of industrialization that people in the north had had to suffer.

Despite this internal and external pressure southern governments never reversed their calls for industrialization. Rather, they responded to such ideas by emphasizing that industrialization had to be undertaken in ways appropriate to a nation's culture and to the physical environment. They reaffirmed their older concern with nurturing the cultural differences between nations and emphasized the new principle of preserving the environment which had come out of the north-south debate in the early seventies. But neither affirmation denied the goal of industrialization. By the end of the seventies, the anti-industrialism of northern NIEO sympathizers had waned as much as that of their southern allies. The debate led to agreement on the position embodied earlier in the Cocoyoc Declaration made by southern leaders and northern nongovernmental supporters. Both southern officials and their northern supporters affirmed that industrialization of the third world was essential and that the south should learn from the north's failure to protect the physical environment and cultural traditions when industrializing.(63)

In summary, some people from the north did have an effect on the way southern leaders conceived of NIEO goals in the late seventies, and those changes in LDC views did result from substantive debate. Yet northern governments rarely debated and the changes in LDC goals that took place were minor. The south never focused on the goals that the most powerful northern governments addressed when they discussed reforming the international economic order. The south only changed its goals to accommodate some of the concerns expressed by northern supporters. But since the realm of disagreement between the south and its northern supporters, both in and outside of government, was so narrow, the substantive debate between those two groups could lead to little new. In the one case where northern supporters of the south insisted upon a goal substantially different than those supported by the Group of 77, the area of basic needs, the debate continues.

THE DEBATE AND NIEO POLICY PROPOSALS

The debate continues over specific NIEO policy proposals as well. Nonetheless, some north-south agreement on controlling yet encouraging transnational investment, facilitating the transfer of technology, eliminating the brain drain, and redeploying northern industrial capacity to the third world has occurred since 1974. Agreement took place after substantial clarification but no substantive change in new order policy proposals. By the end of the seventies international codes of conduct for TNCs and for the transfer of technology appeared imminent. The difference between the DMC view of the primacy of property rights and the LDC view of the primacy of national rights had been clarified. And a few northern nations had started to redeploy industry to the third world.(64)

A small UNCTAD commission concerned with the transfer of technology clarified the south's views on property. The first draft code on the transfer of technology proposed by Brazil in 1975 identified technology as part of the universal human heritage, thus claiming an LDC right to technology higher than the rights of property owners yet not associated with the rights of states per se.(65) Further clarification of this principle found in later UNCTAD versions of the proposed code illustrate a new order position that does not simply place national rights over property above owner's rights, but rather is concerned with having international law -- binding codes of conduct on technology and TNCs, not traditional international law -- define the extent of proprietary rights under the assumption that some property, the resources of the ocean as well as human knowledge, is a common heritage of humankind. Other property belongs to individuals or groups, under the laws of some sovereign nation. To take into account the "primacy" of the national rights of people in developing countries, NIEO advocates want those countries to be given the fullest possible access to technologies whose transfer is not subject to private decision.(66) To put it in simpler language, national governments must give technical knowledge they own to other national governments under the notion of common heritage. Nonetheless, the proprietary rights of private owners of technology should continue to be protected for a fixed period of time by national governments and by international patents. The south wants the principle issue of technology transfer to be one of the duties of states to aid each other, not one of property rights.

Larger UNCTAD meetings also encouraged changes in the south's ideology. At UNCTAD IV in 1976 the LDCs renamed the brain drain the "reverse transfer of technology" to emphasize the similarity between the gain of technically skilled third world people by developed nations and the gain of technical know-how by third world states.(67) Specific policies for combating the brain drain and for redeploying developed industries were left to national governments. Thus, little substance has been added to the new order policy analysis of these issues.

The same is true of the NIEO analysis of techniques for facilitating the transfer of technology and encouraging yet controlling TNCs. The proposed codes of conduct for each continue to emphasize strengthening the bargaining power of LDCs. This would be accomplished by exchanging information more freely and by forbidding investment policies which discriminate against certain groups of states.(68) These points do not bother most northern states, although the idea of binding international codes to assure compliance remains an issue for north-south debate.

The actual north-south debate since 1974 has had a more marked effect on the LDCs' analysis of policies that are meant to encourage industrialization less directly. In response to the debate, the south actually dropped some of its demands.

Of course, most of the NIEO policies for restructuring the financial and monetary systems proposed at the Sixth Special Session continue to be supported by the Group of 77. Many have also received northern support. Since 1974, north and south have agreed on new aid targets. Nations with special development problems -- the least developed, landlocked, and island states -- received greater attention, especially at UNCTAD IV, which agreed to long term measures favoring these states in trade, finance, technical assistance, shipping, and insurance.(69) At CIEC six individual donor nations and the European Community pledged one billion dollars to the LLDCs.(70) The donor nations also supported large replenishments of funds to IDA and to the regional development banks as well as sales of IMF gold reserves and some expansion of SDR liquidity designed to aid poorer nations.(71) Taken together, though, these changes in the aid and financial aspects of north-south relations represented only limited reforms.

Nonetheless, the Group of 77 amended its most radical proposals for restructuring these systems in response to DMC receptiveness to less radical proposals. In 1975 many third world countries were calling for generalized debt relief -- conversion of outstanding aid loans into grants retroactively. The UNCTAD Secretariat provided the analysis justifying a common response to the different debt problems experienced by different LDCs:

> The present debt servicing difficulties of the developing countries are not the result of specific external circumstances peculiar to particular countries . . . The problem clearly has a more general dimension since it springs from maladjustments in the world economy and is beyond the ability of the developing countries to control.(72)

Prior to the late 1970s few of the developed countries and neither the World Bank nor the IMF expressed much sympathy for the long standing third world demands for general debt relief. In 1975 the prospects for generalized debt relief appeared bleak.

They became brighter when financial leaders of the developed nations started to support debt relief.

Although they did not accept the NIEO argument that debt burdens were systemic problems affecting third world states, major private bankers and leaders of national banks in some DMCs felt that prospect of default by many third world debtors would destabilize an already shaky world financial situation. As summarized by the UNCTAD Secretariat in June 1977,

. . . in recent months several authorities have begun to accept the need for some form of official initiative, there being "growing recognition" that private intermediaries may not be able to manage the task.(73)

In August 1977 CIEC approved guidelines for debt relief negotiations on a case by case rather than general basis.(74) With some widespread debt rescheduling a practical possibility after 1977, individual third world nations withdrew their support of general debt relief. Brazil, for example, highly dependent on private credit, realized that it could be jeopardized if the government waged an active campaign for generalized third world debt relief.(75) By mid-1979 British economist and observer of the third world debate Paul Streeten could conclude that the Group of 77 had dropped proposals for generalized debt relief in light of prospects for case by case relief.(76)

Streeten may have spoken too soon. The continuing global economic crisis of the early eighties increased the pressure for debt relief. In 1983 the Brandt Commission issued its second report, giving significant northern support to global solutions to the third world debt crisis.(77) Later in 1983, at UNCTAD VI, the Group of 77 returned to its calls for generalized debt relief.(78) Nonetheless, both exclusion and readmission of this proposal to the south's ideology responded, in part, to northern initiatives in the north-south debate.

In a very different way, northern actions triggered the third world's deemphasis of another element of the NIEO financial package, the Link between new SDR allocations and aid to third world states. The utility of the SDR-Link proposal rests on the assumption that the IMF will periodically and predictably create new SDRs so that there will be a predictable source of new foreign exchange for the governments of poorer nations. Between 1972 and 1979 no new SDRs were created. A date for new allocation, January 1978, even passed without IMF action. Nations with convertible currencies had doubted the need for new allocations. The floating exchange rate system established in response to the U.S. new economic policy of 1971 provided a means for creating new liquidity without new SDR allocations. Because the amount of each of the currencies exchanges in world money markets could be increased by the national decisions of central banks, the potential role of the SDR had been reduced. That meant, as the UNCTAD Secretariat concluded in 1975, the Link was much less feasible.(79)

After 1974 the focus of third world concerns about monetary reform shifted to advocating a greater role for SDRs and to returning to the original Bretton Woods system of fixed exchange rates.(80) By late 1978, when the Managing Director of the IMF was seeking a fifty percent increase in IMF quotas and a new allocation of SDRs, the LDC members of the fund had dropped their calls for the Link. Instead, they concentrated on convincing the fund to relax restrictions upon new LDC borrowing from expanded quotas. They wanted the fund to moderate its requirements affecting the internal and external pricing of LDC commodities and the value of LDC currencies.(81) In a similar distraction from the previous third world focus on the Link proposal, in 1976 the nonaligned states considered new proposals for a third world reserve currency, proposals which have never gone beyond the discussion stage.(82)

As they did with the financial policies they supported, NIEO advocates shifted the trade policies they emphasized in response to northern initiatives of the late seventies. The LDCs changed only the focus of their political action, not the substance of the proposals they supported. In 1976 with the passage of a comprehensive trade act in the United States, tariff preferences to the third world became almost universal.(83) Temporarily, until the conclusion of the next round of GATT negotiations in 1979, this ceased to be the major trade issue for the LDCs. It was replaced by the Integrated Programme for Commodities (IPC), the system of buffer stocks to be purchased from a common international fund and then used to support prices of certain commodities. Despite the fact that DMCs consistently made concessions toward the third world on the IPC, no substantive agreement on new commodity pacts has been reached.

A small group of UNCTAD permanent staff members created the IPC proposal. It reflected Keynes's suggestions for commodity price stabilization as well as the vaguer requirements for giving third world nations control over their external trade found in the 1974 NIEO documents. The invention of the IPC involved dropping one of the south's most radical demands of 1974. Even the earliest versions of the IPC included no proposals for indexing the prices of third world commodities to the prices of DMC goods. Not only did most DMCs find indexing objectionable, the UNCTAD staff could think of no way to make it work in practice.(84) Of course in 1974 the IPC looked only slightly more feasible than indexing. Almost every element of the IPC was anathema to those northern states that acted upon free trade ideologies.

DMC positions moderated. In 1975 the U.S. indicated its willingness to negotiate new commodity agreements. In

1977 the new Carter administration accepted the idea of
the Common Fund.(85) The Eastern European socialist
states, the northern European states, Australia, New
Zealand, and to a lesser extent Japan and other European
Community members have supported the general notion of
the IPC since 1975. While the developed nations supported
the principles of the IPC at UNCTAD IV and V,
disagreements continued over how the Common Fund should
be administered, what commodities could be stabilized by
the program, and whether or not some attempt should be
made to increase commodity prices over the market trend.
Robert Rothstein reports that the simple limitation of
time available to the small group of UNCTAD staff members
familiar with the IPC restricted the extent to which NIEO
advocates could respond to the north's technical
objections.(86)

In addition, the LDCs tended to worry about their
unity throughout the IPC negotiations, and therefore
remained cautious about adopting new positions. They
often failed to respond to northern initiatives.(87)
Conceivably the reluctance of Group of 77 members to
debate the technical problems of the IPC more vigorously
reflected an unwillingness to give those LDCs most likely
to benefit from the pact additional trade advantages so
soon after many of the same states had received the
benefits of the European Community's Lome Pact. That
appeared to be what disturbed some states in the south,
the wealthier nations of Latin America.(88) In any event,
the issue of DMC tariff preferences, especially salient
to Latin America, again became the center of the
north-south trade debate before the IPC could be created.
Despite international agreement on the outlines of the
Common Fund in 1979, no new commodity agreements or
agreements on other elements of the IPC have been
reached. The north-south debate produced a partial
agreement in principle without an active program.

THE DEBATE AND THE GROUP OF 77's POLITICAL ANALYSIS

Despite the lack of progress, and despite the
increasingly radical scholarly analysis being produced by
third world dependency theorists,(89) no significant
radicalization of the third world position took place
between 1975 and 1983. The political analysis acted upon
by LDCs in the late seventies involved no proposals for
projecting third world power beyond the use of Group of
77 unity in international organizations and the use of
"commodity power" of individual developing states through
stricter controls over foreign firms. Even if at the end
of the decade the Saudi oil minister could still tell
reporters that OPEC would refuse to stabilize energy
prices until the DMCs began to be serious about the
NIEO,(90) OPEC states never pressured developed states to

accept the NIEO by cutting off oil.

Obviously, most LDCs consulted more than the NIEO ideology when they made foreign economic policy. OPEC states could not be convinced to sacrifice their interests as oil producers to the cause of the NIEO. Not only would revenues be cut by attempts to use the oil weapon -- a major disadvantage to a few OPEC members like Nigeria -- such action would also invite military retaliation against the oil producers.

In addition, in the late 1970s the positions of the DMCs encouraged continued moderation of third world political analysis. Even the most status quo oriented developed states had become more receptive to specific NIEO policies and to the general idea of a new order. They had not been convinced by the oil price increases. The more conservative DMCs only changed their opinions after months of the discussion that the oil price increases had begun.

Instead of advocating new means to extend third world power, NIEO sponsors concentrated upon proposing and advocating changes in the institutional structure of the U.N. system, redesigning the system to achieve new order goals. A comprehensive plan for restructuring the economic agencies, written for the Seventh Special Session in 1975, became the basis for subsequent NIEO proposals. The report proposed that UNIDO be made a specialized agency with status equivalent to the World Bank and the IMF.(91) Otherwise,the overall structure of global economic institutions envisioned by NIEO advocates otherwise remained as postwar framers of the Bretton Woods system had suggested, including the creation of an ITO out of UNCTAD and GATT. The only other NIEO institutional innovation would be to make the IMF a true global central bank.(92)

The report on restructuring recommended that existing U.N. agencies adopt conciliation procedures when the NIEO is being negotiated.(93) Such procedures, if universally adopted in the U.N. and its specialized agencies, would give the third world a new veto in some agencies including the World Bank, IMF, and Economic and Social Council, without going to the extreme of sanctioning majority rule of states. Nonetheless, neither the advantages of this compromise on rule making, nor its disadvantages in terms of possible delays in making needed decisions, have been widely debated.

Before agreeing on the rules for institutions where the NIEO is to be negotiated, north and south need to agree that there will be an NIEO and that it will be created through negotiation. The northern crossing of ul Haq's philosophical bridge represents agreement on the first point, even though it remains to be seen whether or not the U.S. and its most powerful northern allies are deeply committed to a reformed international economic order. Yet, by itself, the north cannot assure that the

NIEO will be created through negotiation. The south has to agree.

Since 1974 the south has added an understanding of the need for negotiations to its ideology. The Group of 77's earliest political analysis, the views predominant in the group from 1964 through the first years of the seventies, found its justification in utopian principles of international law, "the sovereign equality of states," and in pluralist theories of DMC government. The group later adopted a political analysis taken from realist theories of international relations, emphasizing the projection of power in an essentially heartless, anarchic world, the analysis that led to theories of collective self-reliance and collective economic security as well as to justifications of the OPEC price increases. After 1974 the south adopted a new political analysis, emphasizing what could be done through international negotiation. If pluralist theories of DMC governments and realist theories of international relations can be said to have motivated the first two Group of 77 political analyses, the whole range of theories about negotiation can be said to motivate the group's latest views.

The ideas about rule making taken from the report on U.N. reforms represent a later addition to this analysis. The south's preference for negotiation, rather than direct actions like the OPEC price increases, began in response to the conciliatory northern positions at the Seventh Special Session. The fact that OPEC's success could not be replicated by other commodity producing countries reinforced the third world preference for negotiation.

The LDCs' experience with CIEC made them challenge some of the north's conventional wisdom about what makes for successful negotiations. After the Sixth Special Session, the developed countries, especially the United States, had argued in favor of more intimate negotiating sessions on a limited number of topics. From the south's point of view CIEC, which followed this model, was a near disaster. After CIEC the south emphasized that universal agreement in principle to the NIEO was needed before smaller meetings on specifics could be fruitful. Thus the south adopted something similar to the Club of Rome's suggestion that a framework treaty be worked out by all U.N. members.

The obvious failure of this policy led to reevaluation of what had been wrong with the northern preference for meetings of a few countries on a few topics in the first place. The LDCs reiterated that such meetings could not fully represent the diversity of opinion in the third world. But, at this early stage of negotiation at least, another failure of CIEC proved more telling. Not only had CIEC failed to consider the views of all countries or to integrate all topics, the negotiations began without agreement on a need for an

NIEO.

That, in fact, had been a deliberate decision by the most powerful developed states. Their governments felt that agreement in principle between north and south would prove impossible. The best that could be hoped for was agreements on specific small reforms arrived at through the exchange of concessions between north and south.(94) The most powerful northern states thus acted against William Zartman's dictum that a formula for international agreement has to be arrived at before the details of any successful agreement can be worked out.(95)

The south recognized the usefulness of this dictum only after the failures of the committee of the whole and after the Brandt Commission made alternative suggestions. Cancun's limited size allowed ideas to be shared but unlike CIEC, Cancun aimed at agreement on a general formula for later north-south negotiations. Nonetheless, the choice of participants at Cancun precluded wide-ranging debate on possible formulas for an NIEO. Most of the participants stood with the south. Cancun could only have had one of two outcomes. The U.S., Germany, and the U.K. could agree to the formulas proposed by the south, or else no agreement would occur at all. In fact both occurred.

The overall direction of change in the south's political analysis since 1974 should be clear. The Group of 77 has moved ever closer to a relatively sophisticated analysis of what is needed in order for there to be a successfully negotiated NIEO. The Cancun summit suggests that the south has yet to reach the conclusion that substantive debate on a formula for an NIEO is needed. In such debate the south would have to remain as open to being convinced as it demands that its opponents be. Nonetheless, the Group of 77's thinking has moved in that direction, as evidenced since 1974 by the increasing moderation of some southern economic demands and by the specific moves of north-south negotiations to forums where substantive debate is likely, as well as by the south's support of an increasing role for U.N. conciliation procedures that allow for substantive debate.

Ready explanations for the direction of southern thinking can be found. The theories cited at the beginning of this chapter suggest this direction. My conclusions based on Apter's views about mobilizing ideologies also could be reached by thinking about the conflict resolution needed to created international regimes. The dean of British peace researchers, Adam Curle, demonstrates that, paradoxically, in conflicts between apparently unequal parties, like the north-south conflict, a period of confrontation is necessary before the conflict can be resolved. The confrontation is needed in order for both parties to begin to take the weaker one as a serious partner whose interests will have to be

consulted in resolving the conflict.(96) The oil price
increases were such a confrontation. If they did nothing
else, they made many northern policy makers aware of the
third world's demands for the first time.

At times confrontations between previously weaker
and previously stronger parties can make both equally
powerful on all dimensions, but that is not essential to
conflict resolution. It would be essential if the parties
tried to resolve their conflict simply by exchanging
concessions. A weaker party, with less to exchange, would
find it difficult to get what it wanted from the stronger
and could easily feel aggrieved by any bargained,
temporary resolution.

If, on the other hand, the parties committed
themselves to resolving their conflict by developing a
single view of their mutual interests, rather than by
exchanging concessions to partially satisfy their
separate interests, a weaker and stronger party could, in
theory, resolve their conflict to the full satisfaction
of both. That would mean a commitment to substantive
political debate, to trying to convince each other and to
being willing to be convinced, something a good deal more
complex than just exchanging concessions.(97)

In fact, the conflicts among the states whose
interests have to be satisfied in order to create an
international regime must be resolved, at least in part,
through substantive debate. The actual experience of the
United States in founding the postwar system with its
weaker western European partners illustrates the point.
American policy makers may have tried just to strike
bargains with their weaker partners and never amend U.S.
views, but that was not enough. The U.S. convinced
European leaders of the validity of the basic tenets of
the system it was trying to create. It had to. Regimes
are "principles, norms, rules, and decision-making
procedures around which an actor's expectations converge
in a given area of international relations."(98) While it
is possible for such principles, norms, and rules to be
unconscious, it is unlikely that a regime of unconscious
rules can be created when a conflict over different
possible regimes has made states all the more conscious
of strongly-held, conflicting views. International
regimes can only be created out of a conscious
disagreement over what regimes should be by consciously
resolving that disagreement. That means by substantive
political debate, not by mere bargaining that preserves
the disagreement or by any other strategic action, like
the OPEC price increases, alone.

To the extent that practical concerns continue to
motivate the NIEO ideology, its advocates will be forced
to recognize that substantive north-south debate on a
formula for a new order is needed before international
economic regimes can actually be reformed. The only
significant innovations in the NIEO ideology since 1974

152

already point in that direction.

NOTES

(1)Ul Haq's Sept. 1975 speech quoted in his The Poverty Curtain (New York: Columbia Univ. Press, 1977), p. 147. Brandt quoted in Washington Post, Dec. 18, 1979, p. A20.
(2)This view of substantive debate comes from Anatol Rapoport, Fights, Games and Debates (Ann Arbor: Univ. of Michigan Press, 1960), pp. 245-309.
(3)These characterizations of different northern positions follow those in Robert Cassen et al., eds., Rich Country Interests and Third World Development (London: Croom Helm, 1982).
(4)Selected Documents, Lome Convention, Feb. 28, 1975, pp. 601-19.
(5)Cf. Lima Declaration and Plan of Action, Mar. 1975, quoted in Ervin Laszlo et al., The Objectives of the New International Economic Order (New York: Pergamon Press, 1978), p. 160.
(6)Official Records of the General Assembly Seventh Special Session, Sept. 1, 1975 (New York: United Nations, 1977), p. 1-3.
(7)Ibid., pp. 7-13.
(8)Ibid., p. 14.
(9)Ibid., Sept. 4, 1975, p. 4.
(10)Ibid., Sept. 3, 1975, p. 14-16.
(11)Ibid., Sept. 2, 1975, p. 10.
(12)Just Faaland and Ole Norbye, "Interests of Scandinavian Countries in Third World Development," in Cassen, p. 288.
(13)Catherine Gwin, "The Seventh Special Session: Toward a New Phase of Relations Between the Developed and Developing States," in Karl P. Sauvant and Hajo Hasenpflug, eds., The New International Economic Order: Confrontation or Cooperation Between North and South? (Boulder: Westview Press, 1977), pp. 106-108.
(14)Seventh Special Session, Sept. 1, 1975, p. 12.
(15)E.g. Madagascar, speaking for the Group of 77, Second, 30, Oct. 6, 1975, p. 30.
(16)New York Times, June 6, 1983, p. 23.
(17)Second, 31, Oct. 1, 1976, p. 5.
(18)Phillippines, Second, 31, Oct. 1, 1976, p. 11.
(19)Karl P. Sauvant, "Representing the Collective Economic Interest of the Third World: The Group of 77," Presented at the annual meeting of the International Studies Association, Philadelphia, Mar. 1981, p. 22.
(20)Second, 31, Oct. 15, 1976, p. 2.
(21)Second, 33, Oct. 23, 1978, p. 6.
(22)Jeffrey Hart, The New International Economic Order (London: Macmillan, forthcoming, 1983), chpt. 1.
(23)Jan Tinbergen, coordinator, Reshaping

International Order (New York: E. P. Dutton, 1976).
  (24)Cf. Ibid., pp. 16-69 and Second, 31, Oct.18, 1976, p. 8.
  (25)Second, 31, Oct. 1, 1976, p. 7.
  (26)Second, 32, Oct. 6, 1977, p.13.
  (27)Cf. Tinbergen, p. 176-88, and Second, 32, Oct. 7, 1977, p. 4-7.
  (28)Second, 32, Oct. 13, 1977, p. 10. The fact that Latin American states (Argentina in addition to Brazil, Mexico, and Peru) pushed proposals found in the third Club of Rome report may have something to do with the fact that Colegio de Mexico President Victor L. Urquidi, widely respected among Latin American economists, was part of the Club of Rome team and the only third world member on both the subcommittee dealing with disarmament and the one dealing with negotiations.
  (29)Second, 32, Oct. 7, 1977, p. 4.
  (30)Ibid., p. 7.
  (31)Second, 32, Oct. 18, 1977, pp. 14-20.
  (32)See Robert W. Cox on Trilateralism in "Ideologies and the New International Economic Order," International Organization 33 (Spring 1979): 267-73.
  (33)"Towards a Renovated International System," (New York: Trilateral Commission Triangle Paper #14, 1977), pp. 41-42.
  (34)Second, 34, Oct. 9, 1979, p. 15.
  (35)Cf. Algeria, Second, 33, Oct. 23, 1978, p. 11 on what little the south expected.
  (36)Official Records of the General Assembly Eleventh Special Session, August 26, 1980, pp. 51-55. Global 2000 Report to the President, 3 vols. (New York: Pergamon Press, 1980).
  (37)Quoted in Leonard Silk, "The New U.S. View of the World," New York Times, May 4, 1979, p. D2.
  (38)Independent Commission on International Development, North-South (Cambridge: MIT Press, 1980).
  (39)The Brandt Commission actually envisioned a more authoritative summit than the unstructured discussion that actually took place.
  (40)Secretaria de Relationes Exteriores, Cancun 1981: Framework, Debates, and Conclusions of the Meeting on International Cooperation and Development (Mexico, D.F.: 1982), pp. 65-75.
  (41)See the discussion of the Reagan position by Edward Heath's north-south issues coordinator Duffey Asher, "Negotiations and the Law of the Sea," Senior thesis in political science, Wellesley College, 1982.
  (42)Secretaria de Relationes Exteriores, pp. 72-76.
  (43)"Perspective: The World Economy," U.N. Monthly Chronicle 19 (Oct. 1979): 38.
  (44)See Mexico's summary of the history of the disarmament negotiations in the U.N., Official Records of the General Assembly Tenth Special Session, 1978, p. 43.
  (45)Ibid.

154

(46)North-South, p. 117-25.
(47)Ibrahim Abdel Rahman, "The Most Basic Need: The Will to Develop Rationally," in Anthony J. Dolman and Jan van Ettinger, eds., Partners in Tomorrow (New York: E. P. Dutton, 1978), p. 8.
(48)Ibid., and see Sartaj Aziz, "The Search for Common Ground," in Dolman and van Ettinger, pp. 17-19.
(49)New York Times, Apr. 13, 1979, p. D1.
(50)Washington Post, May 26, 1979, p. A34.
(51)Quoted in New York Times, Apr. 13, 1979, p. D3.
(52)E.g., India, repeating the Group of 77 position, Second, 34, Oct. 1, 1979, p. 8.
(53)See Cox, pp. 260-61 on the influence of the south's social democratic northern supporters.
(54)In addition to the Pearson Report see Robert Packenham, Liberal America and the Third World (Princeton: Princeton Univ. Press, 1973).
(55)Don Mills, "The North-South Dialogue: Background and Present Position," in Dolman and van Ettinger, p. 69.
(56)Gunnar Myrdal, Development and Underdevelopment (Cairo: National Bank of Egypt, 1954).
(57)Hart, chpt. 4.
(58)Michael Harrington, The Vast Majority: A Journey to the World's Poor (New York: Simon and Schuster, 1977), pp. 14-35.
(59)Quoted in Laszlo, p. 151.
(60)Quoted in Laszlo, p. 152.
(61)Washington Post, May 27, 1979, p. A34.
(62)Naipaul's nonfiction exploration of modern India takes him to an institution where these concerns are so directed, V. S. Naipaul, India: A Wounded Civilization (New York: Alfred A. Knopf, 1977), pp. 125-45.
(63)Ignancy Sachs discusses these developments in his excellent account of the north-south agreement on issues of the environment and industrialization beginning with Henry Kissinger's rejection of the Cocoyoc Declaration and ending with the implications of the U.S. rejection of the Law of the Sea Treaty, "Environment and Development: Ten Years After Stockholm Conference," Alternatives 8 (Winter 1982): 369-78.
(64)Laszlo, pp. 120-42.
(65)Brazil's draft is UNCTAD document TD/B/C.6/AC.1/ L.6, Nov. 28, 1975, pp. 1-4.
(66)UNCTAD document TD/CODE TOT/10, Dec. 22, 1978.
(67)Laszlo, p. 10.
(68)Cf. the two codes quoted in Laszlo, pp. 131-32, 138-41.
(69)Summarized in Laszlo, pp. 27-28.
(70)Ibid., p. 29.
(71)Interview with Margaret G. de Vries, Historian of the International Monetary Fund, Washington, June 1979.
(72)Quoted in Laszlo, p. 12.
(73)Quoted in Ibid., p.13.
(74)Laszlo, p. 13.

(75)William R. Cline, "Brazil's Emerging International Economic Role," in Riodan Roet, ed., Brazil in the Seventies (Washington: American Enterprise Institute, 1976), p. 71.

(76)Paul Streeten, "The New International Economic Order," unpublished paper, Washington, June 7, 1979, p. 16. See also his, "Constructive Responses to the North-South Dialogue," in Edwin P. Reuben, ed., The Challenge of the New International Economic Order. (Boulder: Westview), p. 88.

(77)Independent Commission on International Development, Common Crisis (Cambridge: MIT Press, 1983).

(78)New York Times, June 7, 1983, p. 30.

(79)Laszlo, p. 107.

(80)Documents of the Group of 20, quoted in Laszlo, p. 105.

(81)Washington Post, Sept. 24, 1978, p. A4.

(82)Economist, Aug. 21, 1976, p. 121.

(83)C. Clyde Ferguson, "The New International Economic Order," in David M. Kay, ed., The Changing United Nations (New York: Academy of Political Science, 1978), p. 152.

(84)Robert Rothstein, Global Bargaining: UNCTAD and the Quest for a New International Economic Order (Princeton: Princeton Univ. Press, 1979), p. 69.

(85)Ibid., p. 142.

(86)Ibid., p. 69.

(87)Ibid., p. 20.

(88)For the provisions and states included see Selected Documents, Lome Convention.

(89)Cf. Cox, pp. 280-85, 289-300.

(90)Washington Post, Dec. 17, 1979, p. A1.

(91)Laszlo, pp.176-77.

(92)See for example the position of the Commonwealth Group of Experts quoted in Laszlo, p. 186.

(93)Laszlo, p. 178.

(94)C. Fred Bergsten, "Cartel Power to Common Fund," Interdependent, Mar. 1979, p. 17.

(95)I. William Zartman and Maureen R. Berman, The Practical Negotiator (New Haven: Yale Univ. Press, 1982).

(96)Adam Curle, Making Peace (London: Tavistock, 1971), pp. 196-208.

(97)While Rapoport does the most complete job of explaining the complexities, the same message can be found in Roger Fisher and William Ury's popular treatment of "principled negotiation," Getting to Yes: Negotiating Agreement Without Giving In (Boston: Houghton Mifflin, 1981).

(98)Stephen D. Krasner, "Structural Causes and Regime Consequences: Regimes as Intervening Variables," International Organization 36 (Spring 1982): 186.

5
The NIEO Ideology as Ideology

. . . developing countries realize that their
pattern of development will have to be different
from that of the industrialized countries. They . .
. adopt the present criteria of the industrialized
countries as their target -- namely modernization
and catching up with the rich. They pay the price --
a dual society and wide income disparities -- then
frustration and instability. They carefully guard
their recently acquired political independence and
national identity, but they are the weaker partner,
and hence the fear of domination -- not only
politically and economically, but even culturally.

-- Ibrahim Helmi Abdel Rahman

The rejection of irrational constraints by each
state had produced worldwide irrationality. At the
same time the integration of the upper classes of
developing countries into the international system
has contributed to national dualism, national
division, and national disintegration in some
developing countries. Hence the call for "delinking"
and the assertion of a national identity based on
indigenous values.

-- Paul Streeten(1)

    This final chapter recapitulates and summarizes what
the NIEO ideology is before examining the global,
national, and personal interests that the ideology
serves. I reach the same conclusion as Streeten and
former UNIDO Director Abdel Rahman: The NIEO ideology
cannot be fully understood apart from the positions of
developing countries within the international system, the
position of its advocates within developing nations'
domestic social systems, and the position of its

157

advocates within international society. The personal
experiences many NIEO advocates share reinforce their
commitment to the ideology they constructed to explain
and try to transform the Bretton Woods system.
This discussion of the interests the new order
ideology serves leads naturally into a discussion of the
ideology's future. I discuss the most likely developments
throughout this chapter to help illustrate fundamental
elements of the ideology or the interests it serves. I
leave more speculative discussion of the way the ideology
might develop to the afterword.

KEY ELEMENTS OF THE NEW ORDER IDEOLOGY

The NIEO ideology can be thought of as divided into
two parts: A set of principles and a technical policy
analysis. This analysis includes economic goals, factors
affecting those goals, proposed economic policies
designed to manipulate those factors, an analysis of
political impediments to those policies, and political
strategies to overcome those impediments. The new order
technical analysis can be viewed as a rationally
integrated unit, a causal model of the economic and
political factors affecting third world economic
goals.(2) NIEO principles both define the need for and
set moral limits on the NIEO policy analysis.

New Order Principles

Three new order principles have been part of the
ideology since its beginning:

- the need for international management of the
  global economy

- the economic rights and duties of states

- the equality of individual states

The other two arose out of the compromises between more
and less radical third world states when the Bretton
Woods system began to break down at the beginning of the
1970s:

- the moral obligation of past and present
  exploiters to negotiate the reform of existing
  international economic systems

- the duty of current exploiter states to compensate their victims

The most fundamental NIEO principle, the need for
some degree of rational international management of the

world economy, requires the creation of the NIEO policy analysis. It demands that analysis unlike the other NIEO principles which restrict it.

The second fundamental NIEO principle, the south's special version of the economic rights and duties of states, sets limits on that policy analysis. Under this principle the south affirms the rights of national governments to choose their own economic system and to control the natural resources within their territory. The most important duty of states remains to aid the economic development of materially less advantaged countries. The south often links this specific duty with the fundamental rights it affirms in formulas that encompass all elements of the second principle, such as, "the right to develop," "collective self-reliance," and "collective economic security." Other duties include protection of the global environment and other "common heritages."

A final fundamental NIEO principle affirms that separate states are equal in their rights and duties. As an instance of this principle, the south affirms that conflicts about international economic matters that cannot be resolved by appealing to economic science or to prior agreement on principle must be resolved by political means that treat each state as equally powerful, either majority rule of states or consensus.

The two more recent additions to the south's principles incorporate the restitution ethic proposed in the sixties by more radical nations. States that either have benefited from exploitation from third world regions in the past or continue to do so today have a moral obligation to reform the existing international economic system through negotiations. Likewise, those states that have continued such exploitative actions after the adoption of the General Assembly's Charter of Economic Rights and Duties of States have a duty to compensate their victims directly.(3)

New Order Goals

As Abdel Rahman states, the primary new order goal remains industrial development in the third world. NIEO advocates believe that the other benefits of modernization will flow from industry. Many other goals that third world spokesmen cite as elements of the new order program are simply means to encourage third world industry. Thus, meeting the basic needs of people throughout the world, working toward worldwide disarmament, maintaining the economic growth of developed nations, and preventing protectionism among DMC's are NIEO goals to the extent that they contribute to industrialization.

NIEO advocates consider other development goals even less important because proposing them as universals would contradict new order principles. For example, population control can be an NIEO goal of some states because it may contribute to industrialization, but it cannot be a general NIEO goal because some third world states consider it anathema to the economic systems they have chosen.

The New Order Analysis of the World Economy

NIEO advocates consider the prospects for industrialization in the third world to be influenced by one major factor, the power the third world has over north-south economic transactions relative to the power developed countries have. NIEO advocates further divide that factor into three parts. The comparative power of north and south over trade appeared in NIEO analysis first, in the forties. The comparative power of north and south over development financing appeared only slightly later. Finally, new order advocates added a detailed analysis of the comparative power of north and south over TNC investment only after dependency scholars began their studies in the late sixties and early seventies. TNC investment influences the availability of technology for third world industrial development, a factor that NIEO advocates sometimes treat separately.

Economic Policies Advocated as Part of the NIEO

To increase the south's industrial capabilities, NIEO advocates have supported all forms of technical assistance since the foundation of the U.N. Most recently these have included programs to assure the free transfer of technology owned by northern governments. In an effort to assure that TNC investment can be used toward the same end, the south advocates a binding international code of conduct for TNCs. The code would increase the power of third world governments relative to that of firms based in the developed world.

In order to increase the relative power of the third world over north-south trade, the south advocates that tariff preferences continue to be granted to the developing states. The south also supports the IPC's program of commodity agreements backed by a unified system of financing buffer stocks in order to discourage the competition among southern producers of raw materials and thus avoid downward trends in the prices of third world goods (at the expense of dampening upward price movements as well, it should be added). The south also supports any direct action by third world raw material producers to maintain and raise prices whenever possible, although OPEC's successes have yet to be repeated.

In order to increase the relative power of the south over development financing, third world governments have consistently supported channeling all aid through multilateral institutions. Third world concerns for disarmament and for maintaining economic growth in developed countries have to be understood as ways to assure or increase multilateral aid. The SDR-Link proposal serves the same function; the NIEO desire to increase the power of the IMF to that of a global central bank should be understood primarily as a means to make the Link feasible. Southern proposals for both generalized and individual debt relief would increase the power of third world states over development financing more directly. The south's support of compensatory financing for trade income shortfalls and other financial and monetary reforms of the Bretton Woods system also serve the same end of increasing southern power over development financing.

The New Order Political Strategy

Except for direct action on prices by third world commodity producers, all of the major NIEO economic policies require north-south cooperation. Thus, since 1974 the south's political strategy has evolved into one of negotiation. The south has integrated earlier concerns with direct action and attempts to influence northern opinion into an overall strategy for negotiation. Earlier strategies are now used to help build consensus in the north that negotiation is necessary. The south remains wary of conducting negotiations in forums and under rules that do not give it an advantage. Nonetheless, the futility of that position has made NIEO advocates move continually closer to accepting a process of negotiation that would allow the south's new order program to be amended, the system of global negotiations based on a framework consensus in the General Assembly, to be followed by separate negotiations within each of the specialized agencies of the U.N. that deal with economic matters, under rules designed to achieve conciliation between north and south.

Elements of the NIEO Ideology Most Likely to Change

The changes in new order strategy visible in the last decade should not be surprising. The fundamental NIEO commitment to rational policy analysis assures that, within the boundaries established by other new order principles, policies that fail will be discarded. No southern strategy for achieving the NIEO has worked yet. Consequently, we should expect the south to experiment with new strategies.

Likewise, the commitment to rational policy analysis assures that the south will abandon or replace the economic policies if they prove unsuccessful in achieving the south's goals. As of yet, no NIEO policy proposal has been completely abandoned; none has been proven a failure in practice, and economists still disagree over the probable effects of the proposals. Nonetheless, even the economic analysis of critics of the NIEO gives us reason to believe that the south will add new economic policy proposals in the future.

A 1979 Overseas Development Council study of all the NIEO policies then proposed concluded that even if all were enacted, they would assure only a moderate increase in third world per capita income.(4) To the extent that per capita income is a reliable indicator of third world development goals, and (as Abdel Rahman suggests) it probably is, NIEO advocates will have to find additional means to achieve their goals.

Another group of northern economists recently concluded that the NIEO policies would work primarily to the benefit of the most developed third world states.(5) To the extent that the new order alliance remains committed to its principle of the equal treatment of states, such unequal benefits would be unacceptable, assuring that additional policies would have to be adopted.

These probable changes in NIEO strategy and economic analysis would result directly from the confrontation between the new order ideology and reality. Another change in the ideology could arise from a conflict within the ideology itself. Yet it might take substantive debate between north and south to make NIEO advocates worry about that conflict.

The conflict appears in the confused relationships among some of the NIEO principles. New order advocates take a realm of rational management of the world economy to be necessary, but circumscribe that realm by the principle that states are equal in their economic rights and duties. The relationship between the realm of management and the realm of the economic rights and duties of states remains unclear.

Conceivably, the realm of international management could be understood as completely subservient to equal states' rights, meaning that any individual state would have a right to contradict the rational management policies of the NIEO. The south's continual affirmations of state sovereignty and proposals to let any state have effective veto over proposed NIEO reforms suggests that interpretation. But as Keynes pointed out nearly forty years ago, the absolute subjection of international institutions to the will of even one nation-state contradicts the idea that there are global needs that only rational global economic management can meet. An NIEO based on the principle that global management must be absolutely subservient to the policies of national governments would simply institutionalize the system Streeten already sees as existent, a world in which state interventions to rationalize national economies are expected, yet no coherent effort can be made to rationalize the separate policies of separate states.

The south might only wish to affirm that the realm
of equal states' rights creates boundaries on the realm
of economic management. That appears to be what NIEO
supporters argue when they say that specific policies,
like birth control, cannot be adopted as a quid pro quo
for aid from international institutions.

To make that relationship clear the NIEO ideology
would not only have to specify the economic rights and
duties of states, it would also have to specify the
rights and duties of international economic institutions,
thus specifying the boundaries of the realm of rational
management of the world economy. In fact the dialogue
over global negotiations might result in such a
clarification since the northern powers opposed to the
south's formula, the U.S., U.K., and West German, couch
their opposition in terms of support of the integrity of
existing international economic institutions. Agreement
on the specific limits on the autonomous realms of
international economic institutions would overcome the
existing impasse in negotiations.

Elements of the Ideology Likely to Remain Unchanged

Even if some parts of the NIEO ideology might change
as a result of negotiations, the history of the ideology
suggests that others will not change as long as the third
world alliance remains. Some of the elements appear to be
permanent simply because they have been part of the
ideology since its beginning. The third world goal of
industrial development has been affirmed by native
governments in Asia, Africa, and Latin America since the
depression. The goal was part of the ideology of
independent Asian, African, and Latin American
governments at the U.N. even before they adopted NIEO
principles. Similarly, the principles of international
management and the equality of states in their rights and
duties have been part of the ideology from the beginning.
We have no way of conceiving of the ideology without
them.

Recognizing the goal of third world industrial
development and the fundamental NIEO principles as
permanent elements of the ideology, we could conceive
that its adherents might abandon their belief that
differences in power over north-south economic
transactions explain the industrialization of the north
and the lack of industry in the south if further study
(authorized by the principle of rational policy analysis)
proved this assumption false.

Nonetheless, I believe this analysis may be as
fundamental to the new order ideology as any other
element. It does more than help explain the south's lack
of development; it helps define the identity that members
of the third world alliance share. All have similar
grievances with the present economic order. It is not

just that some third world states were colonies when the
present order was created while others were independent
but rarely consulted by those who created the system;
more importantly, all third world states suffered from a
similar position in the world political economy as a
whole. The analysis makes third world countries appear as
natural allies. Appeals to similar grievances, or even to
a similar desire for development, would not suggest the
need for alliance the way a claim to a similar history
does.

The New Internationalism

Many of those who have studied the NIEO ideology
before have tried to capture its most permanent elements
in an even more abstract form than the outline above,
labeling the ideology with the name of an older, more
familiar philosophy. After all, as Clifford Geertz says
when discussing ideology itself, we often expand
knowledge by giving something new an old name.(6)
But none of the old names offered for the NIEO
ideology are quite satisfying. Even calling the ideology
a "new internationalism," and meaning by that that it is
a more coherent expression of the "internationalism"
identified by Sukarno and Nehru in the fifties, would not
be completely accurate. Nonetheless, illustrating the
ways in which the labels do or do not fit can help
clarify what the NIEO ideology is, and even what it might
become.
The NIEO ideology resembles Fabianism, as Daniel
Patrick Moynihan first recognized,(7) in that it supports
social controls on the market. Despite the claims of some
northern economists, the NIEO ideology certainly suggests
no more bureaucratization and control of the global
economy than Fabians advocate for domestic economies in
developed countries. The market remains central. NIEO
trade proposals rely on the market. Third world officials
ignore straightforward proposals for fixing prices, such
as having an international agency empowered to set prices
and penalize violators, the way wage and price controls
work within many countries.
But "Fabianism" fails to capture the NIEO ideology
for the same reason "international Keynesianism" or any
other global form of corporatism does. The role of the
state in the new ideology differs. The NIEO ideology
justifies a compact of states, not a compact of classes,
sectors, or individuals. Keynes's vision of what Fred
Block calls "internationally organized state
capitalism"(8) was designed to overcome the resistance of
national governments to a realm of rational management of
the world economy by creating cross-national class
coalitions. Fabians, who emphasize the political equality
of individuals, might imagine the same possibility. NIEO
advocates, who are concerned more about the equal

treatment of states, could not.

For similar reasons, attempts to justify or criticize the NIEO ideology on the basis of John Rawls's liberal theory of justice fail to correctly characterize the ideology. Rawls argues that if people chose social rules without knowing their own position in society they would meet all basic needs and only let the well off gain when the least advantaged gained as well.(9) But NIEO supporters only advocate basic needs development as a means toward another end, not, as Rawls does, as a goal in itself. Extended to be an ethic of international relations, Rawls's theory justifies duties of individuals in one state to individuals in other states.(10) It does not address the NIEO claims about the rights and duties of states to each other.

Critics who call the NIEO ideology "mercantilism" can deal with the rights of states, at least as they are reflected in the western tradition of international law.(11) But the NIEO ideology defines duties of states that go beyond respecting others' rights. And the central concern of the new order ideology remains the activities of international institutions designed to help manage the world economy, something traditional mercantilists never thought of. Calling the NIEO ideology "mercantilism" also fails to capture the notion of positive duties of states toward one another, something the other proposed names for the ideology ignore as well.

Calling the ideology a "new internationalism" emphasizes the positive duties by recalling the contrast with cosmopolitanism that Sukarno outlined in the 1950s. Sukarno sought to maintain the cultural diversity and cultural autonomy of existing groups. "Internationalism" is even more appropriate to the NIEO ideology than to Sukarno's domestic governing ideology. The NIEO aims to preserve only the cultural diversity and autonomy of nation-states, not of cultures which exist subnationally.

While "new internationalism" does not capture many of the elements of the NIEO ideology, especially the role of government as the sole legitimate definer of culture, it does suggest some new ways to understand the ideology. Just as there is a larger universe of philosophical writings on the ethics of social democracy and liberalism to which the "Fabian" and "Rawlsian" parts of the NIEO debate can be compared, many arguments about the need for maintaining cultural diversity exist.(12)

Even a Rawlsian argument for the ethics of the new internationalism could be constructed: Individuals deciding upon social rules would take into account that their culture will give them their identity. They may choose a world in which cultures, including their own, can die out in competition with others. Or they may choose a world which fosters cultural diversity through collective self-reliance, an NIEO-like alternative. To avoid alienation they would choose the NIEO.

This example is not chosen as the most compelling justification for the ethics of the new internationalism,(13) but because it helps illustrate where potential sources of change in the new order ideology can exist outside the ideology itself. They appear in the interests of the those who advocate the ideology, the interests that the ideology helps them understand. In this case, as Abdel Rahman and Streeten both suggest, for some NIEO advocates, partial integration into the global upper class comes at the cost of cultural alienation, which, like any real concern NIEO advocates have, could become the basis for new ideological innovations.

Yet the personal concerns that NIEO advocates share would not be the first thing to consider when looking for the interests underlying the NIEO ideology. That is why the notion that creating a personal philosophy to deal with cultural alienation might be the primary source of new NIEO innovations does not quite ring true.

I chose this example to illustrate that the new order's third world advocates can be thought of as sharing different interests, each apparent only at one level of analysis. They may share common personal interests based on their personal experience as members of a global elite. They also may share both conflicting and convergent interests as members of the governing elite of separate states. Finally they may share interests as leaders of nations that have a similar position in the world system.

Given the global focus of the new order ideology it make little sense to begin explaining its nature, origin, and future in terms of common domestic interests or similar personal experiences, even though some analysts have tried to explain NIEO doctrine by beginning at one of the less inclusive levels.(14) A more straightforward strategy involves going from the more inclusive to less inclusive levels of analysis, using purely domestic interests to explain only what cannot be explained as a result of common interests created by the world system and using common personal experiences to explain only what cannot be explained at both more inclusive levels. That is the strategy I follow below.

INTERESTS UNDERLYING THE NIEO IDEOLOGY

The explanation for the emergence of the NIEO ideology offered in the introduction emphasizes interests third world officials share due to the similar positions of their states within the world system. It may have only been coincidence that the earliest new order advocates shared an interest in global regimes that would foster their industrial development. Nonetheless, the global process of agreeing upon postwar regimes assured that all of them would become subject to the Bretton Woods system, yet be the only group of states subject to the system to have grievances with it from the very beginning.

To define both those grievances and the reason for their alliance, the early new order supporters adopted the fundamental NIEO principles and the basic NIEO analysis of the world economy while the Bretton Woods system was still being created. Problems NIEO advocates suffered partially as a result of the operation of the Bretton Woods system triggered further amplification of their economic analysis. The alliance began to develop a shared political strategy and an analysis upon which it was based only after its members became conscious of a collective identity.

The first signs of the breakdown of the Bretton Woods system reinforced the alliance's identity, overcoming its members' conflicting national interests and convincing alliance members of the need to become more militant as well as more unified. When the alliance's systemically defined opposition, the north, began to fracture deeply as many northern governments and members of the northern nongovernmental elite began to support the third world program, the alliance slowly began to moderate its views to take some of its former opponents' interests into account and to emphasize more mutual means for resolving the systemic problems that the NIEO ideology identified and by which it was motivated.

The Ideology's Function at a Global Level

As it is summarized above, the emergence of the NIEO ideology was part of the emergence of the third world as a relatively autonomous actor in world politics. Karl Deutsch's way of identifying autonomous actors(15) illustrates how the ideology was able to play this role and suggests the limits of the third world as an actor.

Deutsch says that four functions of "consciousness" must be performed by a person or collectivity -- e.g., corporation, party, nation, alliance -- that acts autonomously. It must have (1) memory and (2) ways to easily recall information from it. The actor must also have (3) ways to learn and (4) means to assure that what is learned can enter memory, what is remembered can influence what is learned, and what has been recalled is remembered. Memory provides the actor with a way to store both its goals and what it has learned about previous attempts to achieve them. The actor's openness to new information assures that it can develop strategies because it will be able to create a record of successes and failures upon which a strategy can be based. Means of assuring the constant transmission of information assure that both memory and learning can play their assigned roles.

The NIEO ideology helps serve two of these functions

for the third world. It is that part of the memory of the third world alliance within international organizations that officials can actually carry with them. At the same time the ideology's principle that rational policy analysis be used to guide global economic decision making helps assure that the third world alliance remains open to new information, that it has the capacity to learn.

Despite the significance of the NIEO ideology, other things contribute to these functions as well: The "memory" of the third world alliance within international organizations, the record of its goals, and what it has learned in the past also depend on the existence of a third world intellectual community including scholars, university officials, and publishers concerned with third world goals. The U.N. Secretariats and regional economic commissions also help play the same role. The research norms of social scientists interested in third world goals help assure that the alliance remains open to new information. The rapidly changing economic environment third world states found themselves in under the evolving Bretton Woods system contributed as well. And the existence of conflicts among third world governments required the alliance to either learn or break apart.

The ability of third world officials to consult the alliance's broader memory and the ease with which they agree upon lessons to be remembered has less to do with the NIEO ideology. Rather, the smooth functioning of these links in the alliance's "consciousness" was facilitated by the existence of the U.N. professional staffs, the development of personal trust among specific third world officials as they worked with each other through repeated conferences, the fact that any two third world representatives in the U.N. system could find at least one language they both knew, and the existence of common genres -- the resolutions and set phrases upon which so much of the debate within international organizations tends to focus.

In summary, the NIEO ideology functions as a key part of the "consciousness" of the third world. But, of course, "the third world" that has this consciousness only acts within certain arenas in the international system, especially in international organizations where economic matters are discussed.

This application of Deutsch's criteria suggests that the reality of the third world as an international actor is a bit different than many opponents of the NIEO have often assumed. For example, the existence of the third world as an international actor dedicated to the goals of the NIEO ideology could not be ended by pulling members out of the alliance. "Graduating" the more developed third world countries, say the OPEC countries and the newly industrialized nations, such as Singapore, into the developed world by giving them the rights and duties that northern states enjoy under Bretton Woods would do nothing to abolish the memory, ways of learning, and links of consciousness which allow the third world to act. Even if officials of graduated states gave up the NIEO ideology, the third world would continue as an actor made up of other states. Convincing LLDC officials to call themselves a "fourth world" would do even less to the integrity of the third world as international actor. It would reinforce some of the conflict within the third world, but that conflict itself may be functional as something that keeps the alliance open to new information.

A concerted attempt to abolish the third world as an international actor, without transforming the system to which the NIEO ideology emerged as a reaction, would have to involve destroying the other factors that contribute to the alliance's "consciousness." Such an effort might include destroying the third world intellectual community, abolishing the international organization staffs interested in NIEO issues, stabilizing the economic environment in which third world states find themselves, reducing the frequency of international meetings on economic matters, and frequently changing the standard procedures for conducting remaining meetings. In sum, the third world probably could not be destroyed as an international actor without either transforming the Bretton Woods system to take into account third world grievances, or else transforming the rest of the postwar system of international organizations that deal with economic matters in such a way that NIEO issues cannot be raised.

This implies that the third world and its NIEO ideology will be a factor in international politics for some time to come. That makes it particularly important to point out the difference between the third world as an international actor and something that that international actor is not, a direct representative of the collective consciousness of all the people in Asia, Africa, and Latin America. Nothing like "third worldism" exists as powerfully as the nationalism that can be found in almost any nation. No third world ideology influences the mass of people within the third world the way the NIEO ideology influences third world elites within international economic organizations. Deutsch's criteria can help illustrate the difference.

Probably most people throughout Asia, Africa, and Latin America have been exposed to the NIEO ideology. Especially in the late seventies, government-sponsored radio throughout the third world constantly discussed the NIEO program.(16) But otherwise, few people in the third world had a source of memories about the third world as a whole. To a certain extent popular music in the south Atlantic basin -- Latin America, Africa, and the Caribbean -- records and retells third world rather than regional or national themes. And Islamic revival

movements from Africa east to the Pacific tell and retell
a history of a single struggle across much of the third
world. Yet neither locus of popular transnational memory
within the third world encompasses all regions and can be
consulted by everyone.

Third world officials who want to remember third
world goals and the lessons of past attempts to achieve
them can consult books, U.N. documents, or the memory of
colleagues. Most people only have access to what they and
those near them remember of government broadcasts. And
since the international forums where third world problems
are discussed provide so few opportunities for popular
input -- especially for people who are poor and distant
-- few people in the third world have any good reason to
spend time trying to learn about changing third world
interests, let alone about changing attempts to achieve
them.

Moreover, those in the third world outside
government who do take the time to learn face impediments
to sharing knowledge. They cannot transform the third
world "consciousness" with what they learn. No systems of
translators, frequent meetings, or standard procedures
exist to let poor people in one part of the third world
share their views with poor people in another. In most
countries no such systems exist even to allow the poor to
share their views with government officials.

The third world as an international actor, then, is
based on a coalition among elites, and the NIEO ideology
is an elite ideology. The possible set of those who could
actually have affected the way the ideology emerged and,
thus, whose interests are likely to be apprehended by it,
is limited to those people within the third world who
have access to at least some of the other factors which
contribute to the alliance's autonomy -- the southern
intellectual community and the resources and meetings of
international economic organizations.

National Interests and the NIEO Ideology

Third world interests generated by the global system
-- the creation, operation, and breakdown of the Bretton
Woods system -- explain most of the history of NIEO
ideology. The Bretton Woods system appeared to thwart
development goals all third world governments shared.
However, that systemic explanation does not tell us why
third world governments tended to share some goals in the
first place. To do that requires going below the level of
the international system and identifying the domestic
interests to which third world governments responded.
Even if the southern states' similar goals have a
"global" source, we can assume that each individual third
world government adopted its goals in response to
domestic pressures.

The goals of a government's foreign policy which

respond to domestic pressure are usually called the "national interest." Wentworth Ofuatey-Kodjoe argues that the most straightforward operational definition of a country's "national interest" would have researchers find out which people foreign policy makers think of as the "nation" when they make foreign policy, and then find out what that group considers to be its interests. Empirically, a country's national interest usually is the self-defined interests of those who keep the government in power.(17)

In most third world countries the governing coalition's interests are expressed in a national development plan. Part of the strength of the NIEO ideology, of course, is that can justify almost any national development plan. The only constants across national development plans that NIEO ideology seems to demand are some affirmation of the desirability of national cultural autonomy (the new internationalism) and some relatively central position for industrial development. These, in fact, are constants across third world development plans.(18)

Superficially, these two constant elements seem to appeal to conflicting domestic interests. Affirmation of the need for industrial development appears to posit development away from rural areas where farmers -- the majority of people in most third world countries -- live, and where "traditional" elites base their power on indigenous customs of land ownership and labor contract. Affirmations of cultural autonomy, on the other hand, appear designed to strengthen the "traditional" elites' power bases and focus development on the countryside.(19)

Yet third world cultural nationalist development ideologies rarely focus on the countryside. Instead of strengthening customary elites the ideologies often weaken them at the expense of central government which acts as the sole definer of the national culture. Even if ideologies of national cultural autonomy were created by people who did not even covertly desire to strengthen the power of the state, they invariably serve that function because the government uses its ability to define the national cultural as a means to reward allies and exclude opponents.(20) In the process, the government need never contradict the interests of the governing coalition based in urban areas and interested in industrialization -- whether that coalition be centered on local or foreign entrepreneurs, industrial workers, merchants, petty wage earners, or even the unemployed.

More rarely, a government can pursue both an overt interest in industrial development and a covert interest in strengthening the state without even being based on a coalition centered in urban areas. As long as its coalition accepts that industrial development is a key to increasing aggregate wealth and that the coalition will gain the benefits of that development, perhaps through the government's redistributive policies, the core of the governing coalition can be any sector, urban or rural. The key is the combination of the two interests served by constants across all the development doctrines the NIEO ideology justifies: industrial development and strengthening the state.

Immanuel Wallerstein argues that unless a region is "invited" to develop by international investors, the only other normal path to the "core" of the world economy requires both industrialization and strengthening the state. He even argues that to follow the least likely to succeed of the three available paths is to honestly pursue self-reliant development.(21) For governments that do that, affirmations of cultural nationalism need not become simply a means to strengthen the state.

Wallerstein imbeds his view within a complex theory of the development of the world economy, but his whole theory need not be accepted to accept the centrality of these two goals. Even if development is taken to mean simply increasing wealth, the labor savings that come from the introduction of industrial techniques make that possible. And, as E. B. Ayal argues, industrialization no longer can be carried out solely in the interests of individual entrepreneurs. Demands for redistribution of new wealth are too all pervasive. Only very rare third world governments, even those governing the most dualistic society with the widest income disparities, can govern without the occasional backing of at least some of the nation's poorest sectors. Development in modern states has to be something of a collectivist process. And the cultural nationalist doctrines which the NIEO ideology justifies help the state create the specific form of collectivism its own supporters demand.(22)

Thus, an excursion into domestic interests underlying the NIEO ideology takes us back to the international system, not to the Bretton Woods system, but to the older "world economy" characterized by development in some regions and underdevelopment in others. The development goals the NIEO ideology supports may be politically astute throughout the third world. Unless third world governments choose to rely on "development by invitation," they may well have interests in industrialization and strengthening the state no matter what specific coalition of social forces maintains the government in power.

There are other ways to explain those domestic interests shared by third world governments and expressed by the NIEO ideology. Some critics of the new order argue that third world governments offer it to their domestic supporters in lieu of development. Such arguments run parallel to John Nellis's convincing assessment of the functions of Tanzania's domestic ideology; it lets rural Tanzanians participate in a social experiment they can tell is of world historical significance even though it has little chance of success. The governing elite in Tanzania, Nellis argues, has used the opportunity created by the way the ideology reduced material demands to secure a more prominant position.(23)

Certainly the NIEO ideology helps strengthen the state and its functionaries, just as did the domestic ideology that Nellis studied. But the words of the NIEO ideology would not be as readily acceptable in lieu of real development as the Tanzanian development doctrine is. The NIEO ideology, even when publicly promulgated over government radio, can offer very few people a sense of participation in something historically important. It invites no public participation. It does not require third world publics to uproot villages, change habits of production, or even to continue to listen to the radio. Perhaps the NIEO ideology offered some third world diplomats at international conferences a sense of participation in world historical changes in lieu of the sense of competence that might come from successfully negotiating north-south agreements. That trade off might have been in the interests of central governments opposed to the kind of north-south agreements that have actually been possible up to now. But the same process could not work to quell the demands of any other group within a third world country in the same way, simply because the NIEO ideology does not offer participation to anyone else.

Of course, it could be that the NIEO ideology's only real function within a third world country is to deflect criticism from the government, to, as Caribbean dependency theorist Havelock Brewster puts it, blame the developed countries for the third world government's inherent inability to control the economy. Certainly, in an extremely facile sense, that is true. Adherents to the NIEO ideology do blame the international system for their inability to set and meet national development goals, just as Brewster says.(24) But the persistence and the ubiquity of the new order ideology throughout the third world argue against explaining it solely as a tool to deflect domestic criticism. It could not be used successfully for that purpose for long. As Ofuatey-Kodjoe says, in a world of ubiquitous dependence third world citizens judge their governments on the basis of what they have done with the cards the international system deals them; a Ghanaian is less interested in the dependence both Ghana and the Ivory Coast equally suffer than in the reasons why the Ivorian government seems to have done better than any Ghanaian government has.(25) To believe that the NIEO ideology has existed for nearly forty years merely as a tool to deflect domestic criticism from third world governments is to have little faith in the intelligence either of third world officials or of third world citizens.

Having some faith in both, I doubt that attempts to

deflect domestic criticism can explain everything in the
NIEO ideology, or even those few common elements in all
third world development doctrines that are not explained
by the NIEO ideology's history as a reaction to Bretton
Woods. Instead, I suspect the desire for industrial
development and the desire to strengthen the state appear
to have been almost universal lessons of mid-twentieth
century domestic politics throughout the south. If we
could compare the process of government formation in
state after state -- sequences of parties formed by or
forming coalitions of domestic social forces, coming to
power and then remaining, or perhaps reorganizing or
falling -- we should expect to find that any stable
government, no matter what groups make up its governing
coalition, would be one that wanted these things that the
NIEO ideology supports. Unfortunately, investigation of
that hypothesis has to await further research.(27)

The Personal Experiences of Third World Officials

Given that no one has done research to determine if
the new order ideology responds to third world domestic
concerns other than the typical government's desire to
deflect public criticism, I may have passed over that
hypothesis too quickly. The argument really is less about
pressures on third world governments from domestic
politics than it is one about common personal
characteristics of third world leaders, in this case, a
common desire to deflect criticism rather than to accept
it and respond to it directly. I now turn to personal
characteristics new order advocates may have in common.
As I argued above, given the global focus of the NIEO
ideology, we should begin to look for its explanation at
more inclusive levels of analysis. Little of the
ideology's history remains to be explained below the
level of the world system. What remains can be explained
as the coordination of domestic interests, which have a
systemic source as well. The following summary of some of
the personal concerns that many third world advocates of
the NIEO share simply reinforces this explanation of the
nature and rise of the NIEO ideology.
The desire to deflect popular criticism of failed
development policies may, indeed, be a trait third world
advocates of the new order share. It may be one way of
coping with the peculiar position in world society in
which they find themselves, the position mentioned in
both quotations at the head of this chapter. Political
and economic leaders recognize they are part of a global
elite, yet have good reason to consider themselves
victims within global society. They identify with the
vast majority of people around the world who are the most
victimized by the present structure of global society,
yet third world political and economic leaders recognize
themselves as contributing to the victimization of the

least advantaged. Before suggesting how this peculiar position might generate beliefs and actions which could influence the NIEO ideology, let me justify the way I characterized it.

That third world economic and political leaders are part of a global elite should not be controversial. The dualism within most third world economies assures that the advantages of the most advantaged people in the south are similar to those of most advantaged people in the north. Third world leaders have had access to the same education that leaders of wealthy states have. Economists meeting to discuss north-south matters may represent all the countries of the world, but they are likely to represent only the most prestigious handful of the world's universities.(27) And, to a certain extent, to understand the personal dynamics of the General Assembly meeting on economic matters involves understanding the concerns of one of the most privileged classes in the city at the center of the world economy, New York.

That third world economic and political leaders are victims might be less apparent. But the victimization of the most frequent promoters of the NIEO ideology, the representatives of third world governments at international economic meetings, can be demonstrated easily. C. Clyde Ferguson, an American representative at the United Nations during the Carter years, points out that the vast majority of representatives at any north-south conference will have grown up in colonial societies. "Some even have vivid memories of signs -- 'No Natives, No Dogs.'"(28) Even many of those who grew up in independent states lived through periods when their nation was wracked by military interventions from countries in the north. And despite the very similar education that all the people who take part in economic debates within international organizations have, all third world representatives have had to suffer the typical condescension of their colleagues from wealthy nations. As Sidney Weintraub noted even during the cooperative early sixties, northern delegates to global economic conferences have trouble resisting their desire to lecture those who appear to have so much to learn about development.(29) Ferguson adds that most experienced diplomats recognize that a peculiar sort of racism creates tension underneath even the most cooperative north-south meetings on economic matters.(30) The coincidence that most Group of 77 states are populated by nonwhites or dark skinned Caucasians lets northerners, including some sympathetic to the third world, express their normal condescension as racism.

The victimization that third world economic and political leaders have suffered and continue to suffer assures that most will identify with the more completely victimized majority within their own country. In fact, those scholars who argue that third world elite concerns with national cultural autonomy inadvertently lead to a highly functional strengthening of the state, also argue that in case after case throughout the third world the elite's initial concern with national cultural autonomy came from an attempt to identify with the country's least advantaged. That identification, in turn, provided a partial psychological resolution of the conflict created by being both a member of the world's colonial or neocolonial elite and its victim.(31) There is no reason to believe that new members of any third world nation's elite cannot find the same reasons for identifying, in part, with the least advantaged and thus, not incidentally, come to reinforce one of the key principles of the new order ideology.

Unfortunately for themselves, many people who govern third world states cannot retain an unambiguous personal identification with their country's least advantaged. Some officials consciously and actively take part in the victimization of the majority in order to maintain their dominant position. Others, perhaps including the Tanzanian officials whose behavior Nellis explains so well, find that the act of governing condemns them to victimize their fellow citizens (at least at times) with taxes, nonremunerative production prices, high consumer prices, or exclusions from social services that others receive.

Those who try to cope with this contradiction between identifying with the most victimized yet consciously contributing to their victimization might decide to deflect popular criticism of their inability to better control the economy by pointing to the international system as the source of the problem and demanding the NIEO as its solution. Equally, says critic of Caribbean dependency theory G. E. Cumper, they might decide to become academic dependency theorists, retain their position in the global social elite, continue criticizing the world economy, yet also be able to criticize officials of third world governments for their "contradictory" and "self-serving" views.(32)

Parenthetically, even though either of these ideological solutions would be "self-serving" in the sense that it would mean adopting beliefs in order to cope with a personal dilemma without first testing to see if the beliefs are valid, there is no reason why beliefs adopted in that way have to be invalid. That is a separate question. I indirectly addressed it in this book whenever I illustrated that NIEO advocates look for explanations of new problems only among those not excluded by the ideological constraint of their prior consensus. Nonetheless, for the purposes of this book, the influence of personal experiences on the NIEO ideology has significance not as a means to test the ideology's analysis, but as a means to test my own thesis about the ideology's origin.

The test cannot be completely conclusive because the personal interests that third world NIEO advocates have because of their position in international society suggest nothing new. Parts of the new order ideology appear overdetermined. Or, to put it more precisely, third world NIEO advocates may have been able to resolve personal dilemmas as well as solve problems created by systemic forces when they adopted two of the key characteristics of the NIEO ideology, its concern for aiding national cultural autonomy and its focus on systemic rather than domestic impediments to industrial development.

Personal, state, and global interests combine to create the NIEO ideology. The ideology's content and origin are best understood first as a reaction to the positions of third world states both within the Bretton Woods system of institutions managing the global economy since the second world war and within the older, more inclusive world economy as a whole. That is why the ideology's history fits so easily within the frameworks provided by Andrew Scott's theory of the rise and fall of international management regimes and David Apter's theory of how ideologies can develop when opportunities for creating a collective political identity exist among those who have been excluded in any political system. The NIEO ideology was created and has operational meaning only within the political system of intergovernmental management of the world economy first created after the second world war. The ideology contributes to the identity of a political actor, the third world, which, even though it acts only within a limited arena, is likely to be with us as long as the present system of intergovernmental management of the world economy exists. The positions of Asian, African, and Latin American elite advocates of the NIEO ideology, both within their national societies and within world society as a whole, should be understood as contributing to the rise of the ideology only in one sense. By adopting the NIEO ideology, third world political and economic leaders can partially resolve some of the contradictory beliefs they hold as a result of their contradictory position as both victimizers within their own societies and victims within world society.

NOTES

(1) Ibrahim Helmi Abdel Rahman, "The Most Basic Need: The Need to Develop Rationally," in Anthony J. Dolman and Jan van Ettinger, eds., Partners In Tomorrow (New York: E. P. Dutton), pp. 7-8. Paul Streeten, "The New International Economic Order," Unpublished paper, Washington, June 7, 1979, p. 4.

(2) In my doctoral research I kept track of changes

in NIEO policy analysis by making a series of "cognitive maps," representations of stated causal relationships, of the "third world" position in Second Committee debates. See the appendix to "The Emergence of the New International Economic Order Ideology," unpublished dissertation, Dept. of Political Science, Univ. of North Carolina, Chapel Hill, 1980.

(3) The Group of 77 tends to treat the Charter of Economic Rights and Duties of States as international legislation enacted in 1974. It applies the duty of restitution to those states continuing "colonialism" after the charter was adopted. Beginning in 1977 the group has charged Israel and South Africa with duties of restitution under this principle, as reported in Ervin Laszlo et al., The Objectives of the New International Economic Order (New York: Pergamon, 1978), pp. 169-70. The previous year the nonaligned countries reiterated their support of this circumscribed version of the restitution ethic:

> The international community is urged to facilitate the effective exercise of the right of restitution and full compensation for damages for the exploitation and depletion and all damages to the natural and other resources of all states, territories, and peoples subjected to foreign aggression and occupation, alien and colonial domination, social discrimination, and apartheid.

Then, emphasizing that the overarching duty under the NIEO was to be the permanent duty of all states to each other, not the historical duty of the exploiter to the exploited, the nonaligned states added:

> It is, in addition, the duty of all states to extend assistance to these countries, territories, and peoples.

Quoted in Laszlo, p. 171.

(4) William R. Cline, "A Quantitative Assessment of the Policy Alternatives in the NIEO Negotiations," in Policy Alternatives for a New International Economic Order (New York: Praeger, 1979), p. 52. Cline uses this evidence to justify the typical northern criticism of the NIEO ideology in the late seventies. The fact that the new order program will not work means that more emphasis must be placed on the ". . . growth and equity performances of the domestic economies of the developing countries." The evidence suggests to him that the developing countries should quit carping about international impediments to development, search for explanations of their lack of development in domestic policies, and adopt basic needs criteria as their central goal. Once Cline's evidence is accepted, it would be just

as logical to redouble efforts to find new intergovernmental policy proposals that would be more effective than those that are now part of the NIEO doctrine. The ideological constraint of the south's prior agreement that there is a systemic source of the major development problems common throughout the third world assures that Cline's evidence will convince NIEO supporters of this alternative to the conclusion he hopes they will reach.

(5)William Loehr and John P. Powelson, Threat to Development: The Pitfalls of the NIEO (Boulder: Westview Press, 1983).

(6)Clifford Geertz, "Ideology as a Cultural System," in David E. Apter, ed., Ideology and Discontent (New York: Free Press, 1964), p. 61.

(7)Daniel Patrick Moynihan, "The United States in Opposition," Commentary 59 (Mar. 1975): 31-4.

(8)Fred Block, The Origins of International Economic Disorder (Berkeley: Univ. of Calif. Press, 1977), pp. 223-24.

(9)John Rawls, A Theory of Justice (Cambridge: Harvard Univ. Press, 1971).

(10)As Charles R. Beitz argues in Political Theory and International Relations (Princeton: Princeton Univ. Press, 1979), pp. 125-76.

(11)This is the approach taken by Robert W. Tucker in his The Inequality of Nations (New York: Basic Books, 1977).

(12)Such arguments are made in Edward T. Hall, Beyond Culture (Garden City: Doubleday, 1977) and Hannah Arendt, Totalitarianism (New York: Harcourt Brace, 1968). In conversation, Arendt's biographer, Elizabeth Young-Bruehl, informed me that Arendt used "internationalism" and "cosmopolitanism" to make the same distinction Sukarno made except that Arendt defined each concept the way Sukarno defined the other.

(13)Hall's argument is the most compelling of the three.

(14)The usual way involves assuming that third world governments share no systemic interests, that no reality, even the reality of a common reaction to the Bretton Woods system, underlies the notion of a "third world." Analysts who make that assumption are forced to look for coincidences of domestic or personal interests to explain the NIEO ideology; see Craig Murphy, "What the Third World Wants: An Interpretation of the Development and Meaning of the New International Economic Order Ideology," International Studies Quarterly 27 (Mar. 1983): 54-59, 70-72.

(15)Karl W. Deutsch, Nationalism and Social Communication: An Inquiry Into the Foundation of Nationality, 2nd ed. (Cambridge: MIT Press, 1966), pp. 166-70.

(16)I make this assertion based on frequent but not

180

systematic listening to short wave broadcasts.

(17)Wentworth Ofuatey-Kodjoe, "A Model of Foreign Policy Decision Making in Africa," unpublished paper, Queens College, City Univ. of New York, p. 3.

(18)Even countries that emphasize rural development want to apply industrial technologies to the countryside, both labor saving devices and the products of industry such as chemical fertilizers. Consequently, they devote significant resources to industrial development.

(19)E. B. Ayal, "Nationalist Ideology and Economic Development" Human Organization 25 (Fall 1966): 236. Boris Erasov, "Cultural Personality in the Ideologies of the Third World," Diogenes 78 (Summer 1972): 126.

(20)Ayal, p. 236; Erasov, pp. 132-35.

(21)Immanuel Wallerstein, "Dependence in an Interdependent World: The Limited Possibilities of Transformation Within the Capitalist World-Economy," in The Capitalist World-Economy (Cambridge: Cambridge Univ. Press, 1979), pp. 66-94.

(22)Ayal, p. 233.

(23)John R. Nellis, A Theory of Ideology (London: Oxford Univ. Press, 1972).

(24)Havelock Brewster, "Economic Dependence: A Quantitative Interpretation," Social and Economic Studies 22 (Mar. 1973): 90-95.

(25)Ofuatey-Kodjoe, p. 11.

(26)I have tried to begin such research through a close study of three African cases (Ghana, Tanzania, and Guinea-Bissau) and a survey of information on the continent's other states, as reported in "Society, Ideology, and Foreign Policy in Africa," paper presented at the annual meeting of the Canadian African Studies Association, Toronto, May 1982.

(27)The best summary of this pattern in world society suggested by both Streeten and Abdel Rahman remains Johan Galtung's "A Structural Theory of Imperialism," Journal of Peace Research 8, no. 2 (1971): 81-18; also see his "'A Structural Theory of Imperialism' -- Ten Years Later," Millenium 9 (Winter 1980-81): 183-96.

(28)C. Clyde Ferguson, "The New International Economic Order," in David M. Kay, ed., The Changing United Nations (New York: Academy of Political Science, 1978), p. 152.

(29)Sidney Weintraub, "After the U.N. Trade Conference: Lessons and Portents," Foreign Affairs 47 (Oct. 1964): 50.

(30)Ferguson, p. 154.

(31)Ayal, passim; Erasov, p. 126.

(32)G. E. Cumper, "Dependence, Development, and the Sociology of Economic Thought," Social and Economic Studies 23 (Sept. 1974): 465-82.

Afterword: How Ideas
Can Help Resolve
the North-South Conflict

Any historical study leads to conclusions that can
be documented and to others that cannot. This afterword
contains my more speculative conclusions about the new
order ideology. They cannot be supported by a weight of
evidence because they do not concern what the ideology
has been; they concern what it might become. I believe
the NIEO ideology might someday contribute knowledge
needed to resolve the current north-south conflict.

In abstract terms, the conflict will be resolved
when the Bretton Woods system or its successor learns to
deal with the south's economic problems as well as it
deals with the north's. If we can say that the the new
order ideology performs functions of "consciousness" for
the third world, we can similarly say that those who act
for the Bretton Woods system share a consciousness, of
which the dominant ideology is part. What Deutsch's
framework would have us call the "consciousness" of that
system just equals what other scholars would call the
"complex regime" containing the Bretton Woods
institutions. In that regime the dominant ideology
provides rules and guides for behavior and the Bretton
Woods institutions help keep the regime open to new
information. Understood in that way, as Ernst Haas
illustrates, a regime is the locus of a capacity to learn
how to manage fundamentally new problems even while it
remains the consciousness consulted by those who manage a
particular global issue.(1) I believe, then, that the new
order ideology and the experience of its southern
advocates can help the postwar management system learn to
deal effectively with the south's problems. That would
transform the postwar institutions and require
transformation of the dominant ideology.

Two equally speculative arguments suggest the new
order ideology's capacity to contribute knowledge needed
to manage global economic problems more effectively. One
highlights the dilemmas third world advocates often face
as a result of their contradictory positions in world
society and within their home countries. According to one
of the doyens of the policy sciences, Duncan MacRae,

people in such contradictory roles are likely to produce positive social innovations.(2) The NIEO ideology's third world advocates live at the intersection between the cultures of the world's wealthy and the cultures of its most impoverished. They try consciously to resolve the contradictions between the two. More than any other group, they are likely to develop ways to resolve those contradictions.

In an entirely different way, the simple fact that NIEO advocates have been opposing the current system for almost forty years may have given them some of the knowledge the system itself needs. Immanuel Wallerstein, who began his career by looking for the commonalities among all the different successful nationalist movements in Africa, claims that the weaker party in any protracted struggle will know more about their relationship to the stronger than the stronger party will.(3) The NIEO's advocates may know some things about the world economy that adherents to the dominant ideology have never learned.

Whatever wisdom about the world economy the third world may have acquired in its forty year conflict with the north, however, will not influence actual intergovernmental economic management until north and south agree upon their common interests. The current focus of the north-south conflict over the role of existing specialized agencies within the process of global negotiations may help. If both sides treat this disagreement as a substantive debate, and therefore try to convince the other side rather than to get it to make concessions, the result could be agreement on a formula defining the common north-south interests that both sides want international institutions to serve.

Luckily, neither north nor south has anything to lose in this debate. They cannot even lose face by being convinced of the other's position. The north need not be worried about being convinced of the south's position because the south's position on the proper role of intergovernmental economic management institutions remains one of the few incoherent parts of the new order ideology. The south need not worry about being convinced by the north; the north's current position on the subject makes no more sense.

The dominant ideology holds that intergovernmental economic management institutions exist only to do things that no state can do by itself. On this north and south agree. Neither fully accepts the lesson Keynes taught, that total subjection of international institutions to the will of one or many states would make such management impossible. Northerners just argue that international institutions must be subject to the interests of their dominant member states only, while the third world demands that international institutions be subject to the will of all states.

North and south will disagree over what common interest international institutions should have some autonomous responsibility to serve. Nonetheless, both northern and southern views will change if they debate the issue. Those views have to change, even if only to frame coherent opposing positions. That could get each side into a habit of changing its views in order to facilitate resolution of the conflict. If that were to happen, the last pages of the history of the south's new order ideology could be written about how it changed through time to resolve the north-south conflict, rather than to perpetuate it.

That has not happened yet. As I finish writing this afterword, in July 1983, north and south look as far apart as ever. UNCTAD VI has just ended after illustrating many of the themes in the last pages of this history of the NIEO ideology. The south came to UNCTAD VI with a set of proposals for "emergency" assistance to the third world,(4) proposals influenced by the opinions of their northern supporters on the Brandt Commission whose second report argued the need for such a crisis program even if it meant postponing global agreement on more fundamental reforms.(5) The northern states rejected even this seemingly moderate short-term proposal.

While southern delegates to UNCTAD VI may have thought that they had moderated their views by ending their calls for immediate creation of the NIEO and by adopting some of the views of their northern supporters, the major northern nations did not see it that way. The U.S. and its closest allies argued that the south's emergency program was too costly and that UNCTAD did not even have the authority to discuss it since the program involved much more than trade matters. Those northern governments still on the far side of ul Haq's philosophical bridge that I discuss in chapter 4 even denied the south's analysis of the current situation in the world economy. The most conservative northern states contended that while the economic health of the LDCs depended on that of the developed nations, the opposite was not at all true; the south's economic well-being was peripheral to that of the north.

The north's position at UNCTAD VI will not be its final word. Significantly, the day after the UNCTAD meetings ended two of the most important economic policy makers in the U.S. contradicted the analysis their government had been loudly defending for a month. The head of the American Council of Economic Advisors to the President and the Chairman of the Federal Reserve both argued that the economic health of some third world states, those with large debts, was indeed crucial to all developed countries.(6) That change in tune hardly means that the U.S. has accepted the significance of every third world country's economy or that the U.S. would be willing to conduct any substantive negotiations with the

184

south in forums like UNCTAD, but the new U.S. argument
was, in fact, the same one the Brandt Commission's second
report had made. That position, in turn, provides a basis
for substantive north-south discussions of common
interests.

The south's UNCTAD VI position will not be its final
word either, although I would not want to predict what
lessons the south will draw from that meeting. Third
world governments may decide that their recent strategy
of showing more consideration for northern interests has
been failure. The south may come to berate the Brandt
Commission and other nongovernmental allies for
suggesting common north-south interests that the most
powerful northern governments failed to see. The south
may move from its strategy of negotiation and from its
growing interest in substantive debate with the north.

If the south does move away from its recent strategy
the, NIEO ideology probably will contribute nothing to
the resolution of the north-south conflict for some time.
Now, the conflict can be resolved only through
substantive debate. Given the difference in economic
power between north and south, each round of simple
bargaining based on exchanged concessions merely
replicates the existing divisions between rich and poor
and the conflict inherent in them. The path away from
substantive debate will lead to a longer history for the
NIEO ideology as third world governments transform their
views in order to deal with their continuing conflict
with the north.

NOTES

(1)Ernst Haas, "Words Can Hurt You; or, Who Said
What to Whom About Regimes," International Organization
36 (Spring 1982): 242.
(2)Duncan MacRae, The Social Function of Social
Science (New Haven: Yale Univ. Press, 1976), pp. 277-78.
(3)Immanuel Wallerstein, The Modern World-System
(New York: Academic Press, 1974), p. 14.
(4)New York Times, July 3, 1983, p. 1.
(5)Independent Commission on International
Development, Common Crisis (Cambridge: MIT Press, 1983).
(6)New York Times, July 5, 1983, p. 1.

Index

Abdel Rahman, Ibrahim,
  Helmi, 157, 159, 166
Acheson Dean, 16, 19
Adjustment assistance, 129
Africa, 7, 12, 13, 28, 46,
  52, 60, 63, 66-75, 82,
  94, 96, 101, 106-12,
  118, 137, 163, 169, 177
  182
Afro-Asian conference
  1955, Bandung, 46
  1961, Cairo, 64-66
Aid, 12, 16, 25-35, 51,
  67, 78, 80, 84, 138,
  139
  multilateral, 12, 46,
    99, 114, 160, 161
  targets, 60, 65, 79
  See also specific
    program
Amin, Samir, 107, 109, 118
Andean Pact, 104
Apter, David, 6-9, 126,
  150, 177
Arab OPEC members, 112,
  113
Argentina, 11, 35, 133n,
  138
Arusha Declaration, 95
Asia, 7, 12, 13, 25-28, 32
  34, 37, 41, 42, 46, 52,
  66-69, 75, 100, 102,
  109-12, 134, 169, 177
Australia, 21, 30n, 49, 68
  147
Austria, 135, 137
Ayal, E. B., 172
Bargaining, direct, 6, 7,
  24, 151
Basic needs, 131-33, 137-
  42, 159, 162n, 165

Block, Fred, 164
Bolivia, 62n, 63
Boumedienne, Honari, 113,
  115
Brain drain, 81, 81, 142,
  143
Brandt, Willy, 125, 127,
  135, 137
Brandt Commission, 135,
  137, 140, 141, 150, 183
Brazil, 30n, 35, 45, 96,
  128, 133, 143, 145
Bretton Woods system,
  defined, 3
Brewster, Havelock, 173
Brzezinski, Zbigniew, 134
Calvo, Charles, 36n
Campos, Roberto de
  Oliveria, 35, 75
Canada, 30n, 135
Cancun, 135, 136, 150
Cardoso, Fernando, 107-09
Caribbean, 47, 106, 107,
  169, 173, 176
Carter, Jimmy, 133, 134,
  139
Carter administration,
  133, 134, 147, 175
Castro, Fidel, 136
Charter of Algiers, 83, 84
  111, 117
Charter of Economic
  Rights and Duties of
  States, 111, 115, 117,
  127, 159
Chile, 30n, 36, 66n, 103,
  104, 108
China, 34, 94-96, 104
Chinweizu, 110

CIEC, 127, 131, 133, 144,
  145, 149, 150
Club of Rome, 132, 133,
  141, 149
Cocoyoc Declaration, 118,
  142
Collective economic
  security, 103, 104, 149,
  159
Collective self-reliance,
  94, 95, 104, 149, 159
Colombia, 43, 44, 59, 62
Colombo Plan, 46n
Colonialism, 43, 44, 47,
  48, 51, 77, 83, 84, 94,
  106, 164
  See also Decolonization
Commodity agreements, 12,
  15, 27, 45, 60, 64, 67,
  71, 105, 147, 160
Common fund, 131, 146, 147
Common heritage, 143, 159
Commonwealth, 12, 17, 21,
  25, 26
Compensatory financing, 60
  62, 64, 71, 72, 127, 161
Conciliation, 74, 148, 161
Consensus of states, 6,
  61, 73-75, 159, 161
Convertibility, 2, 23, 49-
  51, 65, 97
Cooper, Richard, 133
Corea, Gamani, 109, 118
Corporatism, 164
Cosmopolitanism, 38-40
Costa Rica, 30n
Cuba, 81n
Cumper, G. E., 176
Curle, Adam, 150
Czechoslovakia, 50
Debate, substantive, 9,
  10, 125, 126, 133, 142,
  150, 151, 162
Debt, 45, 65-67, 78, 100,
  114, 144, 145, 161
Declaration on Social
  Progress and Devel-
  opment, 76, 84, 140
Decolonization, 51, 82
Denman, Roy, 138
Dependency theory, 92,
  105-12, 160, 173, 176
Deutsch, Karl, 167-69,
  181

Development economics, 46,
  47,
  See also Dependency
  theory, Modernization
  theory
Disarmament, 68, 132, 137,
  159, 161
Dobb, Maurice, 47
Dominican Republic, 30n
Echeverria, Luis, 111,
  112, 115
ECLA, 32, 34, 44, 62, 63,
  68, 106-10
Economic and Social
  Council, 81n, 108, 148
Economic Commission for
  Europe, 34, 48
Economic Rights and
  Duties of States, 12,
  29-33, 36, 42, 82, 118,
  143, 158, 159, 163, 165
Economist, London, 25,
  51, 80n
Egypt, 45, 6, 100, 101,
  107, 112
Employment, full, 5, 17,
  20-23
Ethiopia, 25
Europe, 14, 22, 25, 27,
  33, 42, 49-51, 66, 84,
  100, 105, 118, 133, 137
  central, 31
  eastern, 12, 14, 29, 30,
    104, 147
  northern, 126-29, 137,
    140, 147
  western, 12, 29, 65, 66,
    97, 132, 151
European Coal and Steel
  Community, 50
European Community, 7, 68,
  127, 129, 134, 138, 144,
  147
Exchange rates
  fixed, 19, 49, 50
  floating, 98, 145
Fabianism, 164-65
Fanon, Franz, 82, 106
  Wretched of the Earth,
  82, 84
Ferguson, C. Clyde, 175
Fourth world, 84, 169,
  See also LLCDs
France, 76, 126, 129
Frank, Andre Gunder, 109

Free enterprise, 19, 20,
  42, 116
Free trade, 14-23, 26-29,
  32, 42, 43, 133, 146
GATT, 2, 3, 7, 12, 14, 23,
  24-29, 39, 48-51, 61-64,
  71, 72, 136, 138, 146,
  148
Geertz, Clifford, 164
Geist, Herman, 16, 17, 19
General Assembly, 14, 28-
  31, 34, 43, 46, 62, 65,
  73, 76, 91, 94, 99-101,
  103, 115, 131, 132, 135-
  37, 140, 175
  Second Committee, 30,
    34, 35, 43
  1974 Sixth Special
    Session, 8, 113-16,
    119, 127-30, 144, 149
  1975 Seventh Special
    Session, 127-30, 148,
    149
Genscher, Hans, 135
Germany, 14
  Federal Republic, 50,
    82, 97, 9, 126, 134-36,
    150, 163
Ghana, 82, 173
Girvan, Norman, 107
Global negotiations, 135-
  37, 161
Global 2000, 134, 135
Group of 10, 104
Group of 20, 104
Group of 77, 2, 8, 60, 61,
  66, 69, 71-77, 81-85,
  101-04, 111-114, 126,
  131-34, 140-50, 175
Growth, 19, 20, 42, 116,
  130, 138, 159, 161
Guinea, 82
Gwin, Catherine, 130, 133
Haas, Ernst, 181
Haberler, Gottfried, 50, 72
Haberler report, 50, 51,
  63, 72
Hakim, George, 34, 35
Haq, Mahbub ul, 109-12,
  116-18, 125, 126, 129,
  148
Harrington, Michael, 140
Havana Charter, 27, 68

Havana conference, 26-28,
  43
Heath, Edward, 135
Hirschman, Albert, 14n
Hull, Cordell, 15, 19, 34
Human rights, 36
Iceland, 30n
IDA, 35, 49, 51, 65, 78,
  131, 144
Ideological constraint, 4,
  9, 33, 162n, 176
Ideology
  dominant, 3, 4, 35, 38,
    39
  nonpejorative meaning,
    3, 4, 33
  operational, 3, 10, 49
IFC, 35, 51
IMF, 2, 3, 12, 14, 20-25,
  28, 29, 39, 48-50, 66,
  71-73, 78-80, 97-99,
  104, 144-48, 161
Import substitution, 15,
  43, 4, 47, 106, 107
India, 27, 34, 37, 46, 47,
  65, 78n, 95, 111, 118,
  131
Indochina war, 99
Indonesia, 37, 38, 76n
Industrialization, 5, 11,
  12, 15, 20, 31, 42-49,
  52, 64, 66, 79, 105,
  114-18, 128-31, 137,
  140-44, 159, 160, 163,
  171, 172
Inglesias, Enrique, 109-10
Inter-American conference,
  27
Internationalism, 38-40
  new, 164-66
International Labor Orga-
  nization, 81n, 131, 132
IPC, 131, 146, 147, 160
Iraq, 99
Iran, 81n, 96, 113, 114
Islamic revival, 169, 170
Israel, 82, 112, 113, 159n
Italy, 49, 129
ITO, 20, 25-28, 42, 50,
  61, 73, 148
I.T.T., 103
Ivory Coast, 41, 99, 173
Jamaica, 131, 134

Japan, 49, 97, 105, 126, 133, 134, 147
Kennedy administration, 51
Keynes, John Maynard, 14, 17, 21-24, 28, 33, 67, 80, 146, 162, 182
Keynesian economics, 1, 2, 17-23, 28, 41-44, 164
Kissinger, Henry, 128-30
Kreisky, Bruno, 135-38
La Guardia, Fiorello, 30-33, 35, 38, 104, 139, 140
Laissez faire economics, 1-3, 13, 21-26, 47, 63, 71
  See also Free trade, Free enterprise
Latin America, 1-3, 21, 23, 26-36, 41-44, 47, 52, 65-75, 83, 92-95, 100-109, 112, 127, 132, 134, 140, 147, 163, 169, 177
Latin American Free Trade Area, 64
Law of the Sea Treaty, 136
Leadership, 93, 112-15, 142
League of Nations, 43
Lebanon, 34
Leninism, 2, 41
Lewis, W. Arthur, 47, 75, 106, 107
Libya, 67, 99-102
Limits to growth, 9, 93, 116, 118, 141
Link, 80, 100, 105, 114, 145, 146, 161
LLDCs, 60, 68, 78, 83, 94-96, 101, 104, 144
Lome agreement, 127, 129, 147
London bankers, 14
MacRae, Duncan, 181-82
Maier, Charles, 19
Majority rule of states, 6, 61, 73, 74, 159
Malaysia, 46n
Management, global, 2-6, 11-14, 17, 23-25, 38, 47, 158, 161-65, 177
  unintended consequences of, 7-9, 115

Marketing boards, 14
Marshall, George C., 27
Marshall Plan, 25-27, 66, 76, 137
McNamara, Robert, 75, 131
Memmi, Albert, 106
Menon, Krishna, 46
Mercantilism, 2, 165
Mexico, 30n, 34, 63n, 100, 101, 104, 111, 133-36
Middle East, 32
Mills, Don, 131, 134, 139
Mirror images, 70, 71
Modernization theory, 105-09
Molinari, Diego Luis, 11, 12, 27
Moynihan, Daniel Patrick, 115, 127, 164
Muskie, Edmund S., 134
Myrdal, Gunnar, 48, 139, 140
Naipaul, V. S., 141
National interest, 170-71
Nehru, Jawaharlal, 37, 62, 164
Nellis, John, 172, 176
Neocolonialism, 83, 92, 105-111
New international division of labor, 66, 68
New York City, 30, 38, 136, 175
New Zealand, 30n, 147
Nicaragua, 30n
NIEO
  concept of, 91
  Declaration and Programme of Action, 114, 115, 127
Nigeria, 63, 100, 110, 148
Nixon administration, 98
Nkrumah, Kwame, 83, 106
Nonaligned countries, 104, 113-17, 146, 159n
  1961 Belgrade conference, 63
  1970 Lusaka conference, 93-95
  1973 Algiers conference, 110
  1979 Havana conference, 136

Nongovernmental organiza-
tions, 127, 137, 141,
142
Nordic countries, 49
See also Europe, north
Norway, 99, 129
Nyerere, Julius K., 1, 3,
41, 96
OECD, 51
Ofuatey-Kodjoe, Wentworth,
171, 173
Oil weapon, 112, 116, 148
One nation one vote, 27
See also majority rule
OPEC, 62, 92, 112-16, 130,
147-49, 160, 168
Overseas Development Coun-
cil, 162
Oxford institute for
statistics, 43
Packenham, Robert, 39
Pakistan, 109
Palme, Olof, 137
Panama, 30n
Panch Shila, 37-38, 46,
68, 95
Paraguay, 30n
Patino, Alfonso, 59, 60-61
Pearson, Lester, 75, 84
Pearson Commission, 76,
135
Partners in Develop-
ment, 75, 111, 18, 138
Peru, 100, 104, 108, 132-
34, 137
Peterson, Peter, 135
Point four aid, 27, 39, 46
Political will, 75
Pollution, 116-18
Population, 75, 93, 116-
19, 131, 160, 163
Portillo, Lopez, 135
Portugal, 77
Prebisch, Raul, 44, 45,
60, 62, 68, 72, 106,
107, 141
Property, private, 5, 47,
70 71, 143
Public opinion, 61, 75,
76, 161
Racism, 175, 176
Rao, V. K. R. V., 34, 35
Rawls, John, 165

Reagan, Ronald, 135
Reagan administration, 136
Reconstruction, 22, 25,
26, 33-35, 42, 48, 49
Reshaping International
Order, 132, 141
Restitution, 8, 61, 77,
81, 93, 95, 158, 159
Ricardo, David, 23
Right to develop, 1, 3,
102, 159
Roosevelt, Franklin, 16
Roosevelt administration,
18, 19
Rostow, W. W., 48, 51
Rothschild, K. W., 1, 3,
17, 18, 21, 22
Rothstein, Robert, 147
Sartre, Jean Paul, 84
Saudi Arabia, 62n, 147
Scott, Andrew, 6-9, 177
SDRs, 79, 80, 144-46, 161
Security Council, 34
Senegal, 99
Shapira, Yoram, 115
Singapore, 168
Smith, Adam, 20, 23
Socialists, 38
democratic, 14, 41, 135,
138, 140
See also Fabianism
east European, 20, 39,
65, 70 71, 126, 147
South Africa, 30n, 77, 159n
Sovereignty, 5, 6, 28, 33
37, 71, 81, 143, 149
over natural resources,
36, 114
Soviet Union, 2, 10, 41,
47, 104, 104
Special Fund, 35, 65, 79
Stamp, Maxwell, 80
State capitalism, 164
Stevenson, Adlai, 30-32,
39
Strategic stockpiling, 45,
63
Streeten, Paul, 145, 157,
162, 166
Sudan, 76, 95, 100
Sukarno, 37-39, 164, 165
SUNFED, 33-35, 48, 49, 65
Sweden, 135, 137
Syria, 79n

Tanzania, 41, 76, 95, 172
Tariff preferences, 63,
  64, 67, 71, 72, 146,
  147, 160
Technical assistance, 12,
  27, 32-35, 42, 47, 79,
  144
Technology
  appropriate, 141
  transfer of, 81-84, 92,
  105, 108, 112, 134,
  142, 143, 160
Terms of trade, 7, 15, 44,
  63, 64, 72, 114
Thatcher, Margaret, 135
Third World Forum, 109,
  110, 116
TNCs, 8, 36, 80, 81, 100,
  101-08, 112, 114, 142,
  147, 160
  code of conduct, 108,
  143, 144, 160
Trickle down, 27
Trilateral Commission,
  133, 134
Truman, Harry, 27, 39, 46
Tunisia, 65n, 129
Turkey, 35, 63n
U.N. Conference on Science
  and Technology for
  Development, 134
UNCTAD, 71, 76, 109, 110,
  114, 136, 143-48
  1964 Geneva, 65-75, 83,
  117, 137
  1968 New Delhi, 75, 83
  1972 Santiago, 102, 103,
  111, 115, 118
  1976 Nairobi, 131, 143,
  144, 147
  1979 Manila, 134, 138,
  147
  1983 Belgrade, 130, 141,
  145, 183, 184
UNESCO, 102
UNICEF, 32
UNIDO, 75, 128, 140, 148
U.N. Institute for Eco-
  nomic Planning, Dakar,
  107, 110
United Arab Emirates, 104

United Kingdom, 17, 21,
  25, 30n, 34, 46n, 68,
  111, 126, 135, 136, 145,
  150, 162
  colonies, 14, 15, 111
United Nations
  See specific agency
United Nations, wartime
  alliance, 30
United Nations Charter,
  28-35, 38, 71, 95, 117
United States, 2, 11-27,
  30n, 32, 36, 39-44, 47-
  51, 59, 68-71, 76, 79,
  80, 82, 103-05, 125-30,
  133-36, 139, 140, 146-
  51, 163, 175, 183
  1971 economic policy,
  92, 96-102
  Senate, 27
  State Department, 15-17,
  19, 42
  Treasury Department, 19,
  98
Universalism, 39-41, 48
UNRRA, 30-35, 38, 65, 66,
  70
Upper Volta, 100
Urquidi, Victor, 133n
Uruguay, 63, 102, 103, 108
Wallerstein, Immanuel,
  172, 182
Ward, Barbara, 91, 111,
  118
Weintraub, Sidney, 59, 69-
  72, 175
Wilcox, 11, 42
Wills, Garry, 39
World Bank, 2, 3, 14, 20,
  22-29, 32-35, 39, 40,
  45-49, 65, 73, 75, 78,
  99, 103, 109, 131, 132,
  136, 139, 144, 148
Yugoslavia, 95, 129
Zanzibar, 41
Zambia, 96
Zartman, I. William, 150

G